Sovereignty, Power, Control
Politics in the States of Western India (1916–1947)

Sovereignty, Power, Control

Politics in the States of Western India (1916–1947)

by

John McLeod

Decent Books
New Delhi

Cataloging in Publication Data — DK
[Courtesy: D.K. Agencies (P) Ltd. <docinfo@dkagencies.com>]

McLeod, John, 1963–
Sovereignty, power, control : politics in the states of western India (1916–1947) / by John McLeod.
xiv, 306 p. 23 cm.
Reprint. Originally published: Leiden : Brill, 1999.
(Brill's Indological library; v. 15)
Includes bibliographical references. (p.)
Includes index.
ISBN 8186921427

1. India — Politics and Government — 1919-1947.
2. India — Kings and rulers. I. Title.

DDC 954.035 22

ISBN 81-86921-42-7
First published in Leiden, The Netherlands in 1999
First South Asian Edition, 2007

Published and printed by:
Decent Books
D-36/A-1, Mohan Garden
Najafgarh Road, New Delhi - 110 059
Ph. (011) 2535 3435

Distributed by:
D.K. Printworld (P) Ltd.
Regd. office : *'Sri Kunj,'* F-52, Bali Nagar
Ramesh Nagar Metro Station
New Delhi - 110 015
Phones : (011) 2545 3975, 2546 6019; *Fax* : (011) 2546 5926
E-mail : dkprintworld@vsnl.net
Web : www.dkprintworld.com

CONTENTS

ACKNOWLEDGEMENTS

This book could not have been written without the help of Dr Lionel Carter, Secretary-Librarian of the Centre of South Asian Studies at the University of Cambridge, and of the staffs of the Jawaharlal Nehru Memorial Museum and Library, New Delhi; the John P. Robarts Research Library at the University of Toronto; the National Archives of India, New Delhi; the Oriental and India Office Collections of the British Library, London; and the William F. Ekstrom Library at the University of Louisville. I should like to thank the following individuals, who in one way or another have all added to my knowledge and understanding of the history of the Western India States Agency: Lieutenant-Colonel (retired) P.W.M. Doyle; Ms Suzanne Falkiner; Professor Milton Israel; Professor Martin A. Klein; Professor T.O. Lloyd; Professor Shannon McSheffrey; the late Mr John S.H. Shattock; Professor N.K. Wagle; and the anonymous reviewer who read and commented on the manuscript of this book for the publisher. Many of my colleagues at the University of Louisville gave me encouragement and support while I was writing the book, but I am particularly grateful to Professor Blake R. Beattie; Professor Robert B. Kebric; and cartographer-extraordinary Professor Justin McCarthy. I owe a special debt of gratitude to His Highness Maharana Sriraj Meghrajji III, Maharaja Sriraj of Dhrangadhara, who in personal discussions and written comments has taught me much about the field that could not be learned from archives; to His Highness Maharana Mahipendra Singh, Maharana of Danta, a kind host and a patient interviewee; to Professor Barbara N. Ramusack, a valued mentor for over ten years; and especially to my wife, Mary Hora, who uncomplainingly read and improved each chapter of the book.

I must also record my thanks to the Shastri Indo-Canadian Institute, which helped fund the research for this book with a post-doctoral fellowship. This made possible my researches in the National Archives of India and the Jawaharlal Nehru Memorial Museum and Library, and my talks with Their Highnesses of Danta and Dhrangadhara.

LIST OF TABLES

ABBREVIATIONS USED IN THE FOOTNOTES

INTERVIEWS

H.H. of Danta. His Highness Maharana Mahipendra Singh, Maharana of Danta, Bhavani Villa, Danta-Bhavangadh, 1994.

H.H. of Dhrangadhara. His Highness Maharana Sriraj Meghrajji III (formerly Mayurdhwajsinhji), Maharaja Sriraj of Dhrangadhara, Ajitnivas Palace, Dhrangadhara, 1994.

ARCHIVAL COLLECTIONS

IOC Oriental and India Office Collections, The British Library (London)

- L/P&S Political and Secret
- L/PO Private Office Papers
- MSS Eur D 998 A.J. Hopkinson Collection
- Photo Eur 84 Watson Collection
- R/1 Crown Representative's Records: Political Department
- R/2 Crown Representative's Records: Indian States

NAI National Archives of India (New Delhi)

- FPD Foreign and Political Department
- PSV Office of the Private Secretary to His Excellency the Viceroy
- WISA Western India States Agency

NL Jawaharlal Nehru Memorial Museum and Library (New Delhi)

- AICC All-India Congress Committee Files
- Nehru Papers Jawaharlal Nehru Papers (used by permission)
- SPC All-India States' People's Conference Papers
- Vyas Papers Jai Narain Vyas Papers

SAS Centre of South Asian Studies, University of Cambridge (Cambridge)

- Barlow Papers

OTHER ABBREVIATIONS

Rulers are referred to by the names of their states; thus, "Kutch" means the Maharao of Kutch. Persons other than rulers are identified by office at their first mention in each chapter.

AGG. Agent to the Governor-General; unless otherwise specified, Agent to the Governor-General in the States of Western India

IO. India Office

PA. Political Agent

PD. Political (Crown) Department, New Delhi (1937-1947)

PD Bombay. Political Department, Government of Bombay

PD India. Political Section, Foreign and Political Department, Government of India (1914-1937)

Political Adviser. Political Adviser to the Crown Representative.

Resident. Unless otherwise specified, Resident for the States of Western India (1937-1944) and Resident at Baroda and for the States of Western India and Gujarat (1944-1947)

Secretary of State. Secretary of State for India and (from 1937) for India and Burma

GLOSSARY OF INDIAN TERMS

This glossary excludes names of places, families and clans–except Gaekwad–and people.

Bania	Member of a merchant caste.
Begum	Muslim title for women.
Bhayat (bhayad)	"Brotherhood," the landholding junior members of a ruling family.
Brahman	A member of the first division of the classical Hindu social hierarchy.
Darbar	A levee; the government of an Indian state; title of a ruler.
Dewan	The prime minister of an Indian state (spelled Diwan in southern India).
Durbar (see *Darbar*)	
Gaddi (*gadi*)	The cushion on which an Indian ruler sits, corresponding to the European throne.
Gaekwad	Family name of the Maharajas of Baroda.
Girassia	A landholding noble in an Indian state, often belonging to the bhayat.
Izzat	Personal honour.
Jagirdar	The holder of a jagir (the right to the revenue of a tract of land).
Jam Saheb	Title of the rulers of Nawanagar.
Karbhari	The chief official in a small Indian state.
Kathi	A group of ruling clans of Gujarat.
Khan	Muslim title for men.
Kumar	A young prince.
Lakh	A hundred thousand.
Lok parishad	Political "people's associations" in the Indian states.
Mahajan	In Gujarat, an assembly of urban caste leaders.
Maharaja	Hindu regnal title for men.
Maharaja Sriraj	Hindu regnal title for men.

Maharana	Hindu regnal title for men.
Maharao	Hindu regnal title for men.
Maharawal	Hindu regnal title for men.
Mahi Maratib	The Insignia of the Fish, a high honour conferred by the Mughal emperors.
Mansab	The military commands conferred on distinguished inhabitants of the Mughal empire.
Maratha	A people originating in Maharashtra.
Mughal	"Mongol." The Muslim dynasty that dominated India from 1526 to the eighteenth century.
Mulkgiri	The yearly expedition sent by the Mughals and the Marathas to collect tribute from the chiefs of Gujarat.
Nawab	Muslim title for men.
Nizam	Title of the rulers of Hyderabad.
Pacca (pakka)	Ripe, permanent, of good quality.
Pathan	An Afghan.
Peshwa	Title of the principal Maratha ruler in the eighteenth century.
Praja mandal	Political organization of subjects in the Indian states.
Raj Saheb	Hindu regnal title for men.
Raja	Hindu regnal title for men.
Rajput	Collective name for the principal Hindu ruling clans of northern India.
Rana Saheb	Title of the rulers of Porbandar.
Rani	Hindu regnal title for women.
Rao	Hindu regnal title for men.
Rupee	The standard coin of India.
Satyagraha	M.K. Gandhi's tactic of non-violent passive resistance.
Sultan	Title of the principal Muslim kings of mediaeval India.
Taluka	In the Western India States Agency, a petty state.
Talukdar (Taluqdar)	The ruler of a taluka.
Thakor	Hindu regnal title for men.

Thakor Saheb	Hindu regnal title for men.
Thana	In the Western India States Agency, a group of petty states.
Uttara	A lodge.
Zamindar	A landholder.

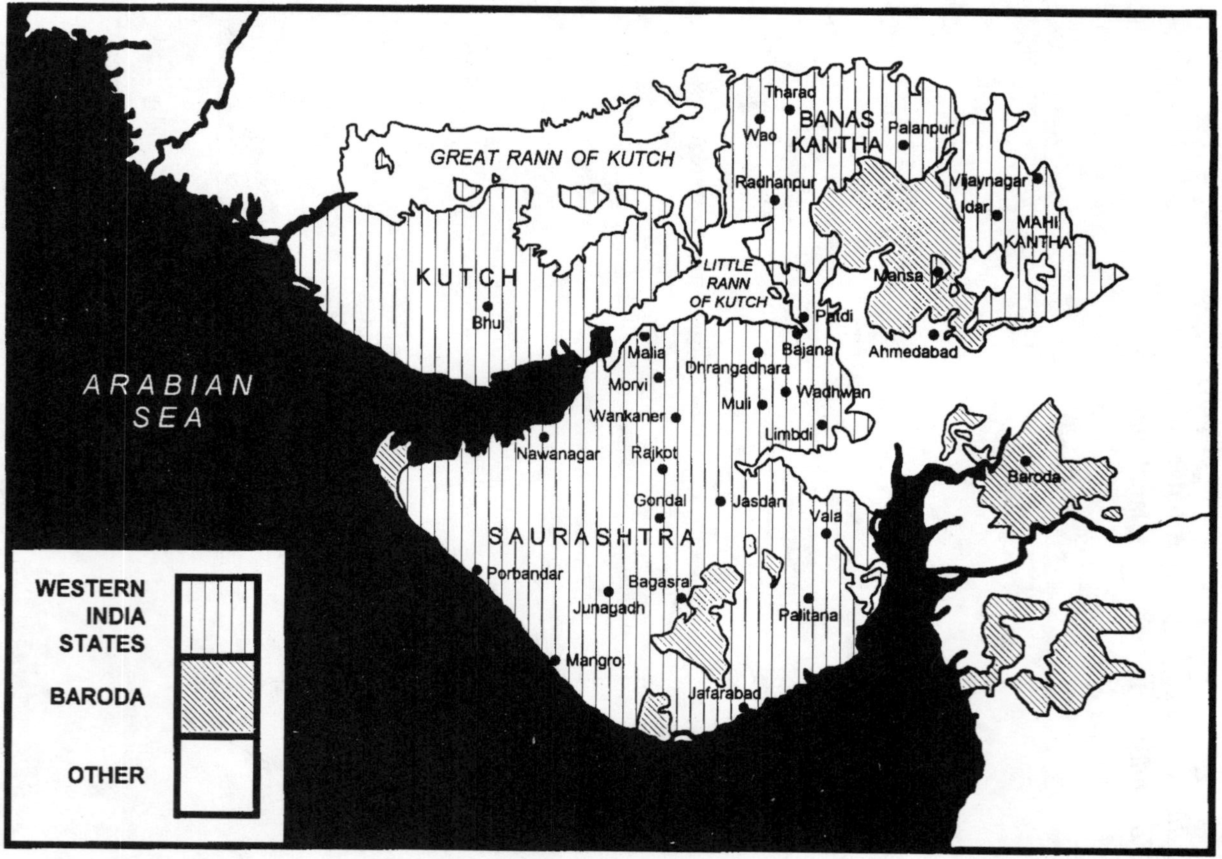
GREAT RANN OF KUTCH
KUTCH
Bhuj
ARABIAN SEA
Tharad
Wao
BANAS KANTHA
Palanpur
Radhanpur
Vijaynagar
Idar
MAHI KANTHA
LITTLE RANN OF KUTCH
Mansa
Patdi
Ahmedabad
Malia
Bajana
Dhrangadhara
Morvi
Wadhwan
Muli
Wankaner
Limbdi
Nawanagar
Rajkot
Baroda
Gondal
Jasdan
Vala
SAURASHTRA
Porbandar
Bagasra
Junagadh
Palitana
Mangrol
Jafarabad
WESTERN INDIA STATES
BARODA
OTHER

PROLOGUE

Few public figures have enjoyed as varied a career as Maharaja Jam Shri Ranjitsinhji. As an undergraduate at Cambridge in the early 1890s, he honed an innate talent for cricket, and for ten years was one of the best-loved cricketers in England. In 1907, he succeeded as Jam Saheb, or ruler, of Nawanagar, a principality in western India, and set about modernising his realm; during a quarter of a century on the throne, he remodelled his capital, constructed roads and railways, and built a great port with modern facilities. In 1914, Ranjitsinhji went to France as an officer of the Indian Expeditionary Force, and while in Europe lost an eye in a shooting accident. During the 1920s, he took a keen interest in the question of disarmament, and served on the Indian delegation to the Assembly of the League of Nations. In 1932, he was elected Chancellor of the Chamber of Princes, the deliberative body through which he and his fellow rulers discussed matters of common interest amongst themselves and with their British overlords.[1]

From November 1930 to December 1932, British and Indian political leaders met in London in three Round Table Conferences to hammer out the details of a new constitution that would launch the next stage of India's progression to self-government. They agreed that the India of the future would be a federation. For the first time in history, Nawanagar and the other semi-autonomous monarchical Indian states would both be represented in, and subject to the authority of, an elected federal legislature and an executive responsible to that legislature. The federation would also include the provinces that covered two-thirds of India and had for generations been under direct British control, but were now to become fully self-governing through elected assemblies. Sir Samuel Hoare, the British Secretary of State for India, assured the rulers of the Indian

---

[1] The official biography is Roland Wild, *"Ranji:" The Biography of Colonel H.H. Shri Sir Ranjitsinhji Vibhaji, Maharaja Jam Saheb of Nawanagar* (London, 1934).

states that their position as autocratic monarchs would not be affected by their accession to the federation, even though the pro-democratic Indian National Congress would definitely be the largest political faction in the federal legislature; but on 25 March 1933, Ranjitsinhji rose in the Chamber of Princes and informed his fellow rulers that

> the present scheme was dangerous to the States and the British connexion. When he entered on the Chancellorship of the Chamber he was favourably disposed to federation, but it became evident that the scheme of his Majesty's Government differed from all modern federations, and that the States were expected to contribute the elements of stability and experience. The Jam thought it was unfortunate that the realization of British India's political ambitions was made contingent on the acceptance of a particular type of federation by the States. He feared that the Federal Court, the Viceroy, and the Upper Chamber would be unable to prevent the Federal Centre from swallowing up the States. In the second place, the proposed constitution would expose Indian kingship to unfair attacks, so that Indian kingship, in an effective form, would be destroyed.[2]

Put bluntly, Ranjitsinhji was calling Hoare's assurances worthless, and hence accusing the Secretary of State of lying. Lord Willingdon, the British Viceroy of India, presided over meetings of the Chamber of Princes, and at this point he angrily broke in to cut off the Chancellor's speech. The following day, Ranjitsinhji left New Delhi for Nawanagar; he arrived in his capital a day later, and was driven from the railway station to his palace in an open car, to greet and be greeted by his subjects. During the ride, he contracted a chill. Six days later, he was dead. It was almost inevitable that many commentators would associate the old prince's death with his treatment at the hands of Lord Willingdon; the leading anti-federation newspaper in Britain went so far as to say that "Feeling himself rebuked by the Power he sought to save, from the moment he left the Chamber he lost all desire to live."[3]

---

[2] *The Times*, 27 Mar. 1933. The newspaper reported Ranjitsinhji's speech in the third person and the past tense.

[3] *The Morning Post*, 19 July 1934.

Whether this was true or not, the scene that took place in the Chamber of Princes was a direct result of disagreement between many Indian rulers and the British as to the best means of holding at bay the third major force in Indian political life in the early 1930s: the politically active members of the various organizations that the British lumped together as "Congress," and modern historians often call "Nationalists."[4] The Jam Saheb believed that federation would lead to the end of monarchical rule in India at the hands of hostile politicians, and hence opposed it; the British Paramount Power considered that only an active princely role could prevent complete Congress control, and therefore urgently desired a federal India.

In 1933, a third of the area of the South Asian subcontinent, and a quarter of its population, were governed by indigenous monarchs, the princes and chiefs of the Indian states.[5] Many historians of India have treated developments in the states as a sideshow at best, or an irrelevancy at worst. But in fact, the size of the states alone gives them a central place in the history of modern South Asia, and other considerations add to their significance. Precolonial governmental structures survived to a much greater extent in the states than in British India (the provinces under direct British rule); this made conflict between Indian and British social and administrative institutions particularly acute in princely India, which is therefore an especially fruitful field of investigation for students of the "modernisation of tradition." Similarly, the division of power between indigenous monarchs and foreign imperialists meant that state-building and nation-making, and the preservation of an Indian identity, took distinctive forms in the states. And the years of separation between princely and British India, and the presence of many articulate and politically-conscious former rulers, have played

---

[4] At the end of the decade, the All-India Muslim League emerged as a fourth force, claiming to speak on behalf of the subcontinent's Muslims. The League grew in importance during and after the Second World War, and in 1947 it triumphed with the creation of Pakistan as a homeland for India's Muslims.

[5] The Government of India Act, 1935, defines "Indian State" as any territory under the rule of an Indian monarch. The designation "Princely State" properly refers only to 140 major units whose rulers were full members of the Chamber of Princes, although it is often used for all of the 735-odd Indian states.

a major role in shaping administration and politics in independent India and Pakistan.

In recent years, a succession of monographs on the history of the Indian states in the twentieth century has shown that every aspect of life in the states was vitally affected by the intersection of the interests of the rulers, the "Nationalist" politicians, and the British Paramount Power.[6] But none of these studies has systematically examined the goals of these three players, or shown how the history of the Indian states and their people was the outcome of a dialogue among them. This book is an attempt to fill that gap. Its central theme is the way in which the rulers, the politicians, and the Paramount Power each pursued their own goals, and thus moulded their relationship. At any given moment, two of the players might collaborate to resist the third, or all three might join together, or again each might pursue separate goals. The resulting dialogue is best observed at the level of what is called the Agency. During the period of British rule in India, an Agency was a group of neighbouring states in the charge of a single British official (variously styled Resident, Agent to the Governor-General, Agent to the Governor, Political Agent, or Political Superintendent). Each Agency included sufficiently few states to permit a detailed exploration of the issues on which rulers, politicians, and Paramount Power confronted one another, and this sets apart a study of the relationship at the level of the Agency from works that examine the interaction of the central authorities with the Indian states as a body, or British relations with all of the states in a single province; the sheer number of states confines works of this type to major issues

---

[6] As will be seen in Chapter One, the term "rulers" is used loosely in this book to include state officials in the service of the princes and chiefs, and, in some ways, the leaders of the Chamber of Princes. The importance of the states in any history of modern India is stressed by Ian Copland, *The Princes of India in the Endgame of Empire, 1917-1947* (Cambridge, 1997). For examples of works on different aspects of the states, see Shamim Aleem, *Personnel Management in a Princely State* (New Delhi, 1985); S.R. Ashton, *British Policy Towards the Indian States 1905-1939* (London, 1982); Bjørn Hettne, *The Political Economy of Indirect Rule: Mysore 1881-1947* (London, 1978); Robin Jeffrey, *The Decline of Nayar Dominance: Society and Politics in Travancore, 1847-1908* (London, 1976); Sobhag Mathur, *Struggle for Responsible Government in Marwar* (Jodhpur, 1982); Robert W. Stern, *The Cat and the Lion: Jaipur State in the British Raj* (Leiden, 1988).

that simultaneously affected numerous rulers, rather than day-to-day questions that arose in individual states. The issues that were important to the rulers and states as an entity were often of a quite different nature from those that affected particular states, which resulted from regional variations in terms of culture, geography or economy. At the same time, an Agency also contained enough states that in examining it, one may distinguish broad policies from reactions to specific questions, whereas studies that explore the British-princely relationship in a single state do not always show whether particular developments resulted from unique local circumstances or general British policies towards princely India.[7] Moreover, while British policies towards the states were normally set in the provincial and central capitals rather than by the staff at the Agency headquarters, it was the latter who implemented them; and it was also through the Agencies that rulers normally fought for or against those policies. This book accordingly takes the position that Agencies not only provide an ideal field in which to study the interaction of rulers, politicians, and Paramount Power, but were actually its focal point.[8]

In 1933, Ranjitsinhji's kingdom of Nawanagar was included in the Western India States Agency, which lay in the northern part of the present Gujarat state. This Agency was established in 1924; its boundaries were altered in 1933 and 1943, and in 1944 it was merged into a larger Baroda, Western India and Gujarat States Agency. At one time or another between 1924 and 1944, about 435 states (three fifths of all the states in India) were included in the Western India States Agency; these "States of Western India," as they were officially (if ambiguously) called, occupied just over half

---

[7] Barbara N. Ramusack, *The Princes of India in the Twilight of Empire: Dissolution of a Patron-Client System, 1914-1939* (Columbus, 1978), examines the princes across India; Ian Copland, *The British Raj and the Indian Princes: Paramountcy in Western India, 1857-1930* (Bombay, 1982), is concerned with rulers in the province of Bombay; and Nicholas B. Dirks, *The Hollow Crown: Ethnohistory of an Indian Kingdom* (Cambridge, 1987), studies the single state of Pudukkottai.

[8] This challenges the view of Michael H. Fisher, *Indirect Rule in India: Residents and the Residency System 1764-1858* (Delhi, 1991), pp. 33-34, who believes that studies of single Agencies do not reveal the "overall patterns" in the relationship between the British and the rulers.

of modern Gujarat, and in 1941 had an area of 39,688 square miles and a population of 5,220,011. Only forty-two of the 435, however, were sufficiently important to be accorded representation in the Chamber of Princes, and only eighteen of them ranked as salute states, meaning that their princes were deemed worthy of being greeted by artillery salutes on state occasions.[9]

The history of the Western India States Agency during the last three decades of British rule in India is particularly illustrative of the three-way dialogue of rulers, politicians, and Paramount Power. This Agency included more states than any other, and its rulers ranged from princes who played central roles in the public life of India, to petty chiefs who rarely ventured beyond the few villages that they governed. At the same time, the small size of many of the states in the Agency was in itself a source of discord among the parties. Moreover, Western India contained a majority of the handful of states with seaports, which led to disagreements over security and the collection of customs duties; such conflicts are not found in other Agencies, but they provide valuable information on the interests and priorities of the princes and the Paramount Power. Finally, Western India was the home of several leading Indian politicians, most notably M.K. Gandhi, and was therefore of particular interest to the nationalist movement.

This book covers the period from 1916 (when the first steps were taken towards the creation of the Western India States Agency) to the lapse of British paramountcy in 1947. These years are particularly significant in the history of the Indian states. As will be seen, they saw two reversals in British policy towards the states, which are important in understanding the evolving relationship between the parties. During this period, too, a shared knowledge of the English language and regular contacts through the Chamber of Princes gave the major rulers a self-confidence and assertiveness not seen since the beginning of colonial rule. As a result, they could now unite to defend their own interests as never before. At the same time, the Indian nationalist movement was being transformed:

---

[9] These forty-two states are listed in Table One. Each of the salute princes of Western India was entitled to a seat in the Chamber; the twenty-four major non-salute chiefs were not members in their own right, but elected two "representative members."

Gandhi became leader of the Congress in 1920, and oversaw the party's adoption of the techniques of non-violent civil disobedience, its transformation from a club of anglicized intellectuals to a mass organization, and its acceptance of the goal of full independence for India; between the World Wars, political bodies sprang up in the Indian states, and from the late 1930s they demanded democratization of the monarchical régimes and sought to bring the states' people into the wider struggle against British rule; and, by 1939, the Congress and the political movements were drawing ever closer in organization and strategy. Finally, the last decades of British rule were the only period in which virtually all of the states were under the supervision of the Political Department in New Delhi; this gave British policy a consistency not seen in earlier days when control was divided between the central and provincial governments.

This book is not a chronicle of the Western India States Agency, and it omits many topics that form part of the connected history of the region (for example, the activities of two successive Jam Sahebs of Nawanagar as leaders of the Chamber of Princes, or Gandhi's campaign for reforms in Rajkot state in 1938-1939). Rather, it is a series of thematic studies that illustrate the workings of the Indian state system under British paramountcy. It examines all of the principal questions on which the interests of the Indian states intersected with those of the Paramount Power during the period under study, a conjunction that in almost every instance was linked in some way to the activities of Indian political leaders.[10] Conflict was an essential part of the relationship between rulers and Paramount Power, despite the stereotypical view of the Indian princes embodied in the words of Jawaharlal Nehru: "The Political Department of the Government of India pulls the strings and the puppets dance to its tune...."[11] For as this book will show, the rulers were

---

[10] Delhi's campaign to secure the states' accession to the proposed Indian federation in the 1930s is frequently mentioned in the book. It has, however, been deliberately omitted from consideration as a separate question, as it was not carried out through the Agency. In any case, the question of federation has been thoroughly studied in Copland, *Princes of India*, pp. 72-182.

[11] Jawaharlal Nehru, *Presidential Address. All-India States' People's Conference February 1939, Ludhiana* (Allahabad, n.d.), p. 6.

not anyone's puppets.[12] They, like the British and the politicians, had their own interests, which they pursued steadfastly and with considerable success. At any given moment, there might be collaboration between rulers and British, or rulers and politicians, as the various parties cooperated to fight groups or trends that seemed to be acting against their interests. The nature of the relationship of rulers, politicians and Paramount Power becomes apparent in an examination of the ways in which these interests brought them into contact with one another.

TABLE ONE

THE PRINCIPAL STATES OF WESTERN INDIA[13]

State:	Dynasty:	Area:	Population 1921:	1931:	1941:	Revenue:
		Salute of 17 guns:				
1 Kutch	Jadeja Rajput	8,461	484,547	514,307	500,800	28.37
		Salute of 15 guns:				
2 Idar	Rathor Rajput	1,668	226,351	262,660	307,798	21
		Salutes of 13 guns:				
3 Junagadh	Babi Pathan	3,337	465,493	545,152	670,719	74.86
4 Nawanagar	Jadeja Rajput	3,791	345,353	409,192	504,006	97.15
5 Bhavnagar	Gohel Rajput	2,961	426,404	500,274	618,429	108.9
6 Porbandar	Jethwa Rajput	642	101,881	115,673	146,648	25
7 Dhrangadhara	Jhala Rajput	1,167	88,406	88,961	94,417	18.35
8 Palanpur	Jalori Pathan	1,794	236,694	264,179	315,855	11.98

[12] Apart from anything else, a slavishly subservient prince would have undercut his own legitimacy as a ruler; Fisher, *Indirect Rule*, pp. 141, 179.

[13] Area is given in square miles, and revenue in lakhs of rupees. The states are listed in order of precedence and arranged according to the salutes enjoyed by their rulers in 1947; for precedence and the gradation of salutes, see Chapter Eleven. There are several English forms of the names of many states and their ruling families. In this book, the forms generally used by the rulers themselves have been adopted: thus, "Kutch" rather than the more correct "Kachchh" or the usual British spelling "Cutch;" "Dhrangadhara" (preferred by the last ruling prince of the state) instead of "Dhrangadhra."

State:	Dynasty:	Area:	Population 1921:	1931:	1941:	Revenue:
		Salutes of 11 guns:				
9 Radhanpur	Babi Pathan	1,150	67,789	70,530	67,691	6.02
10 Morvi	Jadeja Rajput	822	96,697	113,023	141,761	58.53
11 Gondal	Jadeja Rajput	1,024	167,071	205,846	244,514	50
12 Jafarabad	Habshi	53	10,878	12,092	13,837	2.45
13 Wankaner	Jhala Rajput	417	36,824	44,259	54,965	7.37
		Salutes of 9 guns:				
14 Palitana	Gohel Rajput	300	58,000	62,150	76,432	8.21
15 Dhrol	Jadeja Rajput	283	23,460	27,639	33,617	2.67
16 Limbdi	Jhala Rajput	344	35,422	40,088	44,024	7.89
17 Rajkot	Jadeja Rajput	282	60,993	75,540	102,951	13.55
18 Wadhwan	Jhala Rajput	242	37,946	42,602	50,915	5.51
		Non-Salute States:				
19 Vijaynagar	Rathor Rajput	135	5,858	8,491	13,942	0.93
20 Lakhtar	Jhala Rajput	247	23,758	23,754	26,780	n.a.
21 Sayla	Jhala Rajput	222	15,285	15,285	15,352	n.a.
22 Chuda	Jhala Rajput	78	12,942	12,915	15,818	n.a.
23 Vala	Gohel Rajput	190	14,069	14,069	16,197	n.a.
24 Jasdan	Khachar Kathi	296	24,056	34,056	37,679	n.a.
25 Manavadar	Babi Pathan	101	29,061	29,084	26,209	n.a.
26 Tharad	Waghela Rajput	126	52,839	54,311	62,157	n.a.
27 Malpur	Rathor Rajput	97	11,767	13,552	16,568	n.a.
28 Mohanpur	Rehwar Rajput	89	12,565	14,264	15,727	n.a.
29 Mansa	Chavada Rajput	25	15,606	16,942	18,861	n.a.
30 Thana Devli	Vala Kathi	117	15,998	16,005	18,748	n.a.
31 Vadia	Vala Kathi	90	13,719	13,719	16,818	n.a.
32 Lathi	Gohel Rajput	48	9,407	9,404	10,812	n.a.
33 Muli	Parmar Rajput	133	17,129	17,109	16,977	n.a.
34 Bajana	Jat Malek	183	13,481	13,481	13,996	n.a.
35 Virpur	Jadeja Rajput	66	8,052	8,050	8,594	n.a.
36 Wao	Chauhan Rajput	359	22,343	20,721	24,673	n.a.
37 Malia	Jadeja Rajput	103	12,143	12,142	10,788	n.a.
38 Kotda Sangani	Jadeja Rajput	90	10,397	10,420	12,160	n.a.
39 Jetpur	Vala Kathi	120	7,831	7,831	35,145	n.a.
40 Bilkha	Vala Kathi	135	16,011	16,011	31,790	n.a.
41 Patdi	Patidar	39	2,579	n.a.	3,147	n.a.
42 Khirasra	Jadeja Rajput	47	4,663	4,663	5,893	n.a.

PART ONE: SOVEREIGNTY, POWER, CONTROL

CHAPTER ONE

SOVEREIGNTY: THE RULERS

The actions of Ranjitsinhji and the other rulers of Western India during the years from the First World War to independence cannot be fully understood without a consideration of the earlier history of their states, the nature of monarchy in Gujarat in the twentieth century, and the interests that the rulers considered to be important.

I

The Western India States Agency comprised four regions: the peninsula of Kathiawar or Saurashtra on the Arabian Sea, containing thirty-two major states; the single state of Kutch, north of Saurashtra and virtually cut off from the rest of India by salt deserts (the Ranns) and the sea; Banas Kantha, east of Kutch, which included four major states; and Mahi Kantha, with five major states, roughly the present Sabarkantha and Gandhinagar Districts in north-eastern Gujarat.[1] The people of all four regions spoke Gujarati

---

[1] The principal Banas Kantha states were Palanpur, Radhanpur, Tharad and Wao, while Mahi Kantha included Idar, Vijaynagar, Malpur, Mohanpur and Mansa. Other than Kutch, all of the remaining states listed in Table One lay in Saurashtra. The names of these divisions need some comment. The peninsula was anciently called Saurashtra; but the British followed the Marathas in calling it Kathiawar, after the Kathi community which was prominent in the area in the seventeenth and eighteenth centuries, and this remained its official designation until the name Saurashtra was restored after independence. The names Banas Kantha and Sabar Kantha are particularly confusing. From 1816 to 1925, Banas Kantha was known as the Palanpur Agency; to avoid confusion with the Palanpur state, however, the later name is used throughout this section. And until 1933, "Sabar Kantha" was a subdivision of the Mahi Kantha Agency; from 1933 to 1943, the same name was given to a subordinate Agency of the Western Indian States Agency, comprising the petty states of both Banas Kantha and Mahi Kantha; and in 1949, most of the states of Mahi Kantha were formed into the District of Sabarkantha.

dialects and were mostly Hindus; the number of Muslims ranged from virtually none in Mahi Kantha to a quarter of the population in Kutch, and there were also significant numbers of Jains in Saurashtra. Across Western India, the great majority of the population was engaged in agriculture (growing grains and cotton), with important mercantile communities in the coastal towns of Saurashtra and Kutch.[2] The connected history of what became the Western India States Agency goes back almost two thousand years.[3] From at least the eighth century, the region was divided into small kingdoms of the kind that was common across much of northern and western India until the establishment of British rule. In keeping with the pattern, these kingdoms usually recognised the supremacy of the successive overlords of Gujarat: the kings of Anhilwada (942-1304), the sultans of Delhi (1299-1407) and of Gujarat (1407-1573), the Mughal emperors (1573-1753), and the Marathas (from 1753). The states acknowledged this supremacy by paying a tribute in cash or foodstuffs to their overlords; when the overlord was weak, the states might stop paying the tribute and temporarily become independent.[4] The oldest of these kingdoms were ruled by dynasties that came eventually to be recognised as members of the Rajput caste; and the Rajput states of Dhrangadhara, Bhavnagar, Kutch and Vijaynagar all traced their origins to the days of the Anhilwada kings, to whom their early rulers were often connected by marriage.[5] Other

---

[2] The latest account of the people of Western India is Harald Tambs-Lyche, *Power, Profit and Poetry: Traditional Society in Kathiawar, Western India* (New Delhi, 1997). For more detail, see *Gazetteer of the Bombay Presidency* (27 volumes in 35, Bombay, 1877-1904), volumes 5 (Kutch, Banas Kantha, Mahi Kantha) and 8 (Saurashtra).

[3] For an overview, see S.B. Rajyagor, *History of Gujarat* (New Delhi, 1982).

[4] The most recent outline of the traditional political structure in India is C.A. Bayly, *Indian Society and the Making of the British Empire* (*The New Cambridge History of India*, II.1) (Cambridge, 1988), pp. 23-26.

[5] According to Brajadulal Chattopadhyaya, "Origin of the Rajputs: The Political, Economic and Social Processes in Early Medieval Rajasthan," in the same author's *The Making of Early Medieval India* (Delhi, 1994), pp. 57-88, the ancestors of the Rajputs were the chieftains of petty Hindu colonies in the tribal areas of Rajasthan and Gujarat. This explanation better suits the history of the royal families of Gujarat than does that offered in Dirk H.A. Kolff, Naukar, *Rajput and Sepoy: The ethnohistory of the military labour market in Hindustan, 1450-1850* (Cambridge, 1990), especially pp. 71-116. See also Tambs-Lyche, *op. cit.*, pp. 30-

dynasties were subsequently founded in the area as well: the Muslim family of Palanpur, and the Kathis of Jasdan and Jetpur, established themselves under the sultans of Delhi (the Kathis are an aristocratic community of Hindus that, for reasons that are not clear, never gained recognition as Rajputs); and the houses of Idar, Radhanpur and Junagadh, descended from Mughal officials or their relatives who made themselves independent during the realignment of the eighteenth century.

The great majority of the states of Western India, however, began their existence not as separate kingdoms, but as grants of land made to the younger sons of kings. Most Indian states, particularly those ruled by Rajputs or other communities that had adopted Rajput institutions of government (such as the Muslim dynasties of Western India), passed undivided from father to eldest son or whomever else was considered the rightful heir. (The most notable exception was among the Kathis, who traditionally divided the inheritance among all the sons of a ruler.)[6] To ensure that his younger sons could support themselves, a ruler usually gave them a number of villages; the grantees kept the land revenue (a share of the agricultural produce, in cash or kind) from their villages and dispensed justice to the inhabitants. The descendants of these younger sons, however, remained under the suzerainty of the parent state, and were called the *bhayat* or brotherhood.[7] The relationship of the bhayat to their parent states mirrored that of the latter to the overlords of Gujarat: when the parent state was strong, the bhayat enjoyed local autonomy, but were compelled to affirm their subordination through the payment of tribute, and to supply soldiers on demand. When the parent state was weak, however, the more powerful members of the bhayat asserted their independence, becoming kings in their own right. Thus, the Saurashtra state of Rajkot was founded by a bhayat of Nawanagar; and Gondal, by a bhayat of Rajkot. The transformation of the bhayat into independent rulers was accelerated during times of disorder, and particularly in the conditions of virtual anarchy that prevailed in Saurashtra, Kutch and Mahi Kantha

---

95.

[6] See Chapter Ten.

[7] Recent works on this topic include Tambs-Lyche, *op. cit.*, *passim*, especially pp. 63-68, and Stern, *op. cit.*, especially pp. 1-62.

towards the end of the eighteenth century, although during such periods there was also a countervailing tendency on the part of more powerful states, which attempted to annex their weaker neighbours.

As Mughal authority in Gujarat began to decline in the 1690s, the states tried to evade their payments of tribute to Delhi; to force them to remit their dues, the imperial viceroy of Gujarat, backed by an army called the *mulkgiri*, annually visited the peninsula to collect the year's payments. After the death of the emperor Aurangzeb in 1707, many of the rulers became independent, and for a time were freed from paying tribute. By the mid-1730s, however, the Gaekwad, the principal Maratha leader in Gujarat, had begun to bring Saurashtra, Banas Kantha, and Mahi Kantha under his suzerainty. He did not at first levy tribute systematically as the Mughals had done, but occasionally sent troops to extort money or crops from the states; in imitation of the Mughals, he called these expeditions the mulkgiri. Then, in 1753 the Marathas captured the Gujarati capital, Ahmedabad. This event marked the definitive transfer of control over Gujarat from the Mughals to the Marathas, and a Maratha mulkgiri thereafter compelled most of the states of Gujarat to acknowledge their subordination by paying an annual tribute to the Gaekwad and his overlord, the Peshwa. The Maratha mulkgiri was extremely destructive. It entered the country each year at harvest time, commandeering food and fodder wherever it went, and destroying villages and crops in states that refused to pay tribute. The annual pillage impoverished people of all classes and led to a breakdown of order.[8] Under these uncertain conditions, many bhayat began to break away from the control of their parent states; and in 1803, some rulers in Saurashtra went so far as to seek protection against the Marathas by offering to cede their territories to the rising East India Company. At this time, however, the Company had no desire to become involved in the politics of the small kingdoms of Gujarat.

This was soon to change, however. In 1802, a usurper tried to seize the throne at the Gaekwad capital, Baroda; the Company helped the rightful prince to crush the rebellion, but only in return

---

[8] Cf. Bayly, *op. cit.*, p. 22: by the 1760s, the Marathas' "plundering incursions had given way to an efficient form of the Mughal revenue system."

for a series of agreements that placed Baroda under its suzerainty. The Gaekwad, like most rulers who accepted British paramountcy at this time, undertook to subsidise a body of Company troops stationed in his territory. This corps of disciplined, well-armed soldiers was ideally suited for the mulkgiri; but the British had no desire to supply men for a war of extortion against the tributary states, and in 1805 a new treaty between the Company and the Gaekwad stipulated that the subsidiary force "will proceed to Kattywar when there may be a real necessity for it; but the English Government ... must remain the judge of this necessity."[9] The government of Bombay, which conducted the Company's relations with Baroda, wanted to be certain that the Gaekwad would never demand that its troops march into Saurashtra. At the same time, the chaos caused by the mulkgiri threatened the supply of Saurashtra cotton that helped finance the Company's lucrative trade in Chinese tea.[10] There were also problems caused by Gujarati pirates preying on Company shipping; and the requests for protection from Saurashtra, and for help by the Gaekwad, suggested a solution. Several years earlier, the authorities at Calcutta (the capital of the British government of India until 1912, when it was replaced with New Delhi) had proposed that the British mediate a settlement by which the Saurashtra chiefs would promise to pay their tribute without any prompting from the mulkgiri, and Bombay now revived this proposal. The Gaekwad's government gladly agreed to the scheme, which would ensure regular payments without the expense of a great yearly expedition, and in 1807 the Company ordered Colonel Alexander Walker, its Resident at Baroda, to go to Saurashtra and persuade the chiefs to agree to make regular payments in return for

---

[9] Treaty of 21 Apr. 1805, in C.U. Aitchison, *A Collection of Treaties, Engagements and Sanads Relating to India and Neighbouring Countries* (5th edition, 14 volumes, Calcutta, 1929-1933), 6:340-347. For the Company's reluctance to see subsidiary troops used for the collection of revenue, see Bayly, *op. cit.*, p. 90, and Fisher, *Indirect Rule*, p. 199.

[10] The cotton trade is fully discussed in Pamela Nightingale, *Trade and Empire in Western India 1784-1806* (Cambridge, 1970), especially pp. 23-24, 128, 167-168, 182-183, 186-189, 210-213 and 215. See also Bayly, *op. cit.*, pp. 63-64, 77, 104-105.

an end to the mulkgiri.[11] Walker first calculated an appropriate tribute for each chief to pay to the Marathas, based on the mulkgiri's past exactions and the wealth of the state, and promised that this sum would never be changed. The chiefs then engaged to remit their tribute in quarterly instalments. As was noted above, Saurashtra had been in a state of virtual anarchy for many years, with chiefs and bhayat warring against one another. Walker had eliminated the need for the mulkgiri with his revenue engagements, but he knew that the Marathas stood little chance of receiving the tribute, and the British of obtaining their cotton, so long as the peninsula remained unsettled. To end the petty warfare in Saurashtra, he therefore guaranteed that each tribute-payer (as well as those other rulers who did not pay tribute to the Marathas) would retain his existing rights of government. This would deter ambitious rulers from trying to seize the lands of weaker neighbours; and the chiefs cemented the new order with security bonds, promising "That I will not feud with any other (Talukdar) [chief], nor will I harbour the outlaw of any other (Talukdar)..., nor will incite any other person to commit any act of violence."[12]

The Walker Settlement did not bring Saurashtra under British control (the East India Company had merely negotiated a settlement between the Marathas their tributaries).[13] In 1809, the Company

---

[11] Walker's own reports are in R. Hughes Thomas, editor, *Selections from the Records of the Bombay Government* (Bombay, 1856), n.s. 39, pp. 1-315. For short accounts of the Walker settlement, see Copland, *British Raj*, pp. 17-19; Howard Spodek, "Urban Politics in the Local Kingdoms of India: A View from the Princely Capitals of Saurashtra (Kathiawar) under British Rule," in *Modern Asian Studies*, 7, 2 (1973), pp. 253-275; Tambs-Lyche, *op. cit.*, pp. 289-290.

[12] The quotation is from Decennial Security Bond of Sowjee Puttoo, on behalf of Jhala Harisinhji, Aitchison, *op. cit.*, 6:18. See also Perpetual Revenue Engagement of Jhala Harisinhji, Thakor Saheb of Limbdi, *ibid.*, 6:17-18. Not all of the rulers executed security bonds at the time of Walker's visit; 147 were taken between 1807 and 1850, *ibid.*, 6:6. For the Company's insistence on peace between states, see Fisher, *Indirect Rule*, p. 248.

[13] Many chiefs also paid tribute to the Nawab of Junagadh, and in 1807-1808 executed revenue engagements similar to those that they had given for the Gaekwad tribute; A. Walker, "Review of the Proceedings (up to the month of May 1808) of the Honorable East India Company's Government, in the Western Peninsula of Guzerat; accompanied by miscellaneous information connected with the province of Kattywar," in Thomas, *op. cit.*, 39, pp. 267-305, at pp. 272-273.

mediated a similar agreement regarding the payment of the Maratha tribute by the ruler of Palanpur in Banas Kantha; and in 1811-1812, the same was done in Mahi Kantha.[14] The East India Company acquired paramountcy over Western India from the Marathas in several stages. In 1817, the Peshwa transferred to the Company his co-overlordship over Saurashtra and his share of the tribute; and in 1820 the other co-overlord, the Gaekwad, ceded all of his rights in Saurashtra and Mahi Kantha except the tribute, which was thenceforth collected on his behalf by the British.[15] Meanwhile, in 1816, a quarrel between two members of the ruling dynasty led to the collapse of the administration in Palanpur; when the disorder threatened to spread outside the state, the Company intervened and installed one of the disputants on the throne. Palanpur continued to pay tribute to Baroda, but, like the Gaekwad fourteen years earlier, the new ruler was compelled to show his gratitude by agreeing to subsidise a force of Company troops stationed in his territories. This brought the state firmly under British supremacy. Western Banas Kantha, where the leading ruler was the Nawab of Radhanpur, remained independent of the Marathas throughout the eighteenth century. The area came under British paramountcy in 1820, when (in return for help against Sindhi bandits) Radhanpur and the other states of western Banas Kantha agreed to pay tribute to the Company.[16] The government of Bombay grouped all of these states into Agencies, each under the authority of a British official who supervised the states and enforced the Company's paramountcy: the Palanpur Agency was created in 1817, the Kathiawar Agency in 1820, and the Mahi Kantha Agency in 1821.

---

[14] Engagement executed by Dewan Firoz Khan of Palanpur, 19 Nov. 1809, in Aitchison, *op. cit.*, 6:213-214; J.R. Keily, "Memoir on the Mahee Kanta; prepared, in May 1845 ... with subsequent additions," in Thomas, *op. cit.*, 12, pp. 1-53, at p. 6; Aitchison, *op. cit.*, 7:73, 88-100.

[15] Treaty between the East India Company and Bajirao Peshwa, 13 June 1817, Aitchison, *op. cit.*, 7:62-67; treaty between the East India Company and the Gaekwad, 3 Apr. 1820, *ibid.*, 6:361.

[16] Agreement executed by Dewan Fateh Khan of Palanpur, 28 Nov. 1817, Aitchison, *op. cit.*, 6:219-221; agreement executed by the Nawab of Radhanpur, 6 July 1820, *ibid.*, 6:232-233; agreement executed by the town and chiefs of Terwada, 28 July 1820, *ibid.*, 6:265; agreement executed by Waghela Karamsinhji, Thakor of Tharad, 23 Aug. 1826, *ibid.*, 6:266-267.

The establishment of British supremacy in Kutch, the remaining region of the future Western India States Agency, followed a somewhat different pattern. After the collapse of the Mughal empire, Kutch's geographical isolation protected it from Maratha domination, and it was completely independent throughout the eighteenth century. It was therefore spared the mulkgiri; but four Sindhi invasions (1762-1777) and an insane ruler or Rao, Rayadhanji II (1778-1813), meant that by the early nineteenth century, Kutch too was in a state of virtual anarchy, with much of the bhayat effectively independent. The breakdown of central authority made Kutch an ideal base for pirates and brigands, who seized ships and raided Saurashtra. The attacks worsened after the Walker Settlement restored order, and hence a measure of prosperity, to Saurashtra. The pirates preyed on ships belonging to the East India Company and its Indian allies, and the brigandage devastated the tributaries of the Gaekwad, a dependent of the Company. In 1809, the British therefore resolved to take measures against this lawlessness. There was no effective central government in Kutch, but the Company persuaded the two most powerful men in the state, Jamadar Fateh Muhammad (a Muslim officer who controlled the capital, Bhuj) and Hansraj (a former Dewan and now master of the principal port, Mandvi), to promise to eradicate piracy.[17] These arrangements, however, proved utterly ineffective. The mad Rao's son, Bharmalji II, succeeded to the throne in 1813 and restored royal power at Bhuj in 1815; but he too was unable to end his subjects' attacks on ships and on the people of Saurashtra. In December 1815, the Bombay government and the Gaekwad accordingly sent an army that captured Bhuj and compelled the Rao to sign a treaty. The treaty brought Kutch under British suzerainty, Bharmalji accepting a Resident and promising a large annual tribute to the Company; in return, the British undertook to restore the Rao's authority over all of Kutch, so that he could suppress the pirates and bandits. A few months later, it became apparent that Kutch could not afford the tribute, which was therefore remitted.[18]

---

[17] Agreements with Jamadar Fateh Muhammad, 26 Oct. 1809, Aitchison, *op. cit.*, 6:108, and with Dewan Hansraj Samedas Seth, 28 Oct. 1809, *ibid.*, 6:109.

[18] Treaty of 14 Jan. 1816, Aitchison, *op. cit.*, 6:111-113; deed of 16 Jan. 1816, *ibid.*, 6:113-114; supplementary treaty of 18 June 1816, *ibid.*, 6:114-115.

Both the Company and Bharmalji profited from the new treaty. Piracy and brigandage finally ended, and for the first time in a generation the bhayat was subject to the Rao. To ensure that his nobles never regained their independence, Bharmalji began to reduce their extensive privileges, and seized the villages of some of the leading members of the bhayat. The British might have tolerated this, but they would not acquiesce when Bharmalji made it clear that, with his power restored, he had no desire to remain subordinate to them. When several prominent nobles asked for protection against the Rao, the Company was only too happy to oblige, and in 1819 again invaded Kutch. This time, the British took no chances. They deposed Bharmalji, and then turned to the bhayat to elect a new Rao. The choice fell on Bharmalji's two-year-old son, Desalji II. After the election, the government of Bombay concluded a fresh treaty with Kutch, with the leaders of the bhayat signing on behalf of their infant prince.[19] The treaty confirmed British paramountcy, and indeed strengthened it by moving the headquarters of the Resident from the outlying town of Anjar to the state capital. Kutch had joined the rest of Gujarat in subordination to the Company.

II

For more than a century, the states of Western India remained subordinate to the government of Bombay through its political officers in Kutch, Kathiawar, Palanpur and Mahi Kantha, until the four old Agencies were merged into the new Western India States Agency.[20] Over the years, kingship in Western India underwent several changes that resulted directly from British rule, and affected the history of the region throughout the first half of the twentieth century. Although this book is not a general history of Indian kingship under British rule, which has been the subject of several

---

[19] Treaty of 13 Oct. 1819, Aitchison, *op. cit.*, 6:115-119.

[20] The titles of these political officers varied. In Kathiawar, the designation was Political Agent until 1902 and thereafter Agent to the Governor; the earlier Resident in Kutch and Political Superintendent of Palanpur were later both changed into Political Agents; and in Mahi Kantha, the title Political Agent was always used. The best account of the relations between the British and the rulers during this period is Copland, *British Raj*.

excellent studies,[21] these changes must be considered if one is to understand the nature and interests of the rulers of the Indian states.

The most obvious change concerned the relationship between the rulers and the other powerful elements in the state. Historically, all of the rulers–Rajputs, Muslims, Kathis, and others–were to a greater or lesser extent constrained by popular pressure, the *mahajans* or assemblies of urban caste leaders that periodically represented the subjects' viewpoint, and the nobility.[22] The nobility was composed principally of the ruler's bhayat, although it might also include men whose families had been prominent in the state before the establishment of the ruling dynasty, or descendants of companions-in-arms of early rulers. The monarch consulted regularly with his nobles, who besides administering their own villages were his partners in the administration. Few rulers were strong enough to take any step affecting the state without first securing the approval of the nobility.[23] These constraints generally

---

[21] Most recently Joanne Punzo Waghorne, *The Raja's Magic Clothes: Re-Visioning Kingship and Divinity in England's India* (University Park, Pennsylvania, 1994), and Pamela G. Price, *Kingship and Political Practice in Colonial India* (Cambridge, 1996).

[22] See Susanne Hoeber Rudolph, "The Princely States of Rajputana: Ethic, Authority, and Structure," in *The Indian Journal of Political Science*, 24, 1-4 (Jan.-Dec. 1963), pp. 14-32, especially pp. 19-23 and 28; Tambs-Lyche, *op. cit.*, *passim*; James Tod, *Travels in Western India, embracing a visit to the sacred mounts of the Jains, and the most celebrated shrines of the Hindu Faith between Rajpootana and the Indus; with an account of the ancient city of Nehrwalla* (London, 1839), pp. 70-71 and 181; for the mahajans, Tambs-Lyche, *op. cit.*, pp. 236-239.

[23] For almost two centuries observers and scholars have debated whether the relationship between rulers and their bhayat should be termed "feudal." Stern, *op. cit.*, pp. 23-62, gives a good summary of the debate. The earliest reference to it that I have found is in A. Walker, "Report on the districts of Dundooka, Ranpoor, and Gogo; the former condition of Guzerat, &c.," 20 July 1806, in Thomas, *op. cit.*, 39, pp. 43-55, at p. 52. This debate rests on the assumption that there was an objective reality in mediaeval Europe called "feudalism," and that one can easily ascertain whether a given non-European society bears enough of its characteristics to be considered "feudal." This assumption is, however, mistaken, and even historians of mediaeval Europe cannot agree on the characteristics of feudalism. See Elizabeth A.R. Brown, "The Tyranny of a Construct: Feudalism and Historians of Medieval Europe," in *The American Historical Review*, 79, 4 (Oct. 1974), pp. 1063-1088 (I am grateful to Professor Shannon McSheffrey for referring me to this article). This makes the debate on the feudal nature of the traditional Indian state rather pointless–except, perhaps, insofar as nineteenth and twentieth-century British

sufficed to ensure that monarchs ruled in accordance with local custom, and did not resort to exploitation or cruelty. And as has already been noted with regard to the bhayat, the relationship was always fluid: strong kings could keep the other constituents of the state in subjection, while weak ones could not. At the same time, despite the constraints, the traditional ruler was normally very much the ruler, and there was a strong sense that the legitimate king must remain as monarch no matter what. This may be illustrated by an episode from the history of the Jhala dynasty of Dhrangadhara, which in the mid-eighteenth century resided at its old capital of Halvad. Gajsinhji II (1745-1782) had a reputation as a spendthrift and a weakling, and had a constitutional aversion to bloodshed. A great lover of animals, he forbade hunting in the district under his administration when he was heir-apparent; and one of his first acts on becoming ruler was to ban butcher shops from his capital. During a famine in 1747, he opened the granaries and spent freely from his treasury for the benefit of the people and the animals of his realm, admitting all beasts to animal asylums in his major towns. Later in his reign, when his brother Sheshmallji seized the town of Dhrangadhara, Gajsinhji did not stir against him; it was his wife Jijima and her son Jasvatsinhji who assembled the men and arms to recover the town. Gajsinhji was widely seen as a bad king, unable to administer the state wisely or even to protect his throne, and he became known as *bholo*, "the simple." In 1759, Gajsinhji was captured by the Marathas and taken to Ahmedabad. The Marathas demanded a huge ransom of 120,000 rupees before freeing him. One might have expected that no one would miss this incompetent king, and that the ransom would not be paid. But his queen Jijima raised the money, and secured Gajsinhji's release. As Gajsinhji's descendant Meghrajji III of Dhrangadhara says, the reason "would seem to be some unwritten dynastic law and propriety"–a sense that, whatever his shortcomings, Gajsinhji was the legitimate king, whose position must be protected.[24]

---

officials occasionally sought to justify certain policies towards the states on the grounds that they were "restoring" proper relations between a ruler and his nobility, whether feudal or not.

[24] H.H. of Dhrangadhara.

But the establishment of British rule played havoc with the traditional balances. Great changes occurred in the relationship between the ruler and the bhayat, although their nature differed in Kutch on the one hand, and the rest of Western India on the other. It will be recalled that in 1819, an appeal from the Kutch bhayat served to justify the deposition of Rao Bharmalji and the establishment of Company overlordship. The bhayat chose Bharmalji's successor and concluded a treaty with the Company on behalf of their new rao; when the Rao reached adulthood in 1834, he was ordered to take "the constitutional and established advice of ... the members of the Jhareja Bhayad."[25] The bhayat, however, showed no interest in participating in the administration of Kutch; what they wanted was a maximum of autonomy within their estates. This they secured by a provision of the treaty of 1819 that stipulated that "The British Government ... engages to guarantee by separate deeds ... all Rajpoot Chiefs ... in full enjoyment of their possessions...." This included the land revenue from their estates (which covered almost half of Kutch), and civil and criminal jurisdiction over the inhabitants of their villages. The result was that the bhayat of Kutch became semi-autonomous landholders within the state, rather than partners of the Rao in governance. The revenue rights of the bha yat permanently restricted the income of the state treasury, and their jurisdictional powers hindered the administration of justice. All this "prevented the Rulers of Kutch from building up ... the efficient administration which the country needed ... [and] occupied their time and engrossed their activity almost to the exclusion of other matters."[26] It is not clear whether this was an accident, or a deliberate attempt to ensure that no future Rao would be strong enough to challenge British paramountcy. It was not unheard of for the East India Company to favour state nobility to counter the power

---

[25] Treaty of 5 July 1834, Aitchison, *op. cit.*, 6:125-126. The Jadejas are the ruling Rajput clan of Kutch.

[26] L.F. Rushbrook Williams, *The Black Hills: Kutch in History and Legend: A Study in Indian Local Loyalties* (London, 1958), p. 241. See also *ibid.*, pp. 232, 238-239 and 252-253.

of rulers.[27] However, one writer suggests that the British happened to arrive in Kutch at a time of unprecedented disorder and baronial independence; they mistook these unusual conditions for the norm, and sought to safeguard what they wrongly believed was the traditional relationship between the Rao and his bhayat. Yet another interpretation was put forward by the rulers of Kutch, who always claimed that the guarantees were originally intended to do no more than ensure that future princes did not follow Bharmalji's example by infringing on the legitimate rights of the bhayat.[28]

Saurashtra, Banas Kantha, and Mahi Kantha saw change of another kind. The Walker Settlement in Saurashtra in 1807, and similar agreements later executed in Mahi Kantha, guaranteed the rights of all tribute-payers in the region. Since the bhayat generally paid tribute separately from their parent-states, this gave them a status somewhat like that enjoyed by the Kutch bhayat after 1819. During the next half-century, however, British policy gradually recognised even the pettiest chiefs of the bhayat as completely independent of their parent states. The result of this was the fragmentation of Saurashtra, Banas Kantha, and Mahi Kantha. It is unlikely that more than about three dozen states in those regions were truly independent of any overlord other than the Marathas before 1800; but by 1900, British rule recognised over four hundred states, many of them ludicrously small and with no historical justification to any status higher than that of subordinate noble estates of the major states.[29]

British policy therefore completely transformed the relationship of ruler and bhayat, whether by making the latter into a landed

---

[27] See, for example, Manohar Malgonkar, *Chhatrapatis of Kolhapur* (Bombay, 1971), especially pp. 397-414 and 418-420; Susanne Hoeber Rudolph and Lloyd I. Rudolph, "Rajputana Under British Paramountcy: The failure of indirect rule," in Susanne Hoeber Rudolph and Lloyd I. Rudolph, *Essays on Rajputana: Reflections on History, Culture and Administration* (New Delhi, 1984), pp. 3-37, at pp. 9-11; Stern, *op. cit.*, especially pp. 15-16.

[28] Rushbrook Williams, *op. cit.*, pp. 204-207. Tod, *op. cit.*, suggests (pp. 483-491) that the Kutch bhayat had always enjoyed an unusual degree of independence, which was enhanced by British intervention. In 1945, the Paramount Power did allow the state to strip the bhayat of their judicial powers; see IOC R/1/1/4006, 4291 and 4319.

[29] See Chapter Six.

aristocracy whose activities centred on its own estates (as in Kutch) or by severing all connection (as in the rest of Western India). In either case, the result was that the bhayat–hitherto the most important counterbalance to the ruler within the state–ceased to play that role. The other checks (caste leaders, lesser nobles, and so on) also lost their old function, since over the years the new Paramount Power gave the rulers to understand that it would protect them from any discontent among their subjects. As the last ruling Maharaja of Kolhapur (a large state in Maharashtra) noted, by preventing rebellion, the British eliminated that sense of responsibility to their people, which had been essential to the rulers' survival.[30] And this meant that by the beginning of the twentieth century, the rulers enjoyed a more autocratic power over their subjects than ever before. In place of powerful nobles who functioned as partners in the administration, princes and chiefs were surrounded by subordinate bureaucrats whose function was to implement the monarch's wishes or to give advice.[31] Another change strengthened the rulers still further. For almost a hundred years before the establishment of British rule, the rulers had of necessity devoted themselves principally to defence:

> Apart from sustaining the rudiments of a civil administration their incomes went to keeping their defence works in good repair, in buying

---

[30] Adrian C. Mayer, "Perceptions of Princely Rule: Perspectives from a Biography," in *Contributions to Indian Sociology*, n.s., 15, 1 and 2 (1981), pp. 127-154, at pp. 138-139.

[31] This needs to be qualified in two ways. In the first place, officials might run the states with little or no input from the ruler. This could be because the ruler preferred to leave the administration to others (during the period under study, this was true of two successive Maharajas of Baroda, who allowed their Dewans to govern virtually as they saw fit); or because the ruler was a child or had been forcibly removed from the government by the Paramount Power (see Chapters Eight and Nine). In the second place, the power of rulers was occasionally limited by, for example, bureaucrats who used their positions to pursue private interests; see Susanne Hoeber Rudolph and Lloyd I. Rudolph, "Oligopolistic Competition Among State Elites in Princely India," in Rudolph and Rudolph, *Essays*, pp. 141-173, at p. 150. This book seems to emphasize the rulers' autocratic power when they are referred to by the names of their states–"Kutch" for the prince of Kutch. But while the implication that the ruler *was* the state is correct in many cases, it is done here simply for shorthand without any intention of suggesting more.

> sturdy war-worthy mounts, and weapons and artillery, in keeping a host of paid men constantly under arms and strings of healthy horses eating their heads off in the stables, a camel corps for patrolling the borders and carrying despatches, etc. And in building up a "provident fund" to buy off the Vikings from Pune and Baroda [the Marathas]![32]

The coming of peace that followed the establishment of British rule eliminated the need for such military expenditures, but the rulers continued to collect revenue at the same rates as before, and this left them a far larger disposable income than their predecessors had enjoyed. Not only were the counterbalancing elements of society gone: the other main internal limit on a ruler's power, the restricted finances, had also disappeared. The result was that during the period under study, the rulers of the Indian states were real kings, far from Nicholas Dirks's bearers of a Hollow Crown who ruled theatre states empty of all real content.[33] Even those who saw the princes as in some way illegitimate holders of power had to recognise that they did indeed possess real power, although its nature was changed from pre-colonial days. The same thing must be admitted by modern scholars. While the works of the subaltern school have emphasized the degree to which even the humblest elements of Indian society exercised their own agency, the fact remains that an individual ruler could affect all aspects of the lives of his subjects.

At the same time, a new external limit had come into being. The British were far more prone to interfere in the internal affairs of the states than any of their predecessors as Paramount Powers had been, and at any rate by the second half of the nineteenth century, they had the power to do so almost at will. This means that during the period under study, the rulers' ability to pursue their own interests was to a very great extent constrained by the degree of freedom that the British were prepared to allow them. From the time of its establishment in 1921, the Chamber of Princes also occasionally limited the rulers' freedom of action, particularly when an interventionist prince was Chancellor of the Chamber. For example, under Nawab Hamidullah Khan of Bhopal, Chancellor in 1931-1932

---

[32] H.H. of Dhrangadhara.

[33] Dirks, *op. cit.*

and from 1944 to 1947, the Chamber's Standing Committee regularly dispensed advice on the conduct of administration to rulers, often with the expectation that they would heed it.[34] Yet the Standing Committee was elected by the rulers themselves, and despite occasional friction, it is (as is noted below) best to see the Chamber's actions as expressive of a consensus among the princes, rather than as an agency external to them.

III

Just what were these interests of the rulers? A longstanding stereotype has the Indian princes as devoted solely to their own pleasure, and exploiting their people either to finance their enjoyments, or out of cruelty, at any rate to the extent permitted by current British policy.[35] And indeed, the changes wrought by British rule might well produce

> a chief with power and with little to fear and more ready money and more free time on his hands than his predecessors or he had ever known. Earlier, in the interludes of peace, surplus money, as after a plentiful harvest, was habitually used for sinking wells, damming rivers, digging lakes and on their masonry, for building castles, temples, and silos, *pathshalas* or *madrasas* (seminaries), *dharamshalas* (almshouses), and *pinjarapols* (animal asylums), and on founding new villages and on pilgrimages. Now, ... the Indian rulers had every temptation and opportunity to give themselves up to enjoyment, to extravagance, and to let others rule for them.[36]

---

[34] See Copland, *Princes of India*.

[35] The stereotype appears in propaganda, such as K.L. Gauba, *His Highness, or the Pathology of Princes* (Lahore, 1930) and in popular histories, for example Diwan Jarmani Dass, *Maharaja: Lives, Loves and Intrigues of Indian Princes* (Delhi and Bombay, 1970); but it is also hinted at in scholarly treatments, among them Ashton, *op. cit.*. Its pervasiveness is noted in Copland, *Princes of India*, pp. 3-5.

[36] H.H. of Dhrangadhara.

Such a man was Surag, who succeeded as chief of Jetpur in Saurashtra in 1936. He was accused of attempted kidnapping, of rape, and of theft; was arrested for assaulting police constables who stopped him for drunken driving in Delhi; oppressed his subjects with extortionate taxes; and during the Second World War diverted the rationed sugar intended for the people of his state, and sold it for personal gain on the black market.[37] But despite the stereotype, such bad rulers were very much a minority. In many states, a limited revenue base did mean that the level of public services was at a lower level than in British India. Nevertheless, the great majority of princes and chiefs in India took their duties seriously, and ruled their people accordingly. This is apparent from many pieces of evidence, ranging from the perusal of thousands of archival documents, to the attitude that, even fifty years after the end of monarchical rule, the ordinary people of many former Indian states still obviously hold towards their erstwhile royal families.[38]

The real interests of the rulers, then, did not centre on freedom to misgovern their people. It would obviously be ridiculous to claim that every prince held the views ascribed to them in this book. Nevertheless, the actions of the leading rulers of the Western India States Agency, most of whom were active in the Chamber of Princes, show that on the whole they shared common interests and goals.[39] And as far as these men, and comparable princes elsewhere in India are concerned, one word repeatedly turns up as being central to the rulers' interests. For example, in 1935, following the publication of the proposed new federal constitution for India, the Chamber of Princes passed a resolution on the same topic as had led to Ranjitsinhji's last speech two years earlier:

---

[37] See IOC R/1/1/4135, R/2/597/20 and R/2/599/33, and NAI WISA, C-44-13/1947.

[38] This point is noted by Copland, *Princes of India*, p. 285.

[39] The existence of a relatively small group of leading princes and ministers who to a large extent spoke for, and acted as representatives of, the whole princely order, is central to Copland, *Princes of India*, especially pp. 11-12.

> the inauguration and success of federation will depend entirely on the goodwill and co-operation of all the parties concerned, and upon the clear recognition of the Sovereignty of the States....[40]

And it is one of the main contentions of this book that the pursuit of "sovereignty" was the overriding interest of the rulers of the Indian states as a body throughout the last three decades of British rule in India. To them, the practical and symbolic aspects of sovereignty were inseparable. Certainly they wanted minimal British interference in the way they ran their states; in the words of the Maharaja of Patiala, one of the leading princes between the World Wars, "in the sphere of sovereignty which remains to us, however great or small that may be, we should in truth be masters."[41] But the symbols of sovereignty were equally important: "The Rajas prize the prestige attached to their position almost as highly as the powers pertaining to their sovereignty."[42] As a result, they treasured internationally-recognised "symbols of statehood or sovereignty," from office buildings to armies.[43] Indeed, the various manifestations of the concern for sovereignty are so closely linked by this underlying unity that it is difficult to separate them from one another. Nevertheless, an attempt may be made to classify the principal elements in the rulers' concept of sovereignty into five broad categories. First, there was ensuring that the Indian states continued to exist: if their kingdoms disappeared, the rulers would simply cease to be sovereigns. Secondly, there was minimising British intervention in state affairs; if all aspects of life and administration in the states were controlled by the Paramount Power, princely sovereignty would be a mere fiction. Thirdly, there was securing recognition as partners of the British in the government of India, as an hereditary right to play a part in questions of national

---

[40] K.M. Panikkar, *The Indian Princes in Council: A Record of the Chancellorship of His Highness the Maharaja of Patiala 1926-1931 and 1933-1936* (London, 1936), p. 114.

[41] Panikkar, *Indian Princes*, p. 156.

[42] St Nihal Singh, *The King's Indian Allies: The Rajas and their India* (London, 1916), p. 146.

[43] John Hurd II, *Some Economic Characteristics of the Princely States of India 1901-1931* (dissertation, University of Pennsylvania, 1969), pp. 121-122. See also Fisher, *Indirect Rule*, pp. 13, 441-454.

importance is the prerogative of sovereign monarchs. Fourthly, there was preserving those princely rights that symbolized sovereignty. And fifthly, there was the concept often expressed with the word *izzat*, or personal honour, which is especially strong among the Rajputs.[44] The traditional duties of the Indian king include safeguarding the izzat of his family and state. He must fight bravely, avenge all insults, and generally earn respect. This is not unconnected with a phenomenon in precolonial South India, where honour as demonstrated through symbols granted by superiors in court ritual and in temples played a central role in holding together society and "personal honor was a major preoccupation in political contexts."[45] Among the princes of the twentieth century, izzat took at least three forms. First, there was their izzat as monarchs: the rulers' dislike of British intervention in state affairs was partly motivated by a desire to administer their own people without outside interference, but it was also influenced by the view that intervention constituted an attack on their izzat, as it presupposed that they were unable to perform their hereditary function of ruling. Closely related to this was the izzat of the princes as a class, which had to prove itself worthy of the respect that it demanded; and a third izzat was that of the individual ruler or state, rather than of all the princes.

The attitudes of the rulers to the other two main players in Indian politics between the World Wars, the forces of organized politics and the British, are the subject of a stereotype as persistent as that of the hedonistic, exploitative prince. This is the image of the slavishly pro-British ruler, who joins with his country's foreign oppressors to crush the independence movement. There may have been some rulers of this stamp, but it was certainly not applicable to most. Rulers frequently made clear their support for the independence of India: in 1917, the Maharaja of Bikaner (like Patiala a leading ruler of the day) played a central role in securing a promise

---

[44] See John T. Hitchcock, "The Idea of the Martial Rajput," in Milton Singer, editor, *Traditional India: Structure and Change* (Philadelphia, 1959), pp. 10-17, and Tambs-Lyche, *op. cit.*, pp. 104-106. For the general context, see Julian Pitt-Rivers, "Honor", in *International Encyclopedia of the Social Sciences* (19 volumes, New York, 1968-1991), 6:503-511.

[45] Pamela Price, "Revolution and Rank in Tamil Nationalism," in *The Journal of Asian Studies*, 55, 2 (May 1996), pp. 359-383, at p. 362.

from the British government that India would one day attain responsible government; in 1933, the Maharaja of Patiala declared himself willing to devote his life to obtaining Dominion status for his country, and in 1940 the Chamber of Princes passed a resolution supporting the same objective.[46] And the British learned by hard experience that no number of concessions to the princely demand for sovereignty would lead the rulers to accede to demands from the Paramount Power that undercut their own interests. Two factors did, however, qualify this, and perhaps contributed to the stereotype. In the first place, there were the political realities of the day. As the present head of the royal family of Danta observes, "Congress accused the princes of being pro-British. This was not true; but the British were the Paramount Power, and if the princes wanted to serve their subjects, they had to establish a rapport with the British."[47] This required the rulers, for example, to make frequent declarations of loyalty to the British connection, or to phrase their pursuit of their own interests in terms that would suit the British–even when those interests actually involved reducing British control. The other qualification was the growing anti-monarchical tone of the leaders of the Indian National Congress, which would obviously assume control in Delhi after the departure of the British; as the transfer of power became imminent, many rulers emphasized their belief in British paramountcy as the lesser of two evils, without ever regarding it as a good thing in itself:

> M[other]'s enthusiasm over the loyalty of the Indian Princes is based on partly biased information. Some of them have a genuine regard for the West, but I don't suppose any of them like being controlled by us. The reason they support us is that when British control is removed the reactionary states will disappear faster than the kings in Europe after

---

[46] Copland, *Princes of India*, p. 37; Panikkar, *Indian Princes*, pp. 89-90; *India and the War: Communiqué issued by the Governor-General and Resolutions by the Indian National Congress, the All-India Moslem League and the Chamber of Princes*, Cmd 6196 (London, 1940), p. 8. Political calculation may have entered into these declarations, but Copland, *Princes of India*, pp. 76-77, notes that the rulers were by and large sincere Indian patriots.

[47] H.H. of Danta. Identical sentiments are expressed in N.R. Khadgawat (Director, Bikaner State Archives) to Raj Bahadur (Union Minister of Transport and Shipping), 25 Aug. 1965, NL Vyas Papers, file 2.

> the French Revolution. The newspapers mislead the public with stories of loyalty to the empire.[48]

The rulers' attitude to the political movements in India was similarly complex. It has already been noted that, at least in principle, many of them favoured the independence of India. One result of this was that the British were occasionally surprised at the rulers' lukewarm response to demonstrations of nationalist sentiment. This was striking in the 1930-1933 Civil Disobedience campaign, when many rulers neither suppressed their own people nor prevented their states from being used as bases for activities in British India. And once the assumption of power by Congress became imminent, many rulers naturally sought to ingratiate themselves with the incoming masters, and cooperated with them to the utmost extent possible.[49] Still, as far as their own states were concerned, the rulers' insistence on their sovereignty meant that they believed that they alone could decide what form of government their people should enjoy; thus, to their minds, the Raja of Aundh in Maharashtra was constitutionally free to establish Gandhian responsible government in his state, as he did in 1939, while other rulers were just as entitled to rule as autocrats if they felt it suited the circumstances.[50] Rulers were not oblivious to genuine grievances among their subjects; in 1927, the Maharaja of Patiala, then Chancellor of the Chamber of Princes, addressed a letter to his fellow rulers, in which he urged upon them the establishment of a "minimum of good government." His definition of that term accords closely with the demands of many of the political leaders in the states: limiting the ruler's privy purse (personal annual expenditures) to no more than ten percent of

---

[48] James Gibson (housemaster, Doon School, Dehra Dun), private letter, 14 Oct. 1938, in James Gibson, "Glimpses of a Passing Landscape," in *Indo-British Review*, 18, 2 (n.d.), pp. 27-48, at p. 29. For the rulers' growing feeling that British paramountcy was preferable to Congress rule, see Copland, *Princes of India*, pp. 131, 157-158, 206, 216-217.

[49] For the Civil Disobedience campaign, see Shiv Kumar Prasad Singh, *The Indian Ruling Princes and the National Movement: 1927-47* (New Delhi, 1991), pp. 33-37. The rulers' need to stay on the good side of the Congress is noted by Copland, *Princes of India*, p. 77.

[50] See Apa Pant, *An Unusual Raja: Mahatma Gandhi and the Aundh Experiment* (Hyderabad, 1989).

the state revenues; transfer of his judicial powers to an independent judiciary, and replacement of his arbitrary legislative powers with codes of law based on those in force in British India.[51] At the same time, as will be seen, the "popular movements" were by no means as representative as they claimed to be, and by giving in to their demands, the rulers would have done a disservice to the bulk of their people.

---

[51] Panikkar, *Indian Princes*, pp. 18-20. For the context of Patiala's proposals, see Copland, *Princes of India*, pp. 62-64. Copland notes, *ibid.*, pp. 229-232, that if the rulers had been more enthusiastic in implementing such reforms in the last days of British rule, they might have fared better in their efforts to preserve their sovereignty after independence.

CHAPTER TWO

POWER: THE POLITICIANS

It is difficult to propose a suitable name for the second player in politics in the Indian states in the interwar years, which called itself the "people" and sought to transfer some or all of the power of the monarchical rulers to men drawn from its own ranks. The term "people" has been adopted by some scholars, but it is not really an adequate designation, since this segment formed only a small part of the population of the states. There was a longstanding community of interest between the rulers on the one hand, and the cultivators, pastoralists, and service castes that made up the bulk of their subjects, on the other. Those who called themselves the "people" were almost invariably drawn from a different and much smaller segment of society, the urban Brahmans and mercantile communities, who in the twentieth century adopted modern political language to express their longstanding economic, cultural, and religious opposition to the monarchs and rural populace that dominated the political order.[1] Some scholars use the term "public" for this educated, generally wealthy group, but this still suggests a larger body than actually existed.[2] As for the British, they were wont to lump together as "Congress" all but the most moderate or

---

[1] There is a debate regarding the notion of a traditional hostility between rulers and their rural subjects, on the one hand, and urban Brahmans and merchants on the other. It is discussed in Tambs-Lyche, *op. cit.*, pp. 15, 143, 228-230, 233-234, 253, 256-274, 303, 304-306. For another aspect of the relationship between monarchs and merchants in the Rajput state, see Lawrence A. Babb, *Absent Lord: Ascetics and Kings in a Jain Ritual* (Berkeley, 1996).

[2] The rise of this "public" is a major theme of Price, *Kingship and Political Practice*. John R. Wood, "Rajkot: Indian Nationalism in the Princely Context: The Rajkot Satyagraha of 1938-9," in Robin Jeffrey, editor, *People, Princes and Paramount Power: Society and Politics in the Indian Princely States* (Delhi, 1978), pp. 240-274, notes (p. 272) that "less than a dozen of the 220-odd [*sic*] W[estern]. I[ndia]. S[tates]. A[gency]. states experienced any [political] agitation before 1947, most of it weak and prompted externally."

most communal political movements in India, but many of these were not connected with the Indian National Congress.[3] The word "Nationalist" is similarly open to objection, since Indian nationalism was often only a secondary concern among the groups that campaigned for political changes in the Indian states. This book opts for the word "politicians" for the members of these groups. This term may be too limiting, but it does convey the fact that these people more or less held a monopoly on non-princely political activity in the states of Western India.

The dominance of analogous groups in British India during the period under study, and their triumph in the states after 1947, may give a misleading idea of the size and impact of the politicians' organizations in the Indian states. Within the states, they were actually always the least important of the three players discussed in this book. This was partly because they represented only a small part of the population, but also because they were fragmented. As far as the Indian states are concerned, the various political movements fall into three distinct groups, which (despite increasing coalescence from the late 1930s) remained separate from one another until after independence: popular movements in individual states or groups of states; the Indian States' People's Conference, afterwards the All-India States' People's Conference (AISPC), which was established in 1927 to coordinate political activities in all the states of India; and the Indian National Congress itself.[4] Each of these groups had its own interests, and the relations of each with the rulers and the British followed rather different lines.[5]

---

[3] For example, the title of a Western India States Agency file (IOC R/2/650/460) on the activities of the Kathiawar Political Conference begins with the words "Congress propaganda," even though there were no formal links whatsoever between the Conference and the Congress.

[4] In 1939, an All-India States' Muslim League was established, ostensibly as a states counterpart of the All-India Muslim League. It seems to have worked mainly to preserve dynastic rule in those states with Muslim monarchs but largely Hindu populations. See V.K. Bawa, *The Last Nizam: The Life and Times of Mir Osman Ali Khan* (New Delhi, 1992), pp. 172, 221, 224.

[5] Manor notes that in Mysore state, there were two political movements, each drawing on a distinct segment of society: the non-Brahman rural landowners who sought to wrest power from the Maharaja and his Brahman officials in the state government; and the largely Brahman urban supporters of the Indian National Congress. In 1937, these two groups merged in the Mysore Congress. The situation

I

The connected history of political activism in the Indian states begins during and immediately after the First World War, with the formation of *praja mandals* and *lok parishads* (subjects' organizations and people's associations) in a number of states, particularly in modern Gujarat and Maharashtra. In what became the Western India States Agency, the Kathiawar Political Conference (Kathiawar Rajkiya Parishad) was established in 1921, ostensibly to lead organizations in individual states in Saurashtra. All of these bodies arose in response to grievances among educated and primarily urban state subjects (the emerging politicians) over such concerns as the lack of representation in government or the dominance of outsiders in official positions (in many states, Brahmans from other parts of India virtually monopolized the higher bureaucracy). In other words, from the beginning, the main concern of these organizations was with securing a share of the power in the state. They were established under the influence of the rise of the organized anti-British nationalist movement in India, often by states' people who had joined in Gandhi's Non-Cooperation campaign of 1920. With the notable exception of the Muslim Conference (later the National Conference) in Jammu and Kashmir, however, these movements were generally small and weak, and many of them consisted of no more than a handful of well-to-do exiles living in Bombay who occasionally gathered to criticize the administration of their home states.[6] By and large, they remained insignificant at least until the

---

was different in the Western India States Agency, where dominant rural groups were generally on good terms with the state administration, and left political activity of all kinds to urban Brahmans and merchants. James Manor, *Political Change in an Indian State: Mysore 1917-1955* (New Delhi, 1977).

[6] For the history of the states' people's movements, see "The All India States' People's Conference: A Brief History," typescript in NL AICC, non-categories file 17/1947; Ian Copland, "Congress Paternalism: The 'High Command' and the Struggle for Freedom in Princely India, c. 1920-1940," in *South Asia*, new series, 8, 1 and 2 (June-Dec. 1985), pp. 121-140; Manor, *op. cit.*; Vishnu Dayal Mathur, *States' People's Conference: Origin and Role in Rajasthan* (Jaipur, 1984); Barbara N. Ramusack, "Congress and the People's Movement in Princely India: Ambivalence in Strategy and Organization," in Richard Sisson and Stanley Wolpert, editors, *Congress and Indian Nationalism: The Pre-Independence Phase* (Berkeley,

mid-1930s, and were rarely seen as worthy of attention by either the rulers or the Paramount Power. This was to a great extent because, in Copland's words, "the vast majority of princely subjects in the 1930s were loyal and submissive."[7] Nor was this loyalty merely due to repression, as political leaders sometimes alleged; the states' people often had a deeply-rooted loyalty to their rulers, and reacted angrily to the sort of anti-princely criticism voiced by the people's movement. Thus, around 1939, the All-India States' People's Conference warned its local activists not to display the Congress flag in the Indian states or to criticize the rulers, as such acts would ensure that state subjects opposed the political movement.[8]

At first, the activities of the people's movements remained uncoordinated. In 1927, however, subjects of seventeen states in Gujarat and Maharashtra met in an Indian States' People's Conference in Bombay, and resolved to constitute the Conference as a permanent body, committed to a self-governing India and "The attainment of responsible government for the people in Indian States through representative institutions under the aegis of their rulers." The Conference sent representatives to the All-Parties' Conference which in 1928 brought together the principal political organizations with the objective of drafting an Indian-made constitution for a self-governing India; and in 1929, the second session of the Conference called for "the cooperation of the political organizations of British India" in the struggle for responsible government. At the same session, however, delegates reiterated that they did not want either the states or their rulers to disappear, noting that "the people of the Indian states are fully prepared to grant to the princes the same status, privileges and prerogatives as are possessed and enjoyed by

---

1988), pp. 377-403; Rudolph and Rudolph, "Rajputana Under British Paramountcy," pp. 17-20; Singh, *Indian Ruling Princes*; and, for Saurashtra in particular, Wood, *op. cit.*, pp. 250-254.

[7] Copland, "Congress Paternalism," p. 125. Indeed, this remained true of the majority of state subjects until after independence; Copland, *Princes of India*, pp. 227-228.

[8] "A brief analysis of the position concerning the display of the Flag of the Indian National Congress in the Indian States," NL SPC, file 186.

the Crown in England...."[9] During the first decade of its existence, this Indian States' People's Conference was, if anything, even less of a representative body than the individual states' people's organizations. It held its meetings in Bombay, and until 1947 every one of its presidents came from British India rather than the Indian states. Its efforts to expand beyond its roots in Gujarat and Maharashtra met with some success in 1931, when it absorbed the members of the defunct All-India States' Subjects' Conference (a parallel body established in South India in 1927), but it was never able even to secure the affiliation of all of the state political organizations.[10] The Paramount Power therefore saw no reason to give in to the Conference's demand that it be allowed to present the states' people's views before the Butler Committee on relations between the British and the princes in 1928, or the Second Round Table Conference in 1931. Rulers similarly saw the Conference as insignificant. Dhairyashil Rao, a son of the Maharaja of Baroda, was a guest at the first session in 1927;[11] but by and large, rulers paid no heed to the Conference, which was too tiny and unrepresentative to stand any chance of success in its bid for power.

II

As far as the British and the rulers were concerned, the only one of the three groups within state political life that was of any significance before the mid-1930s was the Indian National Congress, and even it was important in what might best be seen as a negative way.[12] The Congress was founded in 1885, but for fifty years it concentrated its efforts on British India. In its early decades, Con-

---

[9] For the establishment of the Indian States' People's Conference, see the works cited above, footnote 6, and Resolutions of the Indian States' People's Conference, second session (Bombay, 25-26 May 1929), NL AICC, G-110.

[10] For the AISPC's unsuccessful attempt in 1945 to secure the affiliation of the Kathiawar Rajya Praja Parishad, see NL SPC, file 95.

[11] "The All-India States' People's Conference."

[12] The best short accounts of the development of Congress policy towards the Indian states are in Copland, "Congress Paternalism;" Mathur, *States' People's Conference*, pp. 50-66; and Ramusack, "Congress and the People's Movement."

gress was favourably disposed to the rulers, who proved Indian capacity to rule and often provided employment to the educated administrators and lawyers who dominated the early Congress. Then, in 1920, M.K. Gandhi became leader of the Congress and set about transforming what had been a small club of anglicized intellectuals and professionals into a nationalistic mass party. This necessitated some acknowledgement of the politicians who sought a measure of power in princely India; from 1920 Congress officially supported responsible government in the states, and in 1922 it first admitted state subjects to its annual session.[13] Indeed, many state subjects joined in political affairs of an All-India nature, and the Gujaratis Gandhi and Sardar Vallabhbhai Patel attracted particularly strong support for the Civil Disobedience campaign of 1930 in a number of states in Western India. At the same time, the Congress leadership refused to interfere in state affairs: it rejected calls for men or money from states' people's organizations, and would not even establish Congress Committees in the states (state subjects who joined the Congress had to affiliate with neighbouring Provincial Committees).[14] State politicians were told that if they wished to bring about changes in their states, they must act alone; in 1936, Shantilal D. Shah, secretary of the Dhrangadhara State Praja Mandal, wrote to the Congress president Jawaharlal Nehru to request that the Congress extend its activities to the Indian states if the states' people called for its help in disputes with their rulers. Nehru replied that "I have already issued statements about work in the Indian States. Every kind of Congress work can be carried on there. But it is not our policy to violate laws at present, therefore no

---

[13] See NL AICC, G-35 (Part VII), and the annual resolutions in A.M. Zaidi and S.G. Zaidi, editors, *The Encyclopaedia of the Indian National Congress* (26 volumes to date, New Delhi, 1976-), *passim*. Resolutions regarding the states were passed at the 1920, 1928, 1929 and 1936 Congresses, and the special session of September 1923; by the All-India Congress Committee in October 1927, April 1935, and October 1937; and by the Congress Working Committee in January 1921 and March 1928. Some of these resolutions were of a general nature regarding Congress policy towards the states, while others addressed specific issues.

[14] See the requests for Congress help from states' people's organizations in NL AICC, G-27 (Parts 1-2)/1934.

conflict with the State authorities should be provoked."[15] State subjects who were interested in political activity should rather throw themselves into the national struggle for freedom, as Nehru pointed out to the States' People's Conference: "the time has come when the people of India States should take up a definite and clear attitude on the subject and should work with the rest of India for the realisation of the common goal of full freedom."[16]

This policy was very largely set by Mahatma Gandhi, for a combination of emotional and pragmatic reasons. As a state subject from a family with a tradition of public service to the princes of Saurashtra, the Mahatma was by nature inclined to counsel subjects' loyalty to their rulers. His belief in the value of the Indian past enhanced this inclination into a general support for traditional kingship, which he believed could (with some reforms) play a role in the modern world. At the same time, Gandhi did not wish to overextend Congress resources by entering state affairs: he knew that the states' people's movements were so weak that the Congress would suffer rather than gain by joining with them. Finally, as a lawyer, Gandhi knew that the monarchs were legally autocrats within their kingdoms, and he felt that a British Indian organization such as the Congress had no right to intervene in the affairs of sovereign states.[17] This attitude was shared by many of the Mahatma's colleagues; in 1934, Bhulabhai Desai, a leading member of the Congress Working Committee, raised a storm of protest among state politicians when he declared that the rulers' internal sovereignt-y was unfettered, and that they were free to determine the future of their states without reference to their subjects.[18]

The result of all of this was that while the Congress enjoyed widespread support in British India by the mid-1930s, it had virtually no presence in the Indian states. This was partly due to the party's self-denying policy as far as the states were concerned, but

---

[15] Shantilal D. Shah (Secretary, Dhrangadhara Praja Mandal) to Jawaharlal Nehru (President of the Indian National Congress), 19 Aug. 1936, and Nehru to Shah, undated, both NL AICC, G-27/1936.

[16] Nehru to Provincial Secretary for Kutch and Kathiawar States, Indian States' People s Conference, 2 Nov. 1933, NL Nehru Papers, Part I volume 34.

[17] See M.K. Gandhi, *The Indian States' Problem* (Ahmedabad, 1941).

[18] See NL AICC, G-27 (Part 1)/1934.

even more to the fact that the bulk of the population of most states was prepared to accept the lead of the rulers in political matters. And the majority of rulers during this period had no interest in giving their support to Congress. This was the true significance of Congress as far as the states were concerned: from the First World War until the late 1930s, the Paramount Power sought to make use of popular loyalty to the rulers so as to prevent the contagion of Congress from spreading to the states; and the way to do this was by maintaining the goodwill to Britain of the princes.[19] To the rulers, Congress at this stage posed only a very distant threat, and one that they were often prepared to tolerate; they might criticize it in order to secure some concession from the British, and on occasion actively suppress its few supporters within their dominions (as the Thakor Saheb of Limbdi did with the Civil Disobedience movement of 1930), but by and large saw no more reason to fear it than they did the States' People's Conference.

But all of this was to change. In the late 1930s, the states' people's movements became forces to be reckoned with, the Conference grew much more radical in its orientation, and finally the Congress turned its attention to state affairs. This drew the three strands of state politics together, and transformed the relationship of the politicians, the rulers, and the British. The first step seems to have been a great surge in the membership and activities of the people's movements in the individual states. The reasons for this are not clear, and various explanations have been offered, from the institution of full self-government in the provinces of British India in 1937 (which threw into sharp relief the complete lack of popular participation in the administration of most states) to a call that Jawaharlal Nehru made in 1936 for the politicization of the states' people.[20] The scope of the change was made obvious in 1937 by the outbreak of widespread agitation in support of responsible government in the large South Indian state of Mysore. The disturbances reached Western India the following year, with protests

---

[19] See Chapter Three.

[20] Copland, "Congress Paternalism," pp. 127-128; Manor, *op. cit.*; Mathur, *States' People's Conference*, pp. 36-37; Ramusack, "Congress and the People's Movement," p. 388.

against the unpopular Thakor Saheb of Rajkot and his Dewan.[21] This new militancy was a boon to the Indian States' People's Conference, whose leaders saw the opportunity to transform their relatively unimportant organization into a major player in Indian politics, indeed the states' counterpart of the Congress in British India. A step in this direction had already been taken in 1936, when the Conference revised its constitution with the goal of enlarging its membership, signified its desired role by renaming itself the All-India States' People's Conference or AISPC, and sought to build links with Congress by choosing the veteran Congressman Dr Pattabhi Sitaramayya as its president. The AISPC pursued, with considerable success, the affiliation of the praja mandals that were founded, revived, or enlarged across India during the agitation of 1937-1938.

Meanwhile, the attitude of Congress to involvement in state affairs had begun to change. To a large extent, this was because of the rise to positions of power in the party of leftists who opposed monarchy in any form. Thus, in 1934, the newly-organized Congress Socialists resolved that

> Inasmuch as the Indian States constitute a principal political and military support to British Imperialism and a source of feudal backwardness and reaction, this Conference declares that the abolition of Indian Princes can alone assure complete independence for the whole of India, and invites the people of the Indian States to fight side by side with the people of British India in the struggle for independence.[22]

These sentiments were shared by Jawaharlal Nehru, although for the time being his acceptance of Gandhi's leadership meant that he had to acquiesce in Congress's policy of non-interference. Nevertheless, Nehru admitted to being "a little too fond of running down kings and princes. I see little in their kind to admire or do reverence to," and in 1933 he commented that "what is really wrong is the whole Indian State system. Anything more incompetent, corrupt and autocratic it is difficult to imagine. I have no doubt in my mind that it must go completely before any proper solution of the Indian

---

[21] See Manor, *op. cit.*; Wood, *op. cit.*

[22] *The Servant of India*, 1 Nov. 1934, NL AICC, G-27 (Part II)/1934.

problem can be found." Nehru's autobiography, written in 1934-1935, included a vicious attack on the states and a denunciation of the Mahatma's policy towards them.[23]

These events posed a threat to the Gandhian old guard of Congress. Some leftists, such as Nehru, might be prepared to accept the Mahatma's dictation, however unwillingly; but there was a strong possibility that others, notably Subhas Chandra Bose, would take advantage of the disturbances in the states to build support for themselves in a constituency excluded by Gandhi's policy, and use that base to take control of the Indian National Congress. With the new constitution, the Government of India Act of 1935, many Congress leaders also concluded that as far as their party was concerned, responsible government in the states had become essential. The problem was that if its support remained confined to British India, the Congress would enjoy a perpetual minority in the projected federal legislature. If, however, it could add control of the state seats, it would acquire a majority. Unfortunately, the constitution provided that state representatives in the legislature would be nominated by the rulers, who would assuredly not appoint pro-Congress members unless the latter had assumed power in the states. These Congressmen were confident that responsible government in the states would give them this power, and thus dominance in the central legislative assembly.[24] The party began to reach out to the state politicians.[25] The last gasp of the old policy came in February 1938, when the Congress held its annual session at Haripura and approved Gandhi's demand that it reiterate its opposition to official party involvement in state affairs.[26] This Haripura Reso-

---

[23] Jawaharlal Nehru, *Glimpses of World History: being further letters to his daughter, written in prison, and containing a rambling account of history for young people* (New Delhi, 1982), p. 61; Nehru to Secretary, Bikaner Political Case Committee, 29 Oct. 1933, NL Nehru Papers, Part I volume 8; Jawaharlal Nehru, *An Autobiography* (New Delhi, 1980), pp. 529-534.

[24] Copland, "Congress Paternalism," pp. 127-129; Mathur, *States' People's Conference*, p. 65; Singh, *Indian Ruling Princes*, pp. 76-91.

[25] Thus, in 1936, the Indian National Congress for the first time endorsed the body that called itself the Mysore Congress; Manor, *op. cit.*

[26] NL AICC, G-35 (Part VII). See also Copland, "Congress Paternalism," p. 123.

lution enraged the states' people's organizations.[27] Some of Gandhi's chief associates now entered state politics, nominally as private individuals (in view of the resolution) but of course bearing with them enormous prestige as Congress leaders. The most notable was the conservative Sardar Patel, who as recently as 1936 had earned the ire of the AISPC with his rejection of Congress involvement in the states.[28] In March 1938, Patel took a leading role in reviving the moribund Kathiawar Political Conference, and the following August he took charge of the ongoing agitation in Rajkot. The Mahatma realised that he was in danger of losing control if he maintained his policy. At the beginning of December 1938, he announced that the Congress would henceforth respond to requests for help from the states' people.[29] The new policy was swiftly confirmed by the Congress Working Committee, and in March 1939 it was approved by the annual session held at Tripuri. Concrete steps were now taken to link the activities of the Congress and the AISPC, which provided the best means for Congress to enter state politics: in March, the Tripuri Congress approved joint meetings of the All-India Congress Committee with the Standing Committee of the AISPC; the same month, the AISPC met at Ludhiana, elected Jawaharlal Nehru as president, and agreed to accept the guidance of Congress; and at the beginning of 1940, the All-India Congress Committee reorganized its Indian States Department in order to bring the states' people into active participation as members of Provincial Congress Committees.[30] The result was growing contact among the Congress, the AISPC, and the state praja mandals, which meant that the longstanding British depiction of the praja mandals and the AISPC as branches of the Congress was becoming increasingly true.

The wave of agitation in the states died down by the end of 1939. In some cases, as in Rajkot, it simply showed itself futile; in others, most notably Limbdi, the majority of the population which

---

[27] See NL AICC, G-35 (Part VII).

[28] Kakalbhai Kothari (Provincial Secretary for Kutch and Kathiawar States, Indian States' People's Conference) to Nehru, 16 May 1936, NL AICC, G-27/1936.

[29] M.K. Gandhi, "States and People," in *Harijan*, 6, 43 (3 Dec. 1938), pp. 360-361.

[30] NL AICC, I.S.-1/1940.

supported the ruler brutally suppressed malcontents; and in still others, it was successfully defused by rulers who made tactical concessions on issues of particular concern to the politicians.[31] The Congress now sought to bring the states' people into All-India activities, rather than addressing local concerns, for example in securing their observance of the Independence Day declared by the Congress Working Committee on 26 January 1940.[32] This may have been partly because of confusion as to what the AISPC's and the Congress's ultimate goal with regard to the states was. On the one hand, from the Ludhiana session of March 1939, the AISPC favoured the merger into British India of all but a few states with very high revenues and large populations. On the other, the organization remained committed to the establishment of responsible government in the states, as it reiterated in the new constitution that it adopted in June 1939.[33] Similarly, while its president Nehru supported the proposed merger of almost all the states into British India, in 1942 the AISPC called on "the Rulers of the States to discard ancient and discarded notions of autocracy and, recognising the people's right to govern themselves, become the real leaders of a free people."[34] But even this was not necessarily sufficient to secure the support of the movement's nominal constituency, the entire population of the states; the Rajasthani people's leader Jai Narain Vyas noted that to gain popular support, the people's movements should emphasize the "actual follies of the ruler of the State" rather than stating any natural right to responsible government: "Ideals and ideologies are infinitely important but there has been a tendency to emphasise them too much to the detriment of the equally important questions of technique and driving power."[35] At the same time, the bringing in of state subjects to the Congress's All-India struggle could only boost the Congress's claim to represent the

---

[31] See the correspondence in IOC R/1/1/3281. Some aspects of the situation in Limbdi are discussed in Chapter Eight.

[32] See NL SPC, file 181(iii).

[33] Mathur, *States' People's Conference*, pp. 172-176. Proposals for the merger of the smaller states are discussed in Chapter Six.

[34] Nehru, *Autobiography*, p. 607; Nehru, Notes [1942], NL Nehru Papers, Notes, S. No. 188.

[35] Jai Narain Vyas, "Political Evolution in the Indian States," undated, NL Vyas Papers, file 8.

whole of the Indian people. This reorientation of the political movement led to changes in the dialogue of rulers, Paramount Power, and politicians. The British swiftly abandoned the policy of conciliating the rulers in favour of direct intervention in state affairs, as the best means of containing the nationalist movement in the states.[36]

The attitude of the rulers to the new political world was more complex. On the whole, they were not as terrified of politicization among their people as the British were. This is partly because the rulers knew that the bulk of their subjects remained loyal, or would at any rate return to their traditional loyalty if specific grievances were eliminated; also partly because even the fiercest firebrands of Congress were prepared to moderate their public pronouncements in private discussions–in 1937, Nehru commented to the Diwan of Mysore, Sir Mirza Ismail, that while civil liberty was essential for the people of the states, responsible government was merely a desideratum to be worked towards after civil liberty had been attained.[37] The result of this was that many rulers enjoyed tolerably good relations with the people's movements throughout the period under study. In the 1920s, for example, the Thakor Saheb of Rajkot adopted that badge of supporters of the political movement, homespun clothes.[38] In 1945 and 1946, the rulers of Udaipur and Gwalior allowed the AISPC to hold its annual sessions in their states; and when in November 1946 the Kathiawar Political Conference met at Dhrangadhara, the Maharaja Raj Saheb of that state hosted a tea party that was attended by some thirty leading members of the people's movement and the Congress, including the future prime minister of India Morarji Desai.[39] The Paramount Power was likely to denounce such behaviour as cowardice; in 1939, the Resident for the States of Western India commented that

---

[36] See Chapter Three.

[37] Nehru to Sir Mirza Ismail (Diwan of Mysore), 19 Oct. 1937 and 4 Nov. 1937, NL Nehru Papers, Part I vol. 34.

[38] Wood, *op. cit.*, p. 252. This Thakor Saheb was the predecessor of the Rajkot prince whose administration was the target of agitation in 1938-1939.

[39] "Extract from Fortnightly Report of the Baroda, Western India, and Gujarat States Agency for the Period ending the 15th November 1946," IOC R/1/1/4350.

> The Rulers of Kathiawar appear to have very little backbone or determination to face the issue, and I doubt if they will ever combine effectively. ... Their attitude is certainly somewhat defeatist and, as one of them told me..., they are all firmly convinced that Congress influence ... will soon be the paramount power throughout India and they are terrified of taking any action which will give offence to Congress.[40]

But even if this is true, it merely shows that the rulers were pursuing their goal of maintaining their sovereignty, in this case by establishing good relations with the future Paramount Power at the price of backing out of the alliance with the outgoing one.[41]

As far as the development of the Western India States Agency is concerned, then, the chief importance of the states' people's movements and the Congress is the way in which, over time, they affected the relations between the other two main players, the rulers and the British. Their quest for power within the states could not succeed until after the accession to power of the Congress in Delhi in 1947, but they continually influenced princely and British policies.

---

[40] E.C. Gibson (Resident) to Sir Bertrand Glancy (Political Adviser), 18 Jan. 1939, IOC R/1/1/3281.

[41] Copland, *Princes of India*, pp. 73-80, 168-169 and 216-217, notes particular efforts by the rulers at rapprochement with the Congress in 1929, 1938-1939, and 1946.

CHAPTER THREE

CONTROL: THE PARAMOUNT POWER

Literally millions of individual Britons (and not a few Indians) were involved in formulating and implementing the policies of the Paramount Power towards the Indian states, from the electorate of the United Kingdom to the political officers who represented the imperial overlords in the states. In this book, however, "the British" refers specifically to those individuals and groups who actually devised and carried out the imperial measures that in some way affected the states of Western India. In a sense, it is even less accurate to use the term "the British" here than it is to call local political leaders the "people," but this use may be defended on the grounds that by and large, the individuals and groups in question were the only Britons who had any significant impact on the rulers and people of the states. Just who these Britons were might vary from year to year and from incident to incident. Some indication of their identity may, however, be obtained through an examination of the structures of authority that carried British paramountcy. The broad outline of policy at any given time (towards not merely the states, but all India) was determined by the Secretary of State for India, a member of the British Cabinet and resident in London. The Secretary of State was a minister of the Crown and thus responsible to the British Parliament; but, as was general in British constitutional practice, his policy towards the states did not normally originate with Parliament. Rather, it was set by the minister himself, perhaps with the advice of his colleagues in Cabinet or of his subordinates, who included the departmental staff of the India Office in London, the Viceroy and the government of India in New Delhi, and the Political Department, also in New Delhi.[1] In practice, the Viceroy and the

[1] The office in Calcutta, from 1912 New Delhi, that was responsible for British relations with the Indian states was known successively as the Secret and Political Department from 1783 to 1843, the Foreign Department 1843-1914, the political section of the Foreign and Political Department 1914-1937, and the Political, or

Political Department usually played the decisive role of determining policy, justifying its adoption to the Secretary of State, and securing his concurrence, though on occasion (as during the abortive efforts to establish a federation in the 1930s) the Secretary of State took a more active role.

Detailed plans for implementing these broad outlines, as far as the states were concerned, were generally worked out by the Political Department, although often with considerable input from the India Office, the government of India, and political officers in the states. It was these last who were actually charged with enacting policy; in the Western India States Agency, the main political officers were the Agent to the Governor-General (called Resident after 1937), his Secretary, and two or three Political Agents. The role of the Political Department and the political officers was simply to effect as best they could the current policies that were set down by their superiors. To a large extent, this explains their apparent conservatism in matters of Indian politics–it seems as if until almost the moment of independence in 1947, these officers carried on as though they were oblivious to impending changes. Their correspondence shows that this impression is mistaken and that they knew full well what was happening around them; but it was simply not their place to develop creative responses to new situations.[2]

I

Even within the limited definition used here, "the British" were never a monolith. Again and again, there were disagreements and debates at all levels as to which policy ought to be followed in any

---

Crown, Department 1937-1947; in this book, all of these are called the Political Department. Until 1937, the Political Department was a branch of the government of India. It was then placed directly under the Secretary of State, but retained close links with the government of India as both were headed by the Viceroy–in the Political Department as Crown Representative, and in the government as Governor-General.

[2] The apparent conservatism of Britons in all walks of life in India is noted in Charles Allen, *Plain Tales from the Raj: Images of British India in the Twentieth Century* (Calcutta, 1992), p. 236. For political officers, see Bawa, *op. cit.*, p. 220.

particular case. In the end, however, one response was of necessity chosen and acted upon. As far as the Indian states were concerned, this response–and indeed, the way many Britons viewed the states in general–usually depended on the current assessment made in London and New Delhi of Britain's interests in India. The princes remained fairly consistent in the means by which they sought to safeguard their position as sovereigns, and the politicians were likewise steadfast in their pursuit of power. The British, on the other hand, periodically changed their policy towards the princes. The result was that

> Unlike relations between decentralized units of local government and a central government, or relations between units in a federal system, Indian princely states under British paramountcy operated under conditions more akin to those found surrounding great powers and client states, in which dependency and independence are relative and ambiguous, the limits on claims and interventions are unregulated by law or binding precedent, and the balance of mutual influence is subjcct to prevailing circumstances.[3]

At any given moment, these "prevailing circumstances" were the dominant attitude in the Political Department, which at bottom controlled the question of which party would be the victor if their interests clashed. This is because ultimate authority always rested with the British,[4] so that apparent successes by the princes actually represent tactical concessions by the Paramount Power during periods when it was seeking their support; when it was not, Delhi could simply ignore the rulers' concerns.

There are obviously grave dangers in ascribing a coherent intellectual system to an entire group of people on the basis of the surviving records of some of its individual members; some scholars have been able to evade this danger only by stating the most obvious truisms, as for example "The primary object of British rule was

---

[3] Susanne Hoeber Rudolph and Lloyd I. Rudolph with Mohan Singh, "A Bureaucratic Lineage in Princely India: elite formation and conflict in a patrimonial system," in Rudolph and Rudolph, *Essays*, pp. 81-140, at p. 126.

[4] This is hinted at in the Butler Report on the relationship between the Indian states and the Paramount Power. *East India (Indian States), Report of the Indian States Committee 1928-1929*, Cmd 3302 (London, 1929), especially pp. 23-32.

to protect and enhance the interests of Britain in India."[5] But there are sufficiently clear patterns in British policy towards the Indian states that some conclusions about its bases may be drawn. At all times, the guiding interest that the Paramount Power pursued was maintaining "control." Just what was to be controlled, and how, changed over time, however. For one thing, there were two broad outlooks on the relationship between the rulers and their subjects, and consequently on the place of the states in the imperial power structure. One group of British administrators saw the rulers as the all-powerful masters of their states, and therefore assumed that as long as the princes accepted British supremacy, their people would do the same; these autocrats could generally be trusted to govern tolerably well, and to stamp out the few outbreaks of disaffection that might appear among misguided subjects. If, then, the Paramount Power secured the support of the rulers, it would automatically enjoy that of their people. The peaceful and loyal states could devote all of their resources to supporting the goals of the imperial overlords; and some of the unimpeachable legitimacy of the princes' rule would be transferred to the foreign masters whose paramountcy they willingly accepted. But according to others, the princes were at heart oppressive tyrants, with little interest in their subjects' welfare; unless the British kept a close watch on affairs in the states, and corrected every abuse that came to their attention, popular discontent would overwhelm not merely the princes, but the Paramount Power that tolerated their misrule. Each of these outlooks contains some measure of truth, although on balance the first is probably a more accurate description of the situation in the great majority of states.[6] In either case, the British pursued control by trying to prevent opposition to their domination from developing in

---

[5] Tapan Raychaudhuri, "British Rule in India: An Assessment," in P.J. Marshall, editor, *The Cambridge Illustrated History of the British Empire* (Cambridge, 1996), pp. 357-369, at p. 365. The danger of trying to go any further is noted by Robert Eric Frykenberg in *The Journal of Asian Studies*, 56, 1 (Feb. 1997), pp. 237-238.

[6] Cf. Chapter One.

the states–under the first scenario, by conciliating the rulers; under the second, by courting their subjects.[7]

II

Within these two schools of thought, British policy towards the Indian states falls into several phases.[8] For over seventy years after the suppression of the great revolt of 1857, the principal objective was keeping control of India itself, where British rule was to be maintained against either fresh revolts or, from 1885, the rising Indian National Congress in British India. This was not seriously affected by either the Secretary of State Edwin Montagu's promise of responsible government in 1917, or the Viceroy Lord Irwin's declaration in 1929 that India would one day become a Dominion. During this period, the balance of opinion as to how that control was to be maintained shifted back and forth between the two camps. Events during the uprising convinced the Crown's first Viceroy of India, Lord Canning, that the states could serve as breakwaters to protect British rule against a tide of Indian opposition. But the princes would not consent to such an alliance until they had been persuaded that British rule was in their own interests. This was to be accomplished by means of judicious concessions to princely sentiment, for example the abandonment of the former policy of annexing states to British India. Nevertheless, Canning refused to give free rein to the rulers' demands for sovereignty, and he warned the princes that his guarantees of their position "will not debar the Government of India from stepping in to set right such serious abuses in a Native Government as may threaten any part of the Country with anarchy or disturbance...."[9] By the time of Canning's successor Lord Lawrence (Viceroy 1864-1869), this belief had translated into a concerted policy of forcing the rulers to implement "reforms." In theory, the reforms aimed to "modernise" or

---

[7] The existence of these two viewpoints is noted in Copland, *Princes of India*, pp. 18, 21-25.

[8] The most recent overview of these phases is Copland, *Princes of India*.

[9] Lord Canning (Viceroy), 30 Apr. 1860, quoted in Sir William Lee-Warner, *The Native States of India* (London, 1910), p. 164.

"develop" the conditions under which the states' people lived; they arose from a belief that western methods meant progress, and that imposing them would fulfil a British duty of improving the lot of the Indian people. This was particularly important because performing this supposed duty was seen as one of the bases of the legitimacy of the British raj in India.[10] This was probably not a conscious attempt to build support for British control among the rulers' subjects. Rather, it reflected the notion that imperial rule in India was secure; the goodwill of the princes was no longer necessary, and the colonial masters could resume their self-appointed task of bringing the supposed benefits of western civilisation to their dependants. It must always be borne in mind that these reforms were of an administrative and social nature, not political: they were aimed at making the administration more efficient, and at providing such elements of a social infrastructure as schools, hospitals, and jails (most of which, cynics might suggest, could function as instruments of social control); but, until the 1930s or even 1940s, there was no idea of increasing popular participation in the government.

Organized Indian nationalism came into its own with the establishment of the Indian National Congress in 1885. Particularly after the partition of Bengal in 1905, many nationalists grew increasingly anti-imperialist in outlook. By the first decade of the twentieth century, the British were therefore actively seeking allies to help them hold their position in India, and they turned to the rulers of the Indian states. The strains of the First World War gave further impetus to this search. The allegiance of the rulers would demonstrate the existence of a group of powerful Indians who rejected militant nationalism and if necessary could assist in suppressing it. Even more important, however, was the assumption that the bulk of the people of the states were loyal to their rulers. This meant that if the rulers remained content with British overlordship, their subjects would too, and the states would therefore serve as regions "uncontaminated" by Indian nationalism. The easiest way for the Paramount Power to court princely support was to give some recognition to the princes' claims of sovereignty, a process that could

---

[10] See Mihir Kumar Ray, *Princely States and the Paramount Power 1858-1876: A study on the nature of political relationship between the British Government and the Indian State* (New Delhi, 1981).

always be justified with the notion that the terms of nineteenth-century treaties meant that the rulers were entitled to some measure of autonomy.[11]

In 1909, the Viceroy Lord Minto launched the new policy with a speech at Udaipur in Rajasthan. While recognising that "the Imperial Government has assumed a certain degree of responsibility for the general soundness of [the princes'] administration and could not consent to incur the reproach of being an indirect instrument of misrule," Minto insisted that his officers "accept the general system of administration to which the Chief and his people have been accustomed. The methods sanctioned by tradition in States are usually well adapted to the needs and relations of the ruler and his people."[12] The announcement of minimal interference in the internal affairs of the states was quickly followed by other concessions to the princes' demand for sovereignty. One man was literally given sovereignty when in 1911 the British Indian landed estate of Benares (now in Uttar Pradesh) was transformed into a full-fledged state.[13] Soon afterwards, a century-old policy was reversed. From almost the beginning of British overlordship, the Paramount Power strictly limited contacts among rulers, who could deal with each other only on such household matters as marriage negotiations. By the early twentieth century, however, several leading princes were demanding an end to this enforced isolation, and the right to participate in the governance of the Indian empire. In 1916, the Viceroy Lord Chelmsford gave in to this demand and convened the first conference of princes and chiefs at Delhi. Five years later, this conference was institutionalised with the inauguration of the Chamber of Princes. The Montagu-Chelmsford Report of 1918, which formed the basis of the Government of India Act, 1919, gave formal recognition to many of the rulers' claims to autonomy. Sir Harcourt Butler's Indian States Committee of 1928, while upholding the all-encompassing nature of British paramountcy over the states,

---

[11] See Ramusack, *Princes of India*, pp. 63-72. For the British attitude to princely sovereignty, see Fisher, *Indirect Rule*, pp. 13, 441-454.

[12] The speech is in Adrian Sever, editor, *Documents and Speeches on the Indian Princely States* (2 volumes, Delhi, 1985), 1:375-377.

[13] The connection between this and the Paramount Power's desire for princely allies is noted by Fisher, *Indirect Rule*, pp. 2, 452.

specified that the rulers' political relations were with the Crown, not the government of India, a definition that represented a major concession to the rulers' claims to sovereignty.[14] It is only with slight exaggeration that the widow of the last ruling Maharaja of Gwalior comments that from this point onwards, "British control had relaxed to the vanishing point and the princes had become real kings."[15] From 1909 to 1930, the Paramount Power was interested primarily in winning the support of the leaders of princely India (generally the men who dominated the Chamber of Princes after 1921), in the hope that if it met their requests they would use their influence to secure the allegiance of the mass of less prominent rulers. This attentiveness retreated somewhat during the viceroyalty of Lord Reading from 1921 to 1926; Reading and his Political Secretary Sir John Thompson were not favourably disposed to the rulers' claims, and wherever possible disregarded them. The Minto policy soon resumed, however, with the arrival in 1926-1927 of the more congenial Lord Irwin as Viceroy and Sir Charles Watson as Political Secretary.[16]

But the Round Table Conferences of 1930-1932, and the resulting 1935 Government of India Act, changed the object that was to be kept under British control. The new constitution transferred a large share of authority from British to Indian hands, including full powers over provincial governments and a large share of authority at the centre. The British could no longer control India as they had done in the past; but they could try to keep the Indian National Congress under control, particularly by securing the participation of the rulers in the Indian federation. The constitution provided that every ruler would accede individually to the federation; and during and after the conferences, the British therefore had to win the goodwill of *all* rulers rather than merely the leaders of the Chamber. This occurred in two main phases: during the runup to the Parliamentary vote on the constitution bill in 1935, when the Paramount Power sought to secure the princes' allegiance so that federation could be presented as a viable option for the India of the future;

---

[14] *Report of the Indian States Committee*, especially p. 13.

[15] Vijaya Raje Scindia with Manohar Malgonkar, *The Last Maharani of Gwalior: An Autobiography* (Albany, 1987), p. 144.

[16] Copland, *Princes of India*, pp. 44-45, 61.

and in 1938-1939, when the Political Department tried in vain to persuade the rulers to accept the terms of accession. Now, concessions were made not merely to the major rulers who ruled large populations or commanded wide support in the Chamber of Princes, but to rank-and-file men who were insignificant except as the rulers of potential member-states of the federation.

In the late 1930s, however, the Paramount Power came to the conclusion that the strategy of securing the friendship of the princes had been misconceived. The federation was initially supported by the leading rulers, and with this in mind the British government expended much time and effort in securing the agreement of all parties in a viable constitution. But the princes' obstructionism during the drafting of the bill in 1932-1935 convinced many Britons that they were unworthy of much solicitude, and this feeling was reinforced when the states rejected the final terms of federation in 1939. In September 1939 the Viceroy Lord Linlithgow accordingly suspended for the duration of the Second World War the efforts to lure in the princes, which eliminated a major reason for conciliating them. Moreover, it was well known that, as has already been noted, the increasing opposition to monarchical government within the Indian National Congress made many rulers more willing to accept British control than they would otherwise have been. The assumption that this acceptance could be taken for granted might easily turn into a greater willingness on the part of the Paramount Power to ignore princely sensibilities.

This was accompanied by the growth of organized political movements in the Indian states in 1937-1939, and the new interest of the Indian National Congress in the states.[17] Despite the existence of the people's movements, the inhabitants of the states had hitherto been largely apolitical; but the agitation seemed sufficiently widespread to suggest that the state subjects could not be counted on to accept their rulers' lead without question. And the role of the Congress leaders Mahatma Gandhi and Sardar Patel in the Rajkot agitation of 1939 raised fears in Delhi and Whitehall that the Congress might resolve popular grievances in the states that the Paramount Power had ignored. Besides spreading Indian nationalism to

---

[17] See Chapter Two.

areas where it had hitherto enjoyed only limited success, this would hand Congressmen a great propaganda victory by confirming their claims that British rule was responsible for oppressing the Indian people. At the same time, it might eventually deprive the princes of their place as the accepted leaders of a large part of the Indian population, which in turn would undercut the rulers' legitimacy as participants in the administration of the country.[18] It did not really matter whether most of the people of the states considered themselves to be misgoverned or not. The fact was that many Britons concluded that the previous thirty years had seen dangerously generous concessions to princely sentiment, which had fostered maladministration in the states without noticeably enhancing British control.

By now, the object of that control had changed again. Despite the firm opposition of Winston Churchill (who became prime minister of the United Kingdom in 1940), it was by this time clear that Indian independence, and a Congress administration, would come sooner rather than later. From 1939 until the end of British rule in 1947, the Paramount Power devoted itself merely to controlling the situation, by preserving order as well as could be done, and by seeking to discharge whatever of Britain's self-defined obligations in India were salvageable. As far as the Indian states were concerned, this meant maintaining stability, and giving the states what it was hoped would be sufficient strength to justify their continued existence in an independent Congress-ruled India (as from 1857, the Paramount Power had asserted a duty of preserving the states). This became particularly urgent during the last year of British paramountcy in India, when the British government recognised the necessity of repudiating the Crown's treaties and other guarantees of protection to the states. As Copland notes, it hoped to erase some of the bad feeling that this must inevitably create by giving the states a fighting chance of survival, which meant striking at what were seen as their main weaknesses.[19]

The result was an abrupt reversal of British policy towards the states, as the needs of the moment seemed to call for extensive

---

[18] Ashton, *op. cit.*, p.198.

[19] Copland, *Princes of India*, pp. 217-222.

interference in state affairs: in the words of the Viceroy Lord Linlithgow,

> we may need very substantially to tighten up our control and to bring pressure to bear on individual Rulers to improve conditions, to meet grievances, to reduce the amount of money spent from the revenues of the State on the Ruling family, and the like. ... we shall find ourselves compelled–in defence of the States as a whole–substantially to raise those standards of administration by which we have hitherto measured performance in the States and the need for direct stimulation of Rulers and Darbars by the Paramount Power.[20]

Princely sovereignty was now overridden to a degree unseen since 1909. The new policy affected virtually all areas of the relationship between the states and the British, and the rulers' protests were largely ignored.[21] In March 1939, Linlithgow informed the Chamber of Princes

> that heavy obligations lay upon the Rulers in these days, and that it was up to them to adjust themselves to changing conditions, to reside in their States, to limit their privy purse, to provide popular institutions, to be active in searching a course for remedying administrative grievances and the like....[22]

Linlithgow and the Secretary of State, Lord Zetland, agreed that if the rulers were unwilling to carry out these measures, the Paramount Power would be justified in stepping in to enforce them. The forms of respect for the rulers' sovereignty were still observed, but in practice that sovereignty was ignored: in 1946, the chief of Lathi in Saurashtra was "advised" to take a particular measure; when he declined to take this advice, the Resident commented that

---

[20] Lord Linlithgow (Viceroy) to Sir Bertrand Glancy (Political Adviser), 27 Dec. 1938, IOC R/1/1/3416(1).

[21] For the origins of the new policy, see Ashton, *op. cit.*, pp. 159-184, and Copland, *Princes of India*, pp. 163-174. Copland, pp. 187-189, suggests a brief resumption of favourable treatment by the Paramount Power in 1940-1942, but this does not alter the general picture.

[22] Linlithgow to Lord Zetland (Secretary of State), 14 Mar. 1939, IOC L/P&S/13/971.

> the Chief knows well enough that when His Excellency the Crown Representative is compelled to issue orders, he describes them in the interests of the States themselves as "advice;" in political practice therefore the words are practically synonyms.[23]

The Paramount Power's desire to control the situation during the last years of British rule in India ensured that from 1939 to 1947, the princes' quest for sovereignty was severely limited by what for the previous three decades had been a friendly imperial overlord.

III

To a great extent, the relationship between the rulers and the British was moulded by the development and resolution of conflicts between the two parties, as the rulers' desire for sovereignty clashed with current British notions of how best to maintain control. Particularly in the context of the change of policy in 1939, it must be noted that while some scholars accept the view that excessive respect for the rulers' sovereignty between the World Wars led to a decline in the quality of government in the states, this reflects British perception rather than reality.[24] Whatever the picture painted by their enemies, most rulers in the states of Western India governed as well as their resources and their abilities permitted; as one Residency official commented, "They are a very decent lot on the whole–I wish all the Princes in India were as good."[25] In any case, a general picture of reformist Britons and reactionary rulers is inaccurate. It is true that the rulers were often conservative, in that they were often disinclined to adopt new forms or practices of government. This was not, however, a sign of a lack of interest in their people's welfare. Rather, it reflected the rulers' notion of the best way to serve their subjects. By and large, the rulers carried out

---

[23] Sir Cyril Hancock (Resident) to L.C.L. Griffin (Secretary to Crown Representative), 20 Sept. 1946, IOC R/2/579/28.

[24] Cf. Ashton, *op. cit.*, p. 198.

[25] H.A.N. Barlow (Under-Secretary to AGG), private letter, 8 Apr. 1934, SAS Barlow Papers, II.34.

such traditional royal good works as the sinking of wells throughout the British period; but they opposed what was seen as the gratuitous adoption of British forms. In 1928, the Maharaja of Patiala commented that

> Western institutions, Western standards, and Western customs, are not necessarily suited to polities where Ruler and ruled who are of one race, and who thoroughly understand one another, are still closely bound together by the ties of traditional sentiment. ... the ancient customs and the long-standing traditions of the Indian States have an intrinsic value of their own, and a part to play even in the world of today....[26]

British "reforms" were not necessarily as disinterested as they sometimes appeared. In the mid-1940s, for example, Sir Cyril Hancock, the Resident for the Western India states, encountered the opposition of the rulers when he promoted a scheme under which the states of Saurashtra would build roads linking all of the towns of the peninsula. The rulers' stance was motivated not by obliviousness to their people's needs, but by the fact that the towns were already connected by rail. It would have been far more useful to construct roads tying villages to the railway towns, and it was widely believed that Hancock's more glamorous project was aimed at securing his own reputation rather that at improving communications in Saurashtra.[27] Nor were the rulers oblivious to the value of some British innovations. It has already been noted that Patiala urged the rulers to enact extensive administrative reforms.[28] At the time, his call was largely ignored, but by the 1940s it was widely heeded. Especially in the wake of the Second World War, many rulers sought to safeguard their position in view of the impending lapse of paramountcy by seeking to "broadbase [*sic*] the administration and associate popular elements with it through internal reforms."[29] It is true that this was partly a response to rising criticism

---

[26] Panikkar, *Indian Princes*, pp. 137-161.

[27] H.H. of Dhrangadhara.

[28] See Chapter One.

[29] Bawa, *op. cit.*, p. 223. For examples, see Copland, *Princes of India*, pp. 212-213, although Copland notes (pp. 277-279) that this reformism did not go far enough to secure mass support for the rulers.

of the princes in British India and occasionally in their own states; but in general, the point at issue was not whether the British or the rulers held a monopoly on good government, but on just what good government was.[30]

[30] For one reformist ruler, see John McLeod, "A model prince? Maharana Bhavani Singh and the end of India's states," in *History Today*, 45, 12 (Dec. 1995), pp. 41-46.

PART TWO: QUESTION, CRISIS, PROBLEM

CHAPTER FOUR

THE QUESTION OF POLITICAL RELATIONS

In 1916, the first conference of princes and chiefs at Delhi assembled major rulers to discuss matters of common interest to the states and British India. The princes also engaged in private talks among themselves, all but forbidden for a century, and here they dealt with many other topics. Among these were the relative merits of political relations with the central and the provincial governments. For at this time, British authority over the Indian states was divided. The territories that later formed the Western India States Agency were grouped into four Agencies subordinate to the government of the province of Bombay. Bombay held charge of a further 101 states in modern Sind, Gujarat, Maharashtra and Karnataka, and indeed most Indian states were under the control of provinces: Madras included five states, Bihar and Orissa twenty-six, Punjab thirty-four, and so on. For historical reasons, however, the central government of India in New Delhi directly supervised British relations with certain other states, including the territories of the four top-ranking princes (the rulers of Hyderabad, Mysore, Baroda, and Jammu and Kashmir) and the states in what are now Rajasthan (the Rajputana Agency) and northern Madhya Pradesh (the Central India Agency).[1] At the close of the 1916 conference, eight prominent rulers from states in Bombay province asked the Viceroy Lord Chelmsford to transfer them to the control of the government of India, on the grounds that "We ... have been impressed, from the experience of this Conference and from the conversations we have had with our Brother-Princes in direct relations with the Government of India, with the

---

[1] See the Agency histories in Aitchison, *op. cit.*, and *Imperial Gazetteer of India* (26 volumes, Oxford, 1908-1909); see also Michael H. Fisher, "Indirect Rule in the British Empire: The Foundations of the Residency System in India (1764-1858)," in *Modern Asian Studies*, 18, 3 (1984), pp. 393-428, and Fisher, *Indirect Rule*.

advantage of being similarly placed."[2] Although they did not explain what these advantages were, it will be seen that the Bombay princes hoped that the end of provincial control would help them to maintain and extend the symbols and the reality of their sovereignty.

Over the previous forty years, the government of India had periodically proposed that, in the interests of uniformity, it should take over some or all of the states that were under the supervision of provinces. This suggestion had always been resisted by the provincial governments, and was repeatedly rejected by successive Secretaries of State in London.[3] Now, however, the Paramount Power heeded the call for transfer, and despite provincial objections, all of the states hitherto under provinces were placed in new Agencies subordinate to the government of India between 1921 and 1936. At the same time, in response to a second demand from the princes, major states were placed in "direct relations" with the government of India, which meant that they were removed from the supervision of local British Political Agents. Then, however, the tightening of British control over the states in the 1930s virtually ended direct relations, despite protests that this constituted an attack on princely sovereignty, although it did not restore provincial control over the states. The establishment of the Western India States Agency in 1924 formed part of the new policy of transfer; and its internal organization over the next two decades reflected the extension and elimination of direct relations. The history of the Agency is therefore illustrative of one aspect of both the rulers' continuing drive for sovereignty, and the changing British view of the relationship between the states and the Paramount Power.

I

When they requested transfer from provincial control in 1916, the princes no doubt hoped that the Political Department in far-off

---

[2] Kolhapur, Rajpipla, Palanpur, Kutch, Nawanagar, Morvi, Gondal and Idar to Lord Chelmsford (Viceroy), 3 Nov. 1916, IOC R/2/572/1.

[3] See I.F.S. Copland, "The Baroda Crisis of 1873-77: A Study in Governmental Rivalry," in *Modern Asian Studies*, 2, 2 (1968), pp. 97-123.

Delhi, dealing with a multitude of rulers from all over India, would be less likely to try to interfere in the internal affairs of their states than the nearby government of Bombay.[4] But this practical consideration was probably less important to the princes than the fact that transfer would raise their status in several ways. Most of the greatest states in India were in political relations with the central government; for besides the four premier ones, such major states as Bhopal and Bikaner came under Delhi because they were included in the Central India and Rajputana Agencies. It therefore seemed to be the mark of an important state to be subordinated to the government of India rather than a provincial government; and the Bombay rulers probably felt that by granting their request for transfer, the Paramount Power would recognise that they ranked among the great princes of India.[5] Moreover, for several years the leaders of the princes had been urging the Paramount Power to treat them as partners in the administration of India, rather than as subordinate chiefs. So long as rulers remained subject to provincial governments, it was clear that they were regarded as mere local administrators, but transfer would recognise that they were indeed partners. Finally, at least some Bombay princes had differences with the provincial authorities, and anticipated more favourable treatment from the central government (perhaps simply because Delhi's record was less well-known than Bombay's). For example, several rulers believed that Bombay was less generous than Delhi in bestowing honours, an important symbol of sovereignty.[6]

---

[4] The following account of the campaign to transfer the Bombay states is based on IOC R/1/1/661, R/1/1/1598(1), R/1/1/1598(2) and R/2/572/1. See also Copland, *British Raj*, pp. 250-260.

[5] In 1924, when he learned that his state would not be transferred with the Western India States Agency, the Maharaja of Kolhapur protested that his subjects would feel that the British had slighted him by leaving him under Bombay. Note by K.S. Fitze (PD India), 20 Nov. 1924, IOC R/1/1/1598(1).

[6] The issue of honours is noted in Sir Samuel Hoare (Secretary of State) to Lord Brabourne (Governor of Bombay), 4 May 1934, IOC L/P&S/13/896. Just two and a half years after transfer took place in 1924, many princes believed that Bombay had in fact been more generous with honours than Delhi was; C.C. Watson (AGG) to G. Cunningham (Private Secretary to Viceroy), 9 Feb. 1927, IOC R/1/4/458. For honours, see Chapter Eleven.

In any case, Chelmsford took the proposal to heart, and in 1918 he and the Secretary of State, Edwin Montagu, recommended in their *Report on Indian Constitutional Reforms* that "all important States should be placed in direct political relations with the Government of India."[7] The Government of India Act of 1919 transformed the Montagu-Chelmsford Report into a new Indian constitution. The Act was concerned with the political institutions of British India and did not deal with transfer; but after it became law in December 1919, the Political Department began to make preparations for taking over at least some states from the provinces. The first task was to decide exactly which states should be transferred. Officers were deputed to the major provincial Agencies to determine whether they should be placed under the control of the central government. The most vocal supporters of transfer were princes from the Punjab and Bombay, and the government of India therefore intended to launch the changes in those provinces. Transfer of the Punjab states was fiercely opposed by its administration; but this was overridden by Chelmsford and his Executive Council (the Indian Cabinet), and in 1921 the thirteen most important states in the Punjab were transferred. The two Bengal states followed in 1922, and the five Madras states in 1923. In the past, the Paramount Power would almost certainly have ignored any princely request for a wholesale reorganization of its relations with the Indian states, particularly when such a proposal was strongly opposed by provincial governments. But transfer had been swiftly approved, and the first stage was implemented within five years of the Bombay rulers' initial proposal. According to the Montagu-Chelmsford Report, transfer was necessary mainly because "the growth of responsibility in provincial Governments will to some extent unfit them to act in political matters as mere agents for the Government of India." In 1917, the provinces of British India were merely administrative divisions, with their governments exercising certain powers delegated by Delhi. But Montagu and Chelmsford planned to make over control of certain subjects to the provinces in their own right, and intended that provincial governments should eventually become

---

[7] *East India (Constitutional Reforms). Report on Indian Constitutional Reforms*, Cd 9109 (London, 1918), p. 246.

wholly responsible to the local legislatures (although for the present they recommended only a system of partial responsibility, which was implemented in the 1919 Act). As the states were not British territory, they would not be represented in the provincial legislatures, and if they remained under provincial control, elected politicians from British India would some day be able to treat the states as they pleased. This might lead to anything from financial discrimination against states to excessive intervention in their internal affairs, and it was quite likely that provincial politicians would be much less solicitous of rulers' rights and privileges than the existing British-dominated administrations. This seemed particularly likely given the rise of the states' people's organizations, whose leaders might well have links with the political leaders who would doubtless eventually come to power in the future autonomous provincial governments.

Montagu and Chelmsford may have regarded the growth of responsibility as the main reason for transfer, but this consideration does not seem to have influenced the government of India when it actually began to take over states from the provinces. The Report had recommended the transfer of "all important States," which it defined as all states whose rulers enjoyed salutes of at least eleven guns. The category may be extended slightly to cover the 108 states that in 1921 were granted full representation in the new Chamber of Princes. Of these, fifty had been in political relations with the government of India before 1918, and thirty-five were transferred between 1921 and 1924; but twenty-three (including Kolhapur, by far the largest state under Bombay) remained under provincial control throughout the 1920s. If the Paramount Power had really wanted to protect the major states from elected governments, it would not have left over a fifth of them under provincial control. This suggests that selective transfer was motivated by another consideration, and it is almost certain that this was a desire to safeguard not the princes, but British control in India. It happened that the princes who had demanded transfer included some of the most vocal and articulate rulers in India, who as leaders of princely opinion could not be safely ignored if the British wished to win the support of the states against the rising force of nationalism. Sir John Wood, the head of the Political Department, admitted as much when he wrote that transfer of the principal Bombay states would accord with "the wishes of the large majority of Chiefs affected.... If the scheme is rejected, it will create bitter disappointment among the leading Bombay States...."[8] Under the circumstances of the day, the Paramount Power had no real need to conciliate all the *members* of the Chamber of Princes. But it did want to win over their *leaders*, the men who took an active role in the Chamber and influenced the thinking of their less prominent brethren. It is striking that the list of these leaders corresponds closely with that of the rulers whose states were transferred from provincial control in the early 1920s. Between 1921 and 1932, twenty rulers served on the executive of the Chamber; eleven of them came from states that had been under the government of India for many years, seven from states that were transferred between 1921 and 1924, and only two from states that remained under provincial control after 1924. It is hard to believe that this was sheer coincidence.[9] This broad picture remains true when one examines the Bombay states in particular. The officers appointed to study the transfer of the Bombay states, J.L. Rieu and S.B. Patterson, submitted their report on 1 May 1920. Their scheme advocated the transfer of all Bombay states whose rulers enjoyed salutes of at least eleven guns. It proposed in addition that Delhi take charge of all the states in the Kathiawar and Palanpur Agencies, salute and non-salute, because these were so intermixed that the nine states that rated eleven guns or more could not be separated from the others; and these nine included four ruled by advocates of transfer (Nawanagar, Morvi and Gondal in Saurashtra, and Palanpur). Similarly, the Mahi Kantha states of Danta and Vijaynagar were to be transferred merely because of their close links to Idar, whose Maharaja had signed the request. Three of the four remaining Bombay states that were earmarked for transfer in the Rieu-Patterson Report (Kolhapur, Rajpipla and Kutch) were also ruled by signatories. It is true that the final state, Cambay, had not demanded an end to provincial control; but it is perhaps significant

[8] Minute by Sir John Wood (Political Secretary India), 10 July 1920, IOC R/1/1/661.

[9] See the list of Chamber officials in Urmila Phadnis, *Towards the Integration of Indian States, 1919-1947* (London, 1968), pp. 214-216. The original members of the Chamber are listed in A.P. Nicholson, *Scraps of Papers: India's Broken Treaties, Her Princes, and the Problem* (London, 1930), pp. 327-329.

that Rieu and Patterson recommended that it not be transferred until its five-year-old Nawab reached adulthood.[10]

But while the India Office and the Delhi Political Department favoured transfer, much of Indian officialdom did not. The Punjab's opposition has already been noted. The government of Bombay, which in the 1870s had thwarted the central government's attempts to take over its states, was perhaps the strongest supporter of continued provincial control; and Sir George Lloyd, the Governor of Bombay from 1918 to 1923, led the fight against transfer. Lloyd mustered an impressive array of arguments against selective transfer, most of them referring to the needs of the states' people.[11] Many, however, alleged that Bombay's chief concern was the reverse side of one of the main princely arguments in favour of transfer. For if the princes thought that transfer from provincial to central control would raise their status, Lloyd and his Council believed that it would lower the prestige of their province. Bombay had charge of more than half of all the states in India, and had as many political officers as all the other provinces put together. It is true that the Rieu-Patterson proposals left many Bombay states under provincial control; but by agreeing to the principle of transfer, and allowing the transfer of some of the most important states, Lloyd would undermine the status of his own province.[12] The Governor objected so strenuously that in 1920, the government of India decided to postpone the transfer of the Bombay states, ostensibly until experience had been gained of the working of the Chamber of Princes and the new constitution but probably actually until Lloyd had left India. Finally, in November 1923, one month before Lloyd's retirement, Delhi announced that it would soon take over

---

[10] J.L. Rieu and S.B. Patterson (PD India), "Report on the Question of the Establishment of Direct Relations Between the government of India and the States in the Bombay Presidency," 1 May 1920, IOC R/1/1/661.

[11] See Colin Forbes Adam, *Life of Lord Lloyd* (London, 1948), pp. 144-145, 157, 175.

[12] *The India Office List 1922*, *passim*, lists 38 officers on the staff of the Bombay Political Department, and a total of forty for the Central Provinces, Bengal, Bihar and Orissa, Assam, United Provinces, Punjab, and Madras Political Departments. Adam, *op. cit.*, p. 157, denies that prestige was a major factor in Lloyd's opposition to transfer; but this is contradicted in Hoare to Brabourne, 4 May 1934, IOC L/P&S/13/896.

the Kathiawar, Kutch, and Palanpur Agencies; the remaining Bombay states would stay under provincial control for the time being, but they too would eventually be taken over, after a trial period for Western India of at least five years. In the early months of 1924, C.C. Watson, a political officer, worked out the details of the transfer; and on 10 October 1924, Saurashtra, Kutch and Banas Kantha were placed under the government of India as a single Agency, headquartered at Rajkot in Saurashtra and christened the Western India States Agency by Watson (who became its first Agent to the Governor-General). Nevertheless, the new Western India States Agency differed in several ways from what Rieu and Patterson had proposed in 1920. The most important change was that Bombay now kept charge of six states that Rieu and Patterson had recommended for transfer (Idar, Danta, Vijaynagar, Kolhapur, Rajpipla and Cambay), and three of them were states whose rulers had signed the request for transfer in 1916. This does not, however, mean that Delhi had abandoned its earlier principles of pleasing the leading princes: since 1920, the rulers of Kutch and of Nawanagar in Saurashtra had emerged as two of the most important princes in India (one of them had represented the Indian states at every session of the League of Nations Assembly since the first in 1920), and this reinforced the need to transfer Kutch and Saurashtra. Similarly, the Nawab of Palanpur (the successor of the signatory of 1916) now ranked among the leaders of princely India, which meant that the Palanpur Agency had to be transferred. On the other hand, the Maharaja of Kolhapur had died in 1922, and the rulers of Idar and Rajpipla had not been as prominent as might have been expected from the size of their states. Several years' experience of intense princely political activity had made it clearer to the Paramount Power who the leaders of the rulers were, and this made it possible to reduce the scope of transfer in the Bombay states.[13]

---

[13] The Nawab of Palanpur served on the Standing Committee of the Chamber of Princes from 1921 to 1923 and in 1928-1929; but neither Idar nor Rajpipla held any Chamber office. Phadnis, *op. cit.*, pp. 214-216.

II

When it announced the impending establishment of the Western India States Agency in 1923, the government of India made it clear that the rest of the Bombay states would stay under provincial control for at least five years, so that any problems raised by transfer could be resolved. Nevertheless, the Chamber of Princes and many of the leaders among the remaining Bombay princes repeatedly urged the transfer of all the Indian states still under provincial control. In 1926, the Chancellor of the Chamber, the Maharaja of Patiala, spelled out the reasons for the demand: "it is inevitable that the States not in direct political relations with the Government of India should experience a sense of disappointment, and an ardent desire for the increased dignity, and other corresponding advantages, attaching to such relations." But the Political Department rejected these requests. It cited opposition to further transfer from several major rulers, including the Maharajas of Baroda and of two leading states still under Bombay, Kolhapur and Idar, as well as the Bombay government.[14] These grounds are not, however, convincing. Delhi could have ignored all of these considerations that militated against transfer, just as it had overridden provincial objections in 1923, and other reasons may be suggested for its unwillingness to take over any more states. By 1924 all the *leaders* of princely opinion had attained their goal of political relations with the central government; however much they might declare their support for the principle of transfer, they would not turn against the Paramount Power merely because *other* states were still under provincial control. Moreover, the British may have been holding the completion of transfer in reserve; they would implement it if a serious threat to their position ever made it necessary to secure further princely support. Then, in September 1931, Delhi announced its intention of taking over the remaining Bombay states after the third

---

[14] The quotation is from Panikkar, *Indian Princes*, p. 62. For Patiala's other speeches on the same point, see *ibid.*, pp. 61-64. See also Resolution of the Chamber of Princes, 1929, NAI FPD, 398-P/1931, and correspondence in IOC L/P&S/13/896 and R/1/1/2357 and NAI FPD, 398-P/1931. Copland, *British Raj*, p. 260, notes that the Maharaja of Kolhapur now opposed transfer, which he had supported in 1924.

Round Table Conference, which was then meeting in London. Within a few weeks of the end of the Conference in December 1932, H. Wilberforce-Bell of the Political Department finished a blueprint for the transfer of the Bombay states; and despite Bombay's protests, his scheme was implemented on 1 April 1933. The Bombay states were divided among existing Agencies; the old Mahi Kantha Agency, including Idar and Vijaynagar, was added to Western India.[15]

Why had the Paramount Power changed its mind about completing transfer? Ostensibly, the roots of the decision went back to 1928, when the Maharaja of Patiala had studied the position of the states under the control of the governments of Bihar and Orissa and of the Central Provinces. He concluded they had been unfairly deprived of their powers, to a large extent because of provincial control, and in 1930 opened a campaign to rectify their position. He persuaded the government of India to make an inquiry into the status of these states, and in due course the resulting Lothian Report recommended transfer. This in turn prompted the reopening of the question of the remaining Bombay states, which were transferred on the same day as the states in Bihar and Orissa and the Central Provinces.[16] But this still does not explain why Delhi agreed to further transfers after rejecting them for several years. The government of India informed the Secretary of State that its main motive had been to save money. It is true that in the early 1930s, Britain and its dependencies sought to reduce their expenditure to cope with the worldwide economic crisis (in August 1931, the

---

[15] The account of the transfer of the Bombay states in 1933 is based on IOC L/P&S/13/896, R/1/1/2241, R/1/1/2357, R/2/634/271 and R/2/634/272. At their rulers' request, two states on the border between Western India and the Rajputana Agency, Palanpur in Western India and Danta in Mahi Kantha, were transferred to Rajputana. Palanpur and Danta both had grievances that their rulers hoped could be eliminated if they were included in the Rajputana Agency: the Nawab of Palanpur had been lobbying for years to secure the removal of the headquarters of the Western Indian Political Agency of Banas Kantha from his capital (see IOC L/P&S/11/281 and R/2/634/280), while the Maharana of Danta was angry at the fact that the British system of precedence ranked him lower than the chief of Vijaynagar, which became part of the Western India States Agency in 1933 (see IOC R/2/168/270).

[16] See IOC R/2/636/300.

British government collapsed over the question of cuts in its spending). Delhi paid Bombay a yearly subvention of 102,000 rupees to cover the costs of administering the states under provincial control, and the Political Department claimed that this sum would be saved if the Bombay states were transferred. But this ignored the fact that Delhi would incur new expenditures when it took over the states; the Finance Department of the government of India and the Secretary of State both doubted that transfer would save money, and according to Wilberforce-Bell the net savings of transfer in Bombay would be 7,914 rupees. Such tiny financial benefits cannot have been a major reason for the resumption of transfer.

Lord Willingdon, the Viceroy, offered another explanation to both the government of Bombay and the Chamber of Princes, relating to the fact that the constitution worked out at the Round Table Conferences provided for full self-government in the provinces of British India, and for a federation of provinces and states. According to Willingdon, this made transfer essential for two reasons. First, fully autonomous provincial governments would be even less suited to exercising authority over states than the partially-responsible administrations established by the Montagu-Chelmsford reforms, as rulers would now be at the mercy of politicians who answered only to provincial electorates, and who might court popularity with their constituents by attacking the interests (economic or otherwise) of the voteless people of the states. For example, some Bombay states had entrusted the administration of their liquor taxes to the provincial government; if a self-governing Bombay adopted prohibition (which was likely, given the teetotaller Gandhi's influence in the province), their revenue from this source might suffer. Secondly, states could not be full members of the federation if they remained under the control of provinces that were themselves members. These considerations certainly contributed to the resumption of transfer, but the Paramount Power was probably motivated more by the need to calm the princes' fears regarding the new constitution than by a selfless desire to protect them from British Indian politicians. For it seems that, as in 1920, Delhi hoped that the removal of states from provincial control would buy goodwill. Willingdon told Sir Frederick Sykes, the Governor of Bombay, that the policy was supported by the rulers of the states, and "refusal to carry it out would be a constant grievance and source of agitation."[17] The British had previously sought to pacify only the leaders of the Chamber. Now, however, they also wanted to avoid "grievance and agitation" among other rulers, whose accession to the federation was so desired by the Paramount Power.[18] It was presumably with this in mind that in the month before the opening of the second Round Table Conference, sixteen Bombay princes asked Willingdon to remove their states from provincial control. A few days later, their requests bore fruit when the Political Department announced that it would resume transfer in Bombay.

III

Besides transfer, the Montagu-Chelmsford Report recommended something else: that the major states be placed in what it called "direct relations" with the government of India. It explained that this did not mean

> that the Durbars [State governments] should write direct to the Political Secretary, but that there should, wherever possible, be only one political officer through whom the States would correspond with the Government of India. ... it will be necessary to revise the existing arrangements by which correspondence passes through a local Political Agent or Resident to an Agent to the Governor General or a local Government and thence to the Government of India.[19]

At that time, only the four premier states of Hyderabad, Mysore, Baroda, and Jammu and Kashmir were in direct relations with the government of India–the sole intermediary between their rulers and the Political Department was the British Resident. In the other Agencies under central control, the various Residents and Political Agents were subordinate to Agents to the Governor-General, creating a two-tier chain of authority between the rulers and New Delhi. Most of the states under provincial control were in direct relations

[17] Lord Willingdon (Viceroy) to Sir Frederick Sykes (Governor of Bombay), 13 Dec. 1931, IOC R/1/1/2241.

[18] See Chapter Three.

[19] *Report on Indian Constitutional Reforms*, p. 247.

with the local government through Political Agents; but as technically the provincial governments merely oversaw state affairs on behalf of the government of India, they were regarded by Montagu and Chelmsford as filling the same intermediary role as Agents to the Governor-General. And the situation was even more complex in Saurashtra, where in 1917 there were *three* levels of officials between each state and the central Political Department: responsibility for the peninsula was divided among four Political Agents, who reported to the Agent to the Governor of Bombay in Kathiawar; he was responsible to the Bombay Political Department, which in turn was subordinate to the government of India.[20]

Unlike transfer, direct relations were rarely discussed before the First World War. Neither the central nor the provincial governments seem to have wished to eliminate any of the levels in the administrative structure of paramountcy. Both doubtless considered the existing system to be well suited to the relationship between the British and the states: local Residents or Political Agents exercised close supervision over the states in their charge, while Agents to the Governor-General and provincial governments coordinated policy in groups of states that faced common problems and situations. But it was for this very reason that the two most vocal rulers of Rajputana, the Maharajas of Bikaner and Alwar, felt that the double-tiered structure should be abolished. They were leading the princes' fight to enhance their sovereignty by minimising British interference in state affairs; one of the best ways of accomplishing their goal would be to remove the Residents and Political Agents, leaving only a distant and busy Agent to the Governor-General whose role would be to act as a diplomatic representative of the Paramount Power rather than its supervisory agent. The two Maharajas were brilliant men with magnetic personalities, fluent in English, and they saw their chance when Montagu and Chelmsford began to study constitutional reform. They were wholly successful in urging the case for direct relations; thirty years later, a top India Office bureaucrat wrote that "it was owing to Mr. Montagu being 'nobbled' [won over] by the late Bikaner and Alwar that the recommendation ... found its way into the Montagu-Chelmsford

[20] Aitchison, *op. cit.*, and *Imperial Gazetteer of India*, *passim.*

Report. It always appeared here [in Whitehall] to be unconvincing and undesirable, but Bikaner was a powerful lever."[21] This is probably true. Nevertheless, Montagu was a capable politician, and Chelmsford an experienced administrator, and they must have had a good reason for recommending direct relations. They claimed to be motivated by the fact that "the necessity of communicating with the central Government through two or even more intermediaries is an obstruction to good understanding and a great obstacle to business."[22] There is force to this explanation, but the telegraph, the telephone and the automobile would have allowed speedy communications and rapid decisions on important matters, even through several tiers of authority. The Montagu-Chelmsford Report actually recommended direct relations for the same reason as had led it to favour transfer: the need for the support of the leaders of princely India. This becomes clear in an examination of the implementation of direct relations after 1921, which was even less systematic than the launching of transfer. Direct relations hardly affected the Agencies that had been under central control before the War: in Central India, Indore been directly subordinate to the Agent to the Governor-General for much of the period since 1854, and in 1921 Gwalior was removed from the Agency altogether so that its Resident reported to Delhi (it joined Hyderabad, Mysore, Baroda, and Jammu and Kashmir as a premier state), but no other states were placed in direct relations; and in Rajputana, only three states (including Bikaner and Alwar) were ever placed under the Agent to the Governor-General. This meant that such great states as Bhopal in Central India, or Udaipur, Jaipur and Jodhpur in Rajputana, remained in the charge of their own Political Agents or Residents. Their rulers were certainly entitled to "good understanding" with the Paramount Power, but they made it clear that they did not want the change; since the whole purpose of direct relations was to win princely goodwill, the British were not prepared to force them on rulers who objected.[23]

But in the states that were transferred from provincial supervision in the early 1920s, the Montagu-Chelmsford principle of direct

---

[21] Note by P.J. Patrick (IO), 14 Feb. 1945, IOC L/P&S/13/896.
[22] *Report on Indian Constitutional Reforms*, p. 246.
[23] The question of direct relations is examined Ashton, *op. cit.*

relations *was* systematically applied. There were several reasons for this. First, it would have made little sense to remove the intermediate level of provincial authority only to replace it with a new two-tier system under the government of India. Secondly, these states were placed in new Agencies, which were without any existing structure to which rulers or political officers had grown accustomed, and could therefore be treated as blank slates where the Political Department could make whatever arrangements it wished. Thirdly, the haphazard institution of direct relations in Rajputana and Central India made it obvious that the Paramount Power was catering to the wishes of certain vocal rulers (Bikaner, Alwar, Gwalior) rather than acting on a definite principle. If direct relations were applied systematically in the new Agencies, this unseemly reality might be hidden; at the same time, the British could grant the wish of the remaining leaders of princely India to be directly subordinated to Agents to the Governor-General.[24] All of the states in the new Punjab and Madras States Agencies were accordingly placed in direct relations. There were, however, too many states in Western India for all to be supervised by the Agent to the Governor-General. The Political Department devised a solution to this problem that preserved the appearance of principle while ensuring that the leading rulers of the new Agency attained their goal. This was to adhere strictly to the Montagu-Chelmsford recommendation that "all *important* states" be placed in direct relations; "important States" were here defined as those whose rulers rated an artillery salute, and Delhi decided to subordinate the salute states directly to the Agent to the Governor-General while leaving non-salute states under their Political Agents, who would in turn report to the Agent to the Governor-General. The civil and criminal system of the Agencies that became part of Western India provided a specious rationalisation for this structure. Salute princes exercised full judicial powers. The jurisdiction of non-salute rulers was limited, however, and cases that lay beyond the competence of their courts

---

[24] Ramusack, *Princes of India*, p. xxi, lists the six leading princes (in terms of political activity on the all-India scene) in the 1920s as Bikaner, Alwar, Nawanagar, Patiala, Gwalior, and Bhopal. Of these, the great Nawab Hamidullah Khan of Bhopal did not come to the throne until 1926. All of the others were in direct relations by 1924.

were decided by the Political Agent.[25] It was explained that this necessitated leaving them under the Political Agent. But this rationalisation confuses the supervisory and judicial duties of the Political Agent, who could have overseen the administration even in a fully jurisdictional state.

The Paramount Power prepared the way for this scheme of partial direct relations even before the establishment of the Western India States Agency. In 1922, the fourteen salute states of Saurashtra were placed in direct relations with the government of Bombay through the Agent to the Governor. And the following year, the four Political Agencies in Saurashtra were reduced to two, Western and Eastern Kathiawar; this was because with the removal of the salute states, the old Agencies were too small for all four to warrant a continued separate existence. On the creation of the Western India States Agency in 1924, the Saurashtra system of direct relations was extended. The Agent to the Governor-General took the place of the Agent to the Governor in supervising the salute states, which besides the fourteen in Saurashtra included Palanpur and Radhanpur from the old Palanpur Agency, and Kutch; the remainder of the Palanpur Agency (or Banas Kantha, as it was soon renamed) became a subordinate Political Agency of Western India, parallel to Western and Eastern Kathiawar. The establishment of direct relations in Western India necessitated special arrangements in the case of Kutch, which became important when direct relations were abandoned twenty years later. In order to ensure that the Rao (later Maharao) would not bar the Company's representative from his capital, the treaty of 1819 that had brought Kutch under British paramountcy stipulated that "The British Resident or his Assistant shall reside in Bhooj" (Bhuj, the state capital).[26] By the beginning of the twentieth century, however, the reason for this clause was misunderstood by both Kutch and the Paramount Power: despite the campaign for direct relations, it was often regarded as a mark of honour for a state to warrant a resident political officer, and the stipulation was interpreted as a guarantee that Kutch would always be entitled to this distinction. But there was simply not enough work

---

[25] See Chapters Six and Eleven.

[26] Treaty of 13 Oct. 1819, Aitchison, *op. cit.*, 6:115-119.

in Kutch to justify a resident Political Agent; in 1920, Rieu and Patterson commented that "it does not ordinarily amount to more than half-an-hour a day."[27] It was therefore necessary to include Kutch in the larger Western India States Agency, but this meant that the guarantee of a resident British representative would have to be withdrawn. Since it had been embodied in a treaty, negotiations were required, and the astute Maharao exacted a price for his consent before, in 1925, he agreed to the change; the Political Department had to replace the old guarantee with a new one that Kutch would not be removed from direct relations unless the Maharao had been consulted.[28]

During the 1920s the Chamber of Princes urged the extension of the principle of direct relations,[29] which was accordingly retained on the enlargement of the Western India States Agency in 1933. As a salute state, Idar was placed under the Agent to the Governor-General, and the petty states of Mahi Kantha were joined with the existing Banas Kantha Agency to form a new Political Agency called Sabar Kantha.[30]

IV

From the beginning, however, some Britons had warned that the lessened supervision of the states implicit in direct relations must inevitably lead to maladministration. The sentiment was to a large

---

[27] Rieu and Patterson, "Report," IOC R/1/1/661.

[28] See NAI FPD, 186(5)-P/1925.

[29] Panikkar, *Indian Princes*, p. 64.

[30] To address the princes' concerns over the future exercise of paramountcy by a hostile central government, the 1935 constitution removed all states from the jurisdiction of the government of India, of which the Political Department ceased to form a part when the new system came into effect in 1937. Relations with the states and responsibility for the Political Department were assumed directly by the British Crown, which exercised its authority through the Crown Representative (in practice the same person as the Viceroy, but in his guise of delegate of the King-Emperor rather than as head of the Indian administration). At the same time, the title of Agent to the Governor-General was changed to Resident.

extent based on the assumption that rulers had a natural tendency to misgovern, which, as has been seen, was on the whole incorrect.[31] Still, there were complaints. In 1939, states' people's leaders in both Orissa and Himachal Pradesh asserted that rulers' oppression of their subjects had greatly increased in the years since their states were removed from the supervision of provincial officials and transferred to non-interventionist political officers from New Delhi.[32] This raised the spectre of popular discontent in the states, and fed into the change in policy that occurred in 1939.[33] But the trend had started several years earlier, when the Paramount Power began to remove states from direct relations. The first step came in 1933, when the British blamed a serious revolt in Alwar on a lack of close supervision, and Alwar (one of the three Rajputana states in direct relations) was promptly put under a Political Agent. By 1943, direct relations had been completely abandoned in the Rajputana Agency. In 1936, all of the Eastern States (a huge Agency, extending from Tripura in the east to modern Madhya Pradesh in the west) were placed under Political Agents; in the same year the Punjab States Agency took over those states that had remained under the government of the Punjab, but most of them (as well as two states hitherto in direct relations) were placed in a new subordinate Political Agency, and in 1939 a second Political Agency was created.[34]

After the changes in the Eastern States, the Resident for the States of Western India had direct charge of more states than did any of his colleagues. The great upsurge in political agitation in that

---

[31] See Chapter One. Sir Michael O'Dwyer, the former Governor of the Punjab, predicted in 1925 that such concessions as direct relations would lead to maladministration; Sir Michael O'Dwyer, *India as I Knew It 1885-1925* (London, 1925), p. 156. But the political officer Sir Terence Creagh Coen notes that the record does not show any decline in administrative standards with reduced British supervision; T. Creagh Coen, *The Indian Political Service: A Study in Indirect Rule* (London, 1971), p. 23.

[32] "A Statement on the Popular Movements in the Orissa States. Historical" (Feb. 1939), NL AICC, G-35/1939; "Report of the Non-Official Enquiry into the Tragic Happenings in Dhami State ..." (30 July 1939), NL SPC, 181(ii).

[33] See Chapter Three.

[34] Many of these changes can be traced in *Memoranda on the Indian States 1940, passim*. See also Ashton, *op. cit., passim*.

Agency in 1938-1939 ensured that direct relations would be abandoned in Western India, and difficulties in seeing that the maritime states of Saurashtra adhered to recently-concluded customs agreements made this reform seem even more desirable than it was elsewhere.[35] The topic was first discussed at the beginning of 1939, when the Political Department and the Resident, Gibson, agreed to place most of the salute states of Western India under Political Agents. There was some debate as to whether any should remain in direct relations. Gibson urged that the three leading Saurashtra states of Junagadh, Nawanagar and Bhavnagar be excused from the changes, but Linlithgow and his Political Secretary, Latimer, felt that these states could be placed under Political Agents. Only Kutch was to stay under the Resident, on the grounds that the agreement of 1925 had guaranteed direct relations to the Maharao.[36] Gibson warned that "The suggested change is unlikely to be welcomed by the States but their objections would have to be overruled."[37] The reasons for these objections were not difficult to find: the rulers still wanted direct relations both as a matter of prestige and because they gave them greater freedom to exercise their sovereignty. More important, they naturally resented the implication that without close supervision they would misrule, and this slur on their izzat was probably the main reason that they opposed proposals to end direct relations. But in 1939, the British concluded that they could ignore all such objections. Nevertheless, soon after the outbreak of the Second World War, Gibson changed his mind and advised the Political Department that direct relations should be maintained for the time being. He offered three reasons: a reorganization would be costly; Delhi proposed to attach the smaller states to larger neighbours, and there was no point in disturbing matters now if the Agency would soon be remodelled in any case;[38] and, at least for the

---

[35] For the customs question, see Chapter Five.

[36] This account of the abandonment of direct relations in Western India is based on IOC L/P&S/13/896, R/1/1/4627 and R/2/598/29, and NAI WISA, A-5-117/1944, A-5-118-A/1944-45, C-35-3/1943 Part I, C-35-3/1944 Part I and E-13-14/1944.

[37] E.C. Gibson (Resident) to Sir Bertrand Glancy (Political Adviser), 4 May 1939, IOC L/P&S/13/896.

[38] For the smaller states, see Chapter Six.

duration of the war, security necessitated a single channel of communication (the Resident) between Delhi and the coastal states. The Political Department was keen to implement the reform immediately; with some difficulty, however, Gibson persuaded Delhi to make no changes until the future of the smaller states had been settled.

The smaller states were finally disposed of in the Attachment Scheme of 1943. This not only cleared the way for ending direct relations in Western India, but gave a new and plausible excuse for doing so. The change in policy towards the states in 1939 had never been formally announced, as the Paramount Power knew that it would incense the princes;[39] the real reason for removing states from the charge of the Residents, the desire to supervise them more closely, could therefore not be publicised. But, as Gibson's successor Gaisford pointed out, many lesser states in Western India had now been attached to Baroda. These territories remained in Gaisford's charge; Baroda, however, was under its own Resident, and the Political Department agreed with Gaisford's suggestion that the resulting administrative difficulties could be remedied by uniting Western India with the Baroda and Gujarat States Agency.[40] This would place thirty states in the Resident's direct charge, which even supporters of direct relations admitted was too many. The Resident at Baroda commented that

> The attachment scheme has not resulted in much diminution of work in my office. I am not at all sure that one man can be expected to run the two Residencies at any rate so long as there are war problems and post war problems.[41]

---

[39] Ashton, *op. cit.*, p. 177.

[40] A senior India Office administrator later noted that the Political Department saved a good deal of money when it amalgamated the two Agencies, and suggested (apparently wrongly) that this was the main reason for the change; minute by Patrick, 9 May 1944, IOC L/P&S/13/896.

[41] L.W. Jardine (Resident at Baroda and for the Gujarat States) to P. Gaisford (Resident), 29 Sept. 1943, NAI WISA, C-35-3/1943 Part I.

Gaisford therefore proposed that the Political Agents, who since the attachment of the non-salute states had had no real work to do, should take charge of the salute states in a unified Agency, leaving only Kutch (because of the Agreement) and Baroda (as one of the five premier states) directly under the Resident. In November 1943, Gaisford met with Sir Kenneth Fitze, the Secretary in the Political Department, to discuss the question:

> At first it was thought that while amalgamation was inevitable, it would be possible to wait till the end of the war before reaching a final decision since owing to the amount of extra work created by the war it was difficult to forecast the amount of work under normal conditions. Also it was felt that by that time some progress might have been made in deciding the fate of the smaller States. After further discussion however it was agreed that the difficulties in dealing with questions affecting the attached areas through two different agencies were such that it was essential to recommend that the amalgamation should take place as soon as possible.[42]

In December 1943 the India Office approved Gaisford's plan to amalgamate the Agencies and end direct relations, adding that the resulting closer supervision would also ensure that the larger states treated their smaller attached neighbours fairly. Gaisford had echoed Gibson's warning that the salute rulers would not want to be put under Political Agents, but he considered that "the needs of the changed situation coupled with the substantial advantages resulting from the closer supervision that Political Agents will be able to exercise must lead us to disregard any protests on the score of lessened prestige and izzat."[43] The protests, however, were furious. The Thakor Saheb of Palitana spoke for many when he stated that "the proposed arrangement is derogatory to any ruler of a Sovereign State of Kathiawar and it will certainly go a long way in lowering the prestige of a ruler in the eyes of his subjects and shall thereby add to the so many existing political anomalies which makes a

---

[42] Aide-memoire on discussions between Gaisford and Fitze (now Secretary to Crown Representative), 12 Nov. 1943, NAI WISA, C-35-3/1943 Part I.

[43] Gaisford to Fitze, 30 Aug. 1943, IOC R/2/598/29.

Ruler's position so very precarious."[44] A worried Resident recommended a stay; but the protests and the Resident's recommendations were to no avail. In July 1944 the salute states of Western India (except Kutch) were placed in the charge of the Political Agents, and in November the two Agencies were amalgamated; the highest official in the new combined Agency bore the cumbersome title of Resident at Baroda and for the States of Western India and Gujarat. Princely anger continued unabated. The Maharaja Jam Saheb of Nawanagar was "not aware of anything that I have done–except my continued loyalty to the Crown as ever and my unsparing, may be humble, efforts and services in everyway for the successful prosecution of the war–to merit this degradation."[45] Besides such general criticisms, the rulers argued persuasively that the changes were unnecessary. They pointed out that the Attachment Scheme should have led to the abolition of the Political Agents, whom it had left without any function, not their assumption of the Resident's work, and that an amalgamated Agency would be too large. Because of such special problems as customs administration, the Saurashtra states needed to be under the direct control of the Resident. As a whole, the new system did little to ease the work of the Political Department, and nothing for that of the state governments; and having Baroda and Kutch directly under the Resident while the other states were under Political Agents "creates an invidious distinction."[46] But with a fatherly "assurance that His Excellency has no intention of doing anything to derogate from their status," the Viceroy, Lord Wavell, replied to the princes that attachment had made amalgamation necessary, and that amalgamation had made Political Agents necessary by making it impossible for the Resident to supervise the salute states.[47] (He did not mention that the Political Department had decided to end direct relations all over India long before attachment or the amalgamation of the two Agencies had ever been considered.) The rulers had lost

[44] Palitana to Gaisford, 4 Mar. 1944, IOC R/2/598/29.

[45] Nawanagar to Gaisford, 25 Aug. 1944, IOC R/2/598/29.

[46] Nawanagar to C.P. Hancock (Resident), 29 Nov./21 Dec. 1944, IOC R/2/598/29.

[47] L.C.L. Griffin (Secretary to Crown Representative) to Hancock, 15 Feb. 1945, IOC R/2/598/29.

to the now-unheeding Paramount Power in their effort to maintain direct relations as a constituent element of their sovereignty.

CHAPTER FIVE

THE CRISIS OF THE STATE PORTS

The altercation that took place between Ranjitsinhji and Lord Willingdon in the Chamber of Princes in 1933 represented the culmination of several years of discord between the Jam Saheb of Nawanagar and the Paramount Power. While the immediate cause of the incident was differing views on the question of federation, its roots lay in disputes over the collection of customs duties on foreign goods that came by ship to state ports. Ranjitsinhji and his fellow princes claimed the right to administer their own customs services, and retain all of the money that they took in. The British, however, asserted that the government of India should supervise the collection of customs, and receive the duty on any imports from foreign countries that were unloaded in states but subsequently went on to British India. A truly satisfactory settlement to this question was never reached, mainly because the two sides were pursuing different objectives: the princes wanted to collect customs partly because this would bring them a large income, but mainly because it was a sign of their sovereignty; Delhi sought to ensure that state ports did not admit banned imports, and more important to safeguard its own customs revenues which formed a significant part of the wherewithal for the maintenance of British control. The situation was complicated by the fact that international law was unequivocal in allowing the princes (as sovereign monarchs) to levy customs at their own ports; this meant that if the British wished to obtain the duty on imports that landed at state ports, they had either to get the princes to renounce their right to customs, or impose customs barriers between British India and the states.[1] Just which solution was adopted varied with the shifts in British policy towards the rulers.

---

[1] See *East India (Constitutional Reforms). Report of the Indian States Enquiry Committee (Financial)*, 1932, Cmd 4103 (London, 1932), pp. 91, 140.

The disputes over sea customs and ports were particularly fierce in the Western India States Agency. From the end of the eighteenth century, the East India Company brought most of the Indian coast under direct British control, for both strategic and commercial reasons. The result was that only fourteen Indian states were left with ports, through which they could import goods directly from foreign countries. No fewer than seven of these (Kutch, Junagadh, Nawanagar, Bhavnagar, Porbandar, Morvi and Jafarabad) were in the Western India States Agency; an eighth, Baroda, was not included in the Agency, but its port, Okha, formed an enclave within Nawanagar.[2] Moreover, the ports in other Agencies did not threaten the trade of British ports; all were relatively near the large and well-developed British harbours at Bombay and Cochin, which meant that importers had no reason to use state ports, except to bring in goods that they intended to sell locally. (Although Cochin was a state, the port city of Cochin formed part of British India.) On the other hand, the Western Indian ports were "the natural outlet of the metre gauge railway system of North-West India," much closer to Delhi and Upper India than were the nearest British ports of Bombay and Karachi. This meant that merchants supplying the north-west would incur lower transportation costs if their imports entered India at Western Indian rather than British ports.[3]

---

[2] Besides Baroda and the Western India States Agency, the maritime states were Travancore and Cochin in Kerala; Sawantwadi and Janjira in Maharashtra; and Cambay and Sachin in Gujarat (the total of fourteen omits the Baluchistan states). The history and trade of the state ports are examined in *Report of the Indian States Enquiry Committee*, pp. 94-134. For the Company's annexation of most of the Indian coastline, see Lord Mornington (the future Marquess Wellesley) (Governor-General) to Court of Directors, 3 Aug. 1799, in Sidney J. Owen, editor, *A Selection from the Despatches, Treaties, and Other Papers of the Marquess of Wellesley, K.G., during his government of India* (Oxford, 1877), pp. 132-159; Nightingale, *op. cit.*

[3] The quotation is from Sir Geoffrey Corbett of the Government of India, "Report on the Conference held at Mount Abu on the 27th, 28th and 29th June, 1927, on the Subject of the Kathiawar Ports," Appendix I, p. 3, IOC R/2/623/118. The question of state customs rights has attracted little scholarly attention. See, however, Ashton, *op. cit.*, especially pp. 140-141.

I

For most of the nineteenth century, few foreign goods entered British India through the Western Indian states; not only were state ports unable to receive anything larger than small coastal boats, but there was no rail line linking them to British India. In theory, the maritime states were treated as foreign territory, that is, all goods that crossed the frontier from the states into British India were subject to the full British tariff. In practice, however, no systematic effort was made to collect duties on the little merchandise that did leave the states.[4] This changed in the 1890s, when railway construction made British India easily accessible from the ports of the Saurashtra states. In order to earn customs revenues, some states began to encourage merchants to land foreign goods at their ports, and then carry them by train to British India. The inducements often included very low duties on imports, on the philosophy that collecting low dues was better than collecting none. Some importers therefore found it profitable to use state ports to land foreign goods intended for sale in nearby parts of British India; this had the additional benefit of saving the costs of transporting cargo the hundreds of miles from Bombay and Karachi. Part of the customs revenue that the government of India had formerly earned at those ports therefore now began to flow into state treasuries. In 1905-1906, the Indian mint found that it did not have enough silver to produce one-rupee coins. The government accordingly used British gold coins to buy silver bullion at a generous price. This was an open invitation to smugglers, who took silver from Oman to Saurashtra and, evading the import duty then charged on silver, crossed into British India where they sold it at a handsome profit. This, however, threatened both India's customs revenues and the stability of the rupee. In 1905, the government of India therefore established a customs cordon around Saurashtra and Kutch. Customs stations were built at every point of entry into British India, and all goods

---

[4] See *East India (Fiscal Commission). Report of the Indian Fiscal Commission 1921-22*, Cmd 1764 (Simla, 1922), pp. 10-15; *Report of the Indian States Enquiry Committee*, pp. 107-108; Kailas Narain Haksar, "The Indian States and the Sea-Customs Duties," in *The Asiatic Review*, 23, 4 (Oct. 1927), pp. 579-584, at p. 582.

leaving the states were required to pay the British Indian import duty. The cordon, called the Viramgam Line (after a town on the border), virtually ended silver-smuggling. By ensuring that all merchandise paid duty at the frontier, in addition to whatever tariffs were collected at state ports, it also eliminated any incentive for importers to choose state over British ports. The government of India promised to lift the Line and cease to collect duty at the frontier if the maritime states would levy customs tariffs at least equal to those charged in British India, and allow a customs officer from British India to conduct periodic inspections of their customs facilities; although the states would continue to receive the duties collected on foreign goods, this would permit proper policing to eradicate smuggling. But the Western Indian princes rejected this proposal. They feared some loss of revenue, as duties raised to the British Indian rate might discourage merchants from using their ports, but their main concern was that by abdicating the right to maintain exclusively their own customs services, they would renounce what was universally recognised as a symbol of sovereignty.[5]

The imposition of the Viramgam Line greatly reduced the customs revenues of the maritime states of Saurashtra, and caused great inconvenience to travellers, as all rail traffic had to stop at the frontier for customs inspection. The affected princes protested vigorously, but only one ruler, the ruler of Bhavnagar, obtained redress, and this was because of what amounted to an historical accident. From 1802 to 1866, Bhavnagar state had been divided into two parts. One portion (tributary to the Gaekwad) ranked as an Indian state, where the monarch enjoyed the status of a sovereign prince; the rest (under the Peshwa until 1802, when the Peshwa ceded it to the East India Company) formed part of British India, and here the prince was a mere landlord. This anomaly was ended by agreements concluded in 1860 and 1866, which gave the ruler full sovereignty over all of his territories. The British Indian territories had included Bhavnagar town, the state's capital and its principal port. The agreements provided that Bhavnagar would continue

[5] For the establishment of the Viramgam cordon, see *Report of the Indian States Enquiry Committee*, pp. 108-109; Abdus Sadeque, *The Problem of the Standard of Indian Currency: Its History and Solution* (Calcutta, 1938), p. 66.

to be treated as a British port (but with its customs revenue going to the state rather than the government of India), as long as the ruler levied duty at the British Indian rates. The main privilege that this conferred was a guarantee by the Paramount Power of free entry into British India for foreign goods that landed at Bhavnagar town. In 1865, the same privilege was extended to the other ports in the state (as well as to the ports of Baroda state). This concession assured Bhavnagar a perpetual income from customs, and was intended to persuade the prince to renounce territorial and financial demands that he had raised against the government of India.[6] The state therefore had good reason to object when the institution of the Viramgam Line denied importers free access to British India. This position eventually secured the support of the Secretary of State, Lord Morley, who in 1910 ordered the government of India once more to allow free entry to goods from Bhavnagar. To ensure that merchants did not evade duty on goods that were re-exported from Bhavnagar into British India, it was stipulated that merchandise crossing the frontier from the state would have to be accompanied by a certificate stating that the proper tariff had already been paid.[7]

The other states could not claim the same rights as Bhavnagar, and the government of India ignored their protests against the Viramgam Line. But the cordon did not stop smuggling. This became a particular problem in 1916, when the British Indian tariff was raised substantially in order to secure more revenue for war needs; smugglers responded by landing foreign goods at ports in Saurashtra where they paid or evaded the low state duties, and then taking the items over the Line. The government of Bombay therefore proposed a new arrangement in the form of an agreement with the states of Saurashtra and with Baroda in regard to its Saurashtra possessions. Besides the concerns over smuggling, such a settlement was desirable for several reasons. In the first place, the railway was about to reach a small Baroda port, and the Gaekwad had declared his intention of building a modern port at Okha. This would lead to a great increase in imports into Baroda. It was to be expected that much of this increase would be re-exported to British India, as

---

[6] See Aitchison, *op. cit.*, 6:90-91, 182-188.

[7] *Report of the Indian States Enquiry Committee*, p. 118.

Baroda (like Bhavnagar) enjoyed the treaty right of free export across the frontier. This in itself did not worry Bombay, but it would anger the administrations of Nawanagar, Porbandar and Junagadh: the three states were currently collecting fees on merchandise that landed at their small ports without paying duty and was immediately transhipped to Bombay where the British Indian authorities received the customs payments. A modern facility at Okha would absorb all of this trade, transferring to Baroda the profits involved in the transhipment. The best way of averting the resulting acrimony would be to reach an agreement that allowed Nawanagar, Porbandar and Junagadh to share in the wealth. It was also noted that maintenance of the Viramgam Line hindered industrial development in the states, something that the Paramount Power supported. Bombay added that there was little chance that the states would break any agreements reached. Two of the states best placed for importing, Junagadh and Porbandar, were ruled by children, and would consequently remain under British administration for the next five or six years. As for the other states, Bombay was confident that their jealousy of one another would be a sufficient safeguard to keep any one state from violating the spirit of the agreement. The Bombay Political Secretary accordingly concluded that "In view ... of the political agitation which has been referred to above, in consideration of the feelings of the Chiefs concerned and seeing that prolonged mal-administration of the ports could not go on without detection, the government of Bombay desire to submit that by far the best course to end this long discussion is to place the ports of the States concerned on the same footing as that of the ports of the Bhavnagar State."[8] Delhi agreed; it renounced the demand for inspection of the state customs facilities, and began to negotiate with the maritime states on the abolition of the Line. In the end, the Saurashtra states signed agreements to levy import tariffs at least as high as the British Indian duty, and to ensure that banned goods did not enter at their ports. The Viramgam Line was promptly lifted, and the states regained free access to British India. At the same

---

[8] L. Robertson (Political Secretary Bombay) to J.B. Wood (Political Secretary India), 13 Nov. 1916, IOC L/P&S/13/897. For the lifting of the Viramgam Line, see IOC L/P&S/13/897, and *Report of the Indian Fiscal Commission*, p. 13.

time, Bhavnagar was freed from the need to accompany goods entering British India with certificates.[9]

The government of India claimed that the reasons for the customs cordon had disappeared when the states agreed to levy high import duties and to maintain security at their ports (moreover, a worldwide rise in the price of silver had eliminated the danger of extensive smuggling of that metal). But the states had not hitherto been trusted to carry out these measures themselves: the central government had demanded the right to inspect their ports, or even to assume full control of their customs services. There is no doubt that the Viramgam Line was actually abolished as part of Delhi's campaign to win the support of the princes for the preservation of British control. The cordon was a major grievance among the rulers of Saurashtra, and by removing it the Paramount Power helped to conciliate such powerful rulers as the Jam Saheb of Nawanagar.[10] Delhi did, however, attach one significant condition to the agreements of 1917: it reserved the right to reimpose the Viramgam Line if "the fiscal interests involved became very important."[11] Before signing the agreement, the Jam Saheb expressed the hope that this vaguely-worded proviso "will not interfere with a healthy development of our resources to the extent of their natural capacity," meaning that the states would lose free access if their import trade grew beyond a certain point; he was assured that "Government have no intention of imposing conditions which will interfere with a healthy development of the resources of your State to the extent of

---

[9] The ruler of Kutch refused to maintain British Indian customs rates, as he believed that low tariffs discouraged smuggling at his ports. Any foreign goods that landed in Kutch therefore remained subject to duties at the Viramgam Line. In any case, there was no rail link between Kutch and British India, and consequently next to no trade.

[10] M.K. Gandhi claimed that the Line was lifted as a result of his intercession with the Viceroy, in response to frequent complaints from passengers. This is not borne out by the records. M.K. Gandhi, *An Autobiography or the Story of My Experiments with Truth* (Ahmedabad, 1992), pp. 314-316, and *Satyagraha in South Africa* (Ahmedabad, 1928), pp. xi-xii.

[11] *Report of the Indian States Enquiry Committee*, p. 109.

its natural capacity," which seemed to be a guarantee that states might import as much merchandise as their ports could handle.[12]

When the Western India States Agency was established in 1924, then, Kutch was cut off from British Indian markets by a tariff wall; goods from Bhavnagar enjoyed free access to British India under the agreements of 1860-1866; and the remaining maritime states (Junagadh, Nawanagar, Porbandar, Morvi and Jafarabad) had entered into a customs union with British India in 1917.

II

So long as the maritime states enjoyed free access to British India, their customs revenues were limited only by the volume of trade that entered their ports. Almost immediately after signing the agreements of 1917, several rulers therefore set about increasing the share of British India's foreign imports that came through their territories. They did this in two ways. First, they encouraged merchants to use their ports by lowering the various incidental charges levied on imports (for example, for warehousing), and the railway charges on goods that were re-exported to British India; the agreements precluded any reduction in duties, but did not affect port charges and other fees. If these were set at rates lower than those levied at Bombay and Karachi, merchants would find it cheaper to use state ports than British ones even if the duties were the same. Secondly, a number of princes sought to remove the main physical barrier to increased trade, the quality of their ports. The Saurashtra ports had primitive docking facilities, and none had a harbour deep enough to receive large ocean-going steamers. The governments of Baroda, Junagadh, and Nawanagar began pouring huge sums of money into the development of their ports, and other states made plans to follow suit. The first port to be modernised was Bedi in Nawanagar, which became fully operational in 1926-1927. In 1917-1918, the Jam Saheb had received 3.6 lakhs of rupees from customs duties; by 1925-1926 this had increased to just under 30 lakhs, and with the

[12] Nawanagar to E. Maconochie (Agent to the Governor of Bombay in Kathiawar), 27 Aug. 1917, IOC L/P&S/13/897; Maconochie to Nawanagar, 13 Oct. 1917, IOC R/2/623/118A.

completion of Bedi it mushroomed to an astounding 78 lakhs the very next year. Part of the gain was caused by India's adoption of protective tariffs in 1923, which raised the duty on some imports, but most of it was due to a great increase in Bedi's trade which was almost entirely at the expense of British Indian ports. The tiny state of Nawanagar would soon earn two percent of the total British Indian customs revenue. With other modern ports about to open in Baroda and Junagadh, Delhi was faced with a serious threat to its customs revenues.[13]

The government of India now felt that it had been wrong to grant the maritime states free entry in 1917. Unfortunately, as far as could be seen, the states had all abided by the terms of their agreements; they levied duty at the British Indian rate, and were vigilant in barring illegal imports. (There were rumours that the states charged duty at the full British Indian rate on goods that entered through their ports, but then granted rebates of up to one third of the amount, although this was never proved.)[14] Fortunately, the Finance Department remembered that the princes had merely been promised that no limits would be placed on the "healthy development" of their ports; and a case (though weak) could be made for seeing the modernisation that had taken place as "unhealthy." This was on two grounds. First, while the states' low port charges had not contravened the letter of the agreements, they might be interpreted as a violation of its spirit. Secondly, the rulers had paid for the expansion of their harbours from customs revenues. Delhi claimed that this gave them an advantage over British Indian ports, which by law could only be developed with money raised by incidental port charges. In the words of C.C. Watson, the Agent to the Governor-General, "Development paid for out of customs

---

[13] For the effects of port development on state customs receipts, see Table Two. For the development of Bedi port, see IOC L/P&S/13/1487. The threat to British Indian customs revenues is explained in the Note prepared for Lord Birkenhead (Secretary of State), July 1927, IOC L/PO/5/9.

[14] For suspicions of smuggling and secret inducements to merchants, see IOC R/2/619/24, R/20/620/84, R/2/621/88, R/2/621/93 and R/2/623/109, and NAI FPD, 210(1)-I/1926 and 210-I/1926, Part 1-A.

revenues could hardly be described as natural or healthy."[15] The charge was not fair. Bombay and Karachi were already able to receive so much traffic that they were assured of a large income from port dues; but so long as the state ports remained small and backward, such charges–even if not deliberately kept low–would never provide sufficient money for modernisation. Any development accordingly had to be funded from other sources. However, in February 1927 Delhi informed the rulers of the maritime states of Saurashtra that "Our revenue losses, owing to the diversion of trade through the Kathiawar ports, have now become so serious that we have been reluctantly forced to the conclusion that the stage has now been reached at which we are bound to reconsider the position."[16] Delhi decided to reimpose the Viramgam Line, although in an effort not to alienate princely India it first made a show of seeking a compromise. In June, the states (including Baroda and Bhavnagar) were summoned to meet representatives of the government of India at Mount Abu (the hot weather headquarters of the Western India States Agency) "to find a new arrangement under which the fiscal and other interests of British India will be reasonably safeguarded with due regard to all similar interests of the states, and without recourse being had to the reimposition of a land customs line between Kathiawar and British India."[17]

The Mount Abu Conference began on 27 June 1927. Delhi clearly hoped to outsmart the princes. The meeting was chaired by Watson, the Agent to the Governor-General in the States of Western India, who was ostensibly neutral but was in fact acting on the instructions of the government of India (and was initially slated to

---

[15] C.C. Watson (AGG), speech at Morvi 1927, IOC Photo Eur 84 (Watson Collection). For the British view, see *Report of the Indian States Enquiry Committee*, pp. 92-93.

[16] Watson to Junagadh, Porbandar, and Morvi, 23 Feb. 1927, IOC R/2/623/118A.

[17] Watson to Junagadh, Nawanagar, Porbandar, Morvi, Sir Prabhashankar Pattani (President of the Council of Administration, Bhavnagar), and J.R. Martin (Political Secretary Bombay), 11 June 1927, IOC R/2/623/118B. For the Mount Abu Conference and the reimposition of the Viramgam Line, see IOC R/2/623/117, R/2/623/118A, R/2/623/118B, R/2/624/120A, R/2/625/127C and R/2/625/127J; NAI FPD, 210-I/1926, Part 1-A; Chimanlal H. Setalvad, *Recollections and Reflections: An Autobiography* (Bombay, n.d. [*ca* 1946]), pp. 485-489.

be a member of the British Indian delegation). British India was represented by Sir Geoffrey Corbett, a top official of the Department of Commerce, and C.R. Watkins, the head of the Bombay customs service. Against these, most of the state delegations merely comprised rulers or their Dewans, who had no specialised knowledge of customs, although Sir Chimanlal Setalvad, a Liberal politician from Bombay and one of India's greatest lawyers, appeared for Nawanagar. But the states argued their case well, and refused to be bullied by the British Indian heavyweights. It is clear that the government of India knew that the conference would fail, justifying the reimposition of the Viramgam Line. Only this explains the outrageous proposal that Delhi made to the states: it undertook not to impose any tariff wall, but only if the states handed over control (either total or supervisory) of their customs services, and the policing of their ports, to British Indian officers. All of the duty collected would go to Delhi. In compensation, the states would receive annual payments based on their customs revenues up to 1925-1926 and on the expenditures that they had already incurred in port development. Given that in 1905 the princes had denounced a similar suggestion as derogatory to their sovereignty, it was a foregone conclusion that they would reject Delhi's scheme; the government of India knew this, having been warned by Watson that "most of the States in Kathiawar value their Customs rights at least as much from the point of view of the Izzat of their States as from that of finances...."[18] Delhi must also have known that, even if the states renounced the right to administer their own customs (Nawanagar seemed prepared to allow British Indian officers to train and inspect, though not replace, its customs services), they would never accept the proposed compensation. By basing the payments on receipts up to 1925-1926, it ensured that Nawanagar would reject the figure, which did not take account of the huge increase in imports at Bedi over the past year (the Jam Saheb was offered 34 lakhs, less than half what he had earned from customs in 1926-1927), while the other states would refuse any compensation that did not include the potential earnings of their ports once they had been

[18] Watson to Sir John Thompson (Political Secretary India), 15 Mar. 1927 (first letter), IOC R/2/623/118A.

developed to the same level as Bedi. The British Indian delegates agreed to revise the compensation to take future expansion into account, but refused to consider the duties collected at Bedi in 1926-1927. Under the circumstances, few delegates can have been surprised when on 29 June, after three days of discussions, Watson announced that the negotiations had broken down. The Viramgam Line was reimposed five days later (though, thanks to the arrangements of 1865 and 1866, it did not affect goods from Bhavnagar). In order to reduce delays to railway traffic, however, the system used from 1905 to 1917 (by which customs had been levied at the British Indian frontier) was not restored. Rather, Delhi ordered that the duty on all imports be collected by state authorities at the port of entry, and goods that afterwards entered British India were subjected to a modified form of the certificates that had covered goods from Bhavnagar from 1911 to 1917: merchandise entering British India was to be accompanied by a certificate stating that the proper duty had been collected in the state. The British Indian customs service would take the certificate at the border, and recover the duty from the state. This certificate system meant that the states could retain only the duty taken on goods that were actually consumed in Saurashtra, losing everything collected on those that were re-exported to British India. Nevertheless, the reimposition of the customs cordon did not end trade into British India through Saurashtra. So long as merchandise from state ports was accompanied by a certificate stating that it had paid duty at the British rates, it was allowed into British India without any additional taxes; the new arrangements merely meant that Delhi now kept most of the customs collected at state ports. As a result, the trade of all the Saurashtra ports continued to grow after 1927: as long as import tariffs were the same everywhere, merchants who sold goods in the north-west did not care who retained the duty; and they naturally pre-ferred Saurashtra to the more distant Bombay or Karachi.

But by reimposing the Viramgam Line, Delhi angered the rulers of all of the maritime states of Saurashtra, and no doubt other princes who interpreted the action as a breach of the agreements of 1917. The Jam Saheb of Nawanagar had especial reason to feel betrayed: on the strength of the assurances he had received from the government of India, he had spent huge sums of money to transform Bedi into a major port of entry for goods destined for markets all over north-western India. He had anticipated that the dues levied at Bedi would assure his state a sizeable revenue; but the reestablishment of the customs cordon restricted him to the dues collected on goods consumed within Saurashtra, and his customs income plunged from seventy-eight lakhs of rupees in 1926-1927 to fourteen in 1927-1928. Perhaps even worse, he was losing a monarch's right to keep all the duties levied at his own ports, and thus an element of his sovereignty. Indeed, there can be no doubt that the Jam Saheb's anger over the customs dispute played a major part in his opposition to federation in the early 1930s. Having seen Delhi break its word and sacrifice his state to safeguard its own finances, he was understandably unwilling to accept an arrangement that could only increase the central government's authority over Nawanagar. The plans for customs collection in the future federation must have angered him still further: they would let each ruler keep only the duty paid by goods that remained in his own state, depriving Nawanagar even of the right to money collected on merchandise consumed elsewhere in Saurashtra. His qualms became public in the angry scene that took place in the Chamber of Princes immediately before his death in 1933, and, as has been seen, opposition to federation spread across princely India.[19] In 1927, of course, any plans for federation were in the future. Still, Delhi was unwise to antagonise the Jam Saheb, one of the most prominent rulers and a leader of the Chamber of Princes. Why, then, did it reimpose the Viramgam Line, which it had already decided to do before the Mount Abu Conference? The cordon was restored at the insistence of the Finance Department of the government of India: the diversion of trade to Bedi posed a very serious threat to the customs income of British India, and Delhi would lose still more money when the other Saurashtra ports were developed. In 1917, the need

[19] For the Jam Saheb's protests over the reimposition of the Viramgam Line, and subsequent customs negotiations between Nawanagar and the government of India, see IOC L/P&S/13/897, L/P&S/13/923-927, R/1/1/2249, R/1/1/4653, R/1/1/4661, R/1/1/4780, R/2/624/119, R/2/625/127F, R/2/627/150A, R/2/639/315 and R/2/642/337A; NAI FPD, 37-I/1932, 101-I/1931, 164-I/1931, 226-IB/1934, 276-I/1932 and 358-I/1931. For the role of the customs dispute in the Jam Saheb's opposition to federation, see Copland, *Princes of India*, pp. 115-116, 122-123. For the proposals regarding customs collection in the federation, see *Report of the Indian States Enquiry Committee*, pp. 141, 164.

for princely support had led the central government to open British India to trade from state ports, overruling any objections that Finance may have raised, but ten years later no one in Delhi saw any reason to jeopardise the country's revenues merely in order to conciliate the states. For in the mid-1920s, the Paramount Power was more secure in its position than at almost any other time in the twentieth century: the constitution of 1919 was functioning reasonably well, and the Congress, the only nationalist organization that the British perceived as a true threat, was quiescent. And although the princes' opponent Lord Reading had left India in 1926, the like-minded Sir John Thompson remained Political Secretary, and persisted in his policy of ruthlessly subordinating the rulers' interests to what he believed were the interests of India as a whole.[20] It therefore seems that the Political Department and the rest of the government of India agreed to Finance's plans (which were necessitated by the serious harm being caused by the diversion of revenues to the state coffers, with the resulting impact on Britain's ability to maintain control) mainly because they saw no need to court the princes with favourable treatment.

The states were not about to submit meekly to so severe a reduction of their revenues, however. In 1928, the rulers of Baroda, Junagadh, Nawanagar, Porbandar and Morvi lodged formal protests with the new Viceroy, Lord Irwin. The Jam Saheb complained that he had undertaken expensive port development after being assured that no limits would be placed on Bedi's trade. He continued that Delhi must have foreseen the effects of this promise, and he could only conclude that it had either misled him into wasting money that he could not now recover, or changed the rules of the game in mid-play. He stated that, as he had loyally adhered to the agreement of 1917, the government of India must do the same and lift the Viramgam Line. If this were not possible, he demanded that the matter be referred to arbitration, perhaps at the Judicial Committee of the Privy Council, or a committee set up under the 1920 rules, to determine whether the government's actions had indeed been justi-

---

[20] For the Reading-Thompson policy and its effects on the states' finances in general, see Copland, *Princes of India*, pp. 56-58.

fied.[21] The other four princes pointed out that, as their ports posed no threat to the customs revenues of the central government, the imposition of a tariff wall against their trade was unjustified.[22] In September 1929, Delhi answered the princes' charges. The Jam Saheb was told that the diversion of trade to Bedi had simply posed too much of a threat to the central revenues to be tolerated, and that the fiscal interests had indeed become important; moreover, by lowering his port charges and paying for harbour development from the state treasury, he had fostered an unhealthy development of Bedi and violated the spirit of the agreements of 1917. The grievances of the other maritime states, however, were largely redressed. So long as duties remained at the British Indian rate, each state would be allowed to retain the money that it collected on goods destined for re-export to British India, provided the total collected did not exceed two lakhs of rupees. Once that figure had been reached, the states would have to hand over all duties taken on goods that crossed the Viramgam Line, but as only Nawanagar and Baroda had attained the limit, the other states (Junagadh, Porbandar, Morvi and Jafarabad) regained free entry into British India. Delhi also promised to reimburse the states for their expenditures on port development. Even Nawanagar and Baroda were given relief: not only an offer of a lump sum to compensate them for the expenses of port development, but, in view of the extent of their loss of anticipated revenue, they (and any other state that reached the maximum of two

---

[21] The 1920 rules, arising from the Montagu-Chelmsford report, concerned the appointment of arbitrators in the case of disputes between, on the one hand, an Indian state, and, on the other, the government of India, a province, or another state.

[22] For the rulers' memorials, and the Paramount Power's response, see IOC L/P&S/13/921, R/1/1/4654, R/2/625/127D, R/2/625/127E, R/2/625/127G, R/2/625/127H and R/2/625/127I. The princes do not seem to have raised the issue of fairness, although they could easily have done so: for while Delhi denied that the states had the right to keep the duties collected on goods imported through state ports but sold in British India, it showed no desire to give up any money collected on imports that went from British ports to landlocked states. In the same vein, Tod, *op. cit.*, pp. 263-264, noted that at the beginning of the nineteenth century, competition from British ports lowered the customs revenues of Bhavnagar state by more than half; but there were then no financial experts to protest that this was unhealthy.

lakhs) could now retain a share of their customs income on re-exports equal to the highest amount allowed to any other state.

The new measures derived from a suggestion that Watson had made on the collapse of the Mount Abu Conference, but at that time had been rejected by Delhi. In the two years since then, however, Indian politics had been transformed. In November 1927, Indians were outraged by the appointment of the all-British Simon Commission to study constitutional reform. Congress revived and Gandhi returned to politics; the renewal of civil disobedience, a resurgence of terrorism, the Nehru Report which demanded Dominion status, and the rise of the radical Jawaharlal Nehru all followed, and the Paramount Power perceived its position to be under a much greater threat than at any time since the end of Gandhi's last campaign. The British were once again in need of Indian allies; they naturally turned to the princes, and very likely implemented Watson's proposal mainly in order to conciliate at least some of the rulers who had been angered by the restoration of the Viramgam Line.

But no compromise would satisfy the Jam Saheb. Even without low incidental charges (which had been abandoned), trade through Bedi to British India continued to expand at a phenomenal rate. This made it clear that the growth of the trade had indeed been "healthy," and that Bedi was a natural port of entry for imports destined for the north-west. Little wonder that the Jam Saheb deeply resented the fact that he was able to keep only forty-four of the 156 lakhs that his customs service collected in 1930-1931. Indeed, he and the Maharaja of Baroda refused to accept the rebate cheques sent to them under the next-highest system. There was the added problem that the strangulation of his revenue meant that the state could not maintain the unfinished port works, which by 1931 were collapsing. In 1931, he appealed to the Secretary of State, repeating his request for an impartial tribunal. The Agent to the Governor-General supported the appeal; but the government of India was only willing to support an appeal if it could be sure of winning, and in the end it recommended that the Secretary of State reject the memorial. The Secretary of State sought the opinion of J.C.C. Davidson, a Conservative Member of Parliament who had recently chaired the Indian States Enquiry Committee into the financial position of the states. He stated his opinion that the government of

India would win an appeal, since the "assurance" given to the Jam Saheb in 1917 was not a binding "promise." Nevertheless, "broader considerations justify the offer of a reasonable compromise," and he proposed the establishment of a forty-year annuity that would pay the Jam Saheb six lakhs a year to compensate him for the expenses incurred in port development, as well as other annuities to offer appropriate compensation to other states. If the Jam Saheb rejected this offer, Davidson recommended a reference to a tribunal, to decide on the legal issues involved.[23] The "broader considerations" were not explained, but Davidson must have been referring to the realisation of the harm that the quarrel with the Jam Saheb might do to the plans for federation.

Delhi opined that the Jam Saheb would reject the annuity, since he had already refused any lump sum compensation, and that in any case the proposal could not be accepted by the government of India. In the first place, a generous annuity for Nawanagar might make negotiations with the other states more difficult, and in the second place it would allow the Jam Saheb to continue to profit at the expense of the central revenues. At the same time, the government concluded that a tribunal would not necessarily end the dispute, as even if it did rule in the Jam Saheb's favour, it could not set the amount of compensation that he should receive, so the question would remain open. The Viceroy instead proposed a fresh conference of the maritime states, as "It should be possible ... to satisfy Morvi, Junagadh & Porbander and thus shorten the front of attack and strengthen the position generally. Nawanagar may refuse to be satisfied, but we should be in a better situation to demonstrate that any further claims from that quarter are unreasonable."[24] But the Secretary of State refused to consider a conference, which might necessitate commitments from Delhi that would render more difficult the ongoing discussions on the financial terms of federation being worked out at the Round Table Conferences (where the Jam Saheb was representing the Indian states). Instead, he ordered that the Jam Saheb simply be offered arbitration by a tribunal regarding the interpretation of the 1917 agreements; confident of victory, the

---

[23] J.C.C. Davidson to Sir Samuel Hoare (Secretary of State), 27 July 1932, NAI FPD, 276-I/1932.

[24] Minute by B.J. Glancy (PD India), 8 Sept. 1932, NAI FPD, 276-I/1932.

Secretary of State said that such a tribunal would have the effect of "dispelling idea of Princes that Government is afraid of an independent verdict or that Princes legal advisers are infallible."[25] He later added that a final settlement of the Nawanagar dispute would also set a precedent that would make it possible to reach agreements with the other maritime states. In November 1932, the Jam Saheb was accordingly told that if he wished, he might leave the matter to a tribunal of one English and two Indian judges. The Jam Saheb was currently in London engaged in the third Round Table Conference; he promised to make a decision on the proposal once he returned to India.

In the event, Jam Saheb Ranjitsinhji died the following April. Just eight days later, his successor Digvijaysinhji accepted Delhi's suggestion that the customs question be referred to arbitration, although he preferred a single British judge rather than a tribunal. The Scottish judge Lord Dunedin was accepted by both parties, and the Jam Saheb selected the experienced princely lawyer Sir Leslie Scott to act as his counsel before the tribunal.[26] Dunedin heard the case in January 1934. He supported the Jam Saheb's contention that the assurance given in 1917 had modified the agreements permitting a reconsideration of the lifting of the line if the fiscal issues became important, and that the reimposition of the Line in 1927 had violated this understanding. He concluded that Bedi was a natural port of entry for goods going to large areas of British India, and that while the government of India was entitled to the bulk of the customs receipts on such goods, Nawanagar too ought to receive a share of the duty, and substantially more than the two lakhs offered by the government of India. Dunedin ordered that Willingdon work out a mutually acceptable figure with the Jam Saheb. In May 1934, they settled at five lakhs of rupees (although Delhi rejected Digvijaysinhji's demand for five lakhs for each year since the reimposition of the Line in 1927). Since Nawanagar was already keeping well over forty lakhs from merchandise consumed in Saurashtra, the compromise assured the Jam Saheb a sizeable customs revenue, although even this was not enough to restore his support for the Paramount

[25] Telegram Hoare to Lord Willingdon (Viceroy), 10 Oct 1932, NAI FPD, 276-I/1932.

[26] For Scott's career as a lawyer for the princes, see Copland, *Princes of India*.

Power. It was perhaps symbolic that Digvijaysinhji was Chancellor of the Chamber of Princes when in 1939 the states definitively rejected the federal proposals.

Even as the customs dispute with Nawanagar was being resolved, however, disagreements with the other maritime states of Junagadh, Porbandar, Morvi and Jafarabad were reigniting. This was because the trade of their ports had continued to grow since the settlement of 1929. By 1934, all were collecting over two lakhs of duty on goods that were re-exported to British India.[27] They therefore had to hand over to Delhi all of the duties collected on merchandise that crossed the Viramgam Line, since the agreement had merely allowed them to keep a sum equal to the highest duty collected by any state that stood under two lakhs. This meant that their customs incomes had dropped even as their share of British India's import trade increased. Like the late Jam Saheb, they now naturally resented the limits that British financial policy placed on their revenues. This was a great danger to the Paramount Power, which was in the midst of trying to secure princely support for federation. But the new disputes threatened to create an even more immediately perilous situation. The maritime states had come to depend on their customs revenues. If a ruler could not retain the duty on goods that were re-exported across the Viramgam Line, his only hope was to increase his ports' share of the foreign imports consumed within Saurashtra (on which he could keep all the customs collected). The easiest way to do this would be to set lower duties and port charges than were levied at other Saurashtra ports. Since 1917, all of the states had levied customs at British Indian rates; but in July 1932, two months after losing the right of free entry into British India, Morvi announced that it would henceforth set its own tariff rates. This could only lead to a tariff war among the maritime states, each struggling to maintain and expand its share of the local trade. The resulting animosities might make the Saurashtra princes unwilling

---

[27] See Table Two. For the customs of Junagadh, Porbandar, Morvi and Jafarabad in the 1930s, see IOC L/P&S/13/15, L/P&S/13/175, L/P&S/13/790, L/P&S/13/897, L/P&S/13/921-922, R/1/1/4654, R/1/1/4781, R/2/597/18, R/2/632/239, R/2/639/319, R/2/640/330, R/2/640/330A; NAI FPD, 56-I/1933, 146-IB/1935 and 171-IB/1936. Junagadh lost the right of retaining all dues in 1931, as did Morvi in 1932, and Jafarabad and Porbandar in 1934.

to enter into the closer ties with one another necessitated by federation. Moreover, those rulers whose revenues suffered in the tariff war would doubtless blame Delhi for provoking the conflict, and perhaps fight its constitutional scheme for that reason; and any chance of a settlement with Nawanagar would be wrecked if Bedi lost much of its trade to other state ports. The Paramount Power had to avoid any lowering of duties, and "persuaded Morvi to hold its hand pending a Conference to be held after decision of the Nawanagar claim."[28] After Dunedin's ruling on the Bedi case, the meeting (attended by representatives of Junagadh, Porbandar and Morvi) duly took place in December 1934. It set the stage for further negotiations with all the maritime states, leading to new customs agreements between the government of India and Junagadh, Nawanagar, Porbandar and Morvi which were concluded in 1936 (and an agreement with Jafarabad in 1940). Both sides made concessions: the states promised to maintain British Indian rates of duty, and undertook to grant no rebates or subsidies to incidental charges; Delhi allowed the states to retain two lakhs out of the duties collected on merchandise that crossed the Viramgam Line for each year since 1927 and in the future, and if Delhi was satisfied that the states were upholding their part of the agreement, five lakhs (the amount already allowed to Nawanagar, which also at last received a refund of two lakhs a year to cover 1927/8-1933/4). Nawanagar also received an assurance "that it is not the intention of the Government of India to issue any prohibition calculated to subject the ports of the Nawanagar State to a differential treatment as compared with the ports of British India or devised with the object of interfering with the legitimate commercial interests of any particular port...."[29]

The Paramount Power and the states both seem to have been satisfied with these agreements, although Delhi was wrong if it thought that by resolving the customs disputes it could win the princes' support for federation.[30] The arrangements made in 1936

---

[28] Note by P.J. Patrick (IO), 6 Nov. 1933, IOC L/P&S/13/921.

[29] F.V. Wylie (PD India) to J. de la H. Gordon (AGG), 15 June 1936, IOC L/P&S/13/922.

[30] For the significance of customs claims in the failure of the federal negotiations, see Copland, *Princes of India*, pp. 154, 283-284.

governed customs collection at the ports of Saurashtra until after Independence (although as late as 1941, the government of India suspected that secret rebates were being granted); in 1946 the Political Department proposed a full customs union between the Saurashtra states and British India, but it made no effort to bring one into being.[31] In January 1948, on the unification of the states of Saurashtra into the United State of Kathiawar, N.M. Buch, the Regional Commissioner at Rajkot (successor to the British Resident), proposed negotiations with the government of India to remove the Viramgam Line, commenting that "This customs examination at Viramgam has been most humiliating and irritating to the travelling public of Kathiawar." This resulted in an agreement that transferred control of customs at the Saurashtra ports to the government of India, in return for compensation.[32]

III

When the Viramgam Line was restored in 1927, Bhavnagar alone of the Saurashtra states retained the right to keep all the duty it collected on merchandise that entered British India through its ports, subject to certification that the correct duty had been paid. The Bhavnagar authorities disliked this system of certificates, which was imposed to ensure that goods did not enter Bhavnagar through other states that did not collect adequate customs duties, and then move on to British India. In 1928, Bhavnagar agreed instead to the erection of a customs cordon against the rest of Saurashtra, and in 1929 the demand for certificates was lifted. By 1934, however, a new concern had emerged. Cheap Japanese cotton goods were being imported into Kutch (which was outside of the British Indian cus-

---

[31] See IOC R/2/596/2, R/2/596/4, R/2/596/5, R/2/597/16 and R/2/597/18.

[32] N.M. Buch (Regional Commissioner for the States of Western India and Gujarat) to V.P. Menon (Secretary, Ministry of States), 27 Jan. 1948, NAI WISA, C-15-1/1948; V.P. Menon, *The Story of the Integration of the Indian States* (New York, 1956), p. 455.

toms system and charged very low import duties) and the maritime states of Saurashtra (which Delhi believed were secretly giving rebates of duty to encourage the use of their ports); they were then smuggled through the rather porous frontier between Bhavnagar and its neighbouring states in the guise of personal baggage, and next carried into British India and sold. The government of Bhavnagar was accordingly informed that unless steps were taken to prevent the smuggling into Bhavnagar, certificates proving that the correct duty had already been paid would be required for all goods entering British India. Sir Prabhashankar Pattani, the Dewan of Bhavnagar, was given the opportunity of suggesting an alternative; but meanwhile, Delhi decided to begin examining the baggage of all rail passengers crossing from Bhavnagar into British India.[33]

But the smuggling of the Japanese goods was only a symptom of what Delhi saw as a larger problem. In February 1934, the Central Board of Revenue had drawn up a vicious denunciation of the incompetence of the customs personnel of all the maritime states, who it claimed could not be trusted to appraise goods correctly even if the British Indian rates of duty were being charged. The Board said that Delhi must assert the right to re-assess all goods that entered British India through Bhavnagar, and ensure that the correct duty had been paid. But the most serious concern was that the volume of goods entering British India through Bhavnagar had greatly increased in recent years. In 1931, the government of India had imposed a duty on imports of raw cotton, and Bhavnagar had taken advantage of this to make an aggressive attempt to lure cotton to its ports. Even if the correct duty was being paid, Bhavnagar offered lower rates through, for example, free insurance and free storage, all permissible under the terms of the treaty. The result was that virtually all of the foreign cotton destined for Ahmedabad mills now entered through Bhavnagar. The losses to British Indian revenues on account of goods entering through Bhavnagar had risen from one lakh in 1927-1928 to forty-five lakhs in 1932-1933, and Bhavnagar had now replaced Bedi as the main threat to the reve-

---

[33] For customs relations between Bhavnagar and the government of India from 1927 to 1947, see IOC L/P&S/13/897, L/P&S/13/1464-1466, R/1/1/4792, R/1/1/4804, R/2/598/21-22, R/2/639/323-326 and R/2/640/327; NAI FPD, 124-IB/1934, 124(3)-IB/1934, 138-IB/1935, 161-IB/1935 and 213-IB/1936.

nues. (Delhi did not mention that Bhavnagar also happened to be much closer to Ahmedabad than any other major port.) The following month, the question was discussed at a joint meeting of representatives of the Finance, Commerce, and Political Departments, and there were calls for the denunciation of the port treaty with Bhavnagar, on the grounds that "the present conditions were never contemplated when the treaty was made."[34] But the Legislative Department noted that the treaty could only be denounced if Delhi had proof that Bhavnagar had violated its terms; and the Political Department pointed out that if a major treaty with a state were repudiated without firm cause, "A general feeling of insecurity would arise which would ruin all chances of negotiation for the future."[35] Rather, Bhavnagar had to be persuaded to make concessions. But the state was most unlikely to do so, since it found the existing situation so profitable. The government of India therefore adopted a rather underhanded technique: it drew up a Bill to impose an excise duty on imported raw cotton to be collected at the cloth mills; but to ensure that this would only affect Bhavnagar's trade, the excise was to be restricted to cotton coming from within the British Empire, as almost all of the cotton arriving at Bhavnagar was from British East Africa rather than from, for example, Iran (another major supplier). There was actually no intention of placing this Bill before the Legislative Assembly, and the whole thing was a ruse to secure Bhavnagar's acquiescence in a new policy. Furthermore, in June 1934, representatives of the Political Department and the Central Board of Revenue met at Simla and concluded that "the position created by the Secretary of State's interpretation of the Bhavnagar treaty [in 1910] was resulting in an intolerable inroad into our customs revenue," and that they must reverse this loss "by all legitimate means consonant with the treaty as interpreted by the Secretary of the State."[36] The government of India even threatened to close the frontier to all goods except those that could be proved to have entered at the port of Bhavnagar itself, ending the conces-

[34] Note by Sir George Schuster (Finance Member, Government of India), 10 Mar. 1934, NAI FPD, 213-IB/1936.

[35] Minutes by L. Graham (Legislative Department), 13 Mar. 1934, and Glancy, 19 Mar. 1934, both NAI FPD, 213-IB/1936.

[36] Minute by R.E.L. Wingate (PD), 10 June 1934, NAI FPD, 124-IB/1934.

sion that had existed since 1865 extending the same rights to the other ports of Bhavnagar state (since the treaty only specifically mentioned Bhavnagar proper). After this heavy pressure from the Paramount Power, Pattani agreed that Bhavnagar would voluntarily place itself in the same position as the other maritime states: it would keep the duties that it collected on imports up to a certain amount, but would then pay the balance over to the government of India. But fixing such an amount proved impossible, as Pattani insisted on retaining the huge sum of one hundred lakhs, which Delhi would not allow; and in any case, the smuggling of goods through Bhavnagar and into British India continued. And on 1 June 1935, after securing a legal opinion that the certificate system did not infringe upon Bhavnagar's rights, Delhi terminated the agreement of 1929 and began to demand proof of duty paid on all goods entering British India from Bhavnagar; if no such proof were forthcoming, the duty was collected at the border. It was soon reported, however, that while goods that had landed in Bhavnagar were accompanied by certificates stating that they had paid the correct duty at British Indian rates, they were often being misappraised and charged a lower duty than was required. In 1936, the Secretary of State agreed to a proposal of the government of India that unless Bhavnagar allowed inspection of the customs arrangements at its ports, the Viramgam Line would be reimposed against the state, in other words all goods entering British India from Bhavnagar would have to pay duty at the border, whether or not they had already paid anything in the state. Not surprisingly, the government of Bhavnagar angrily rejected inspection, and the customs cordon was promptly restored. In 1937 the Maharaja of Bhavnagar submitted to Lord Zetland, the Secretary of State, a formal protest against the closing of the frontier and the imposition of the certificate system; two years later, he received the answer that the customs cordon would be lifted only if he fully cooperated in administering the certificate system. This, however, the Maharaja refused to do, even though it would have benefited the state economically and financially. The British ban on goods from Bhavnagar caused serious damage to the finances of the state, which had been earning from imports a sum equal to 1½ percent of British India's total customs revenue. And because under the 1936 agreements all of the maritime states did in fact maintain the British tariff, the adoption of the certificate system would have had no effect on Bhavnagar's trade. But giving in to British dictation on its customs policy would diminish the state's sovereignty, and such a slur on the izzat of the ruler and people of Bhavnagar far outweighed the economic benefits that acquiescence in Delhi's wishes would assuredly bring. The Paramount Power did not understand this. It thought that three years' experience of the Viramgam Line had made the Maharaja and his new Dewan, Sir Prabhashankar's son A.P. Pattani, desperate to regain entry to British India and willing to accept any conditions that Delhi attached to reopening the frontier. For the central government did not merely hope to secure Bhavnagar's cooperation in the certificate system; it wanted the state to renounce the special status that it had enjoyed for eighty years, so as to establish uniformity in the customs system of Saurashtra. The outbreak of the Second World War in September 1939 led the government to desire tighter control of India's export and import trade in the interests of security, and the following month Zetland accordingly ordered the Resident, Gibson, to try to extort "a new arrangement with Bhavnagar more in accordance with the Agreements made with other Maritime States in Kathiawar."[37] In other words, in return for an end to the British blockade, Bhavnagar was to give up its right to keep all of the duty collected on goods that entered British India.

It soon became clear, however, that while Pattani did want a settlement of the customs dispute, he insisted that it take the form of a restoration of the situation that had existed before 1937: free entry to British India, with Bhavnagar keeping all of the customs duties collected at its ports, and the abolition of the certificate system. Delhi should have known that the izzat of his state would never allow the Maharaja to agree to anything less than this; during two and a half years of meetings and discussions with the Resident and the Political Department, Pattani made it abundantly clear that Bhavnagar found unacceptable the two central elements of the agreements with the other Saurashtra maritime states, a limit on the

[37] C.G. Herbert (PD) to E.C. Gibson (Resident), 7 Oct. 1939, IOC R/2/598/21.

state's share of the duties it collected and the certificate system.[38] No settlement was therefore reached for the duration of the war. The Paramount Power showed that it had indeed abandoned its interwar policy of conciliating the princes. Before 1939, it might well have tried to earn Bhavnagar's goodwill by giving in to Pattani's demands: because the tariff war had not materialised, there was no need to insist that Bhavnagar adopt the certificate system, and Bhavnagar ports had enjoyed special rights for many years without injuring the central government's interests. Now, however, Delhi decided that if Bhavnagar did not yield to its demands, there was no reason to pursue a settlement. Finally, at the end of 1946, Pattani indicated that he was willing to negotiate a solution to the twenty-year-old customs dispute. He may have hoped that their impending departure from India would put the British in a generous mood, or he may have realised that Bhavnagar would never get all that it wanted, and decided to make concessions. But the independence of India was imminent, and the Political Department answered his proposal with instructions to wait "until the Central Government had settled down on a more permanent basis."[39] In January 1948, Bhavnagar became the first state in Saurashtra to institute full responsible government, and the new prime minister promptly requested the cancellation of the certificate system.[40] The following month, however, Bhavnagar was merged into the United State of Kathiawar, and the Bhavnagar customs dispute was absorbed into the wider regional one.

---

[38] Pattani claimed to be willing to limit Bhavnagar's customs receipts to a certain amount and hand the rest over to the central government; but as he insisted that the state should keep a percentage of the central government's total customs revenue equal to the percentage of India's foreign trade that went through Bhavnagar ports, this was no limit at all.

[39] Note by Sir Conrad Corfield (Political Adviser) on talks with A.P. Pattani (Dewan of Bhavnagar), 11 Dec. 1946, IOC R/2/598/22.

[40] Telegram prime minister of Bhavnagar to Buch, 30 Jan. 1948, NAI WISA, C-15-1/1948.

TABLE TWO

CUSTOMS RECEIPTS OF THE MARITIME STATES OF SAURASHTRA

(in lakhs of rupees).

Total Customs Receipts, 1917/18-1926/27 and 1930/31:

	1917/18	1918/19	1919/20	1920/21	1921/22	1922/23	1923/24	1924/25	1925/26	1926/27	1930/31
Bhavnagar	4.53	4.77	5.66	8.22	14.47	14.27	20.74	18.15	17.20	6.36	51.05
Jafarabad	n.a.	n.a.	n.a.	n.a.	0.08	0.07	0.08	0.0007	0.01	0.006	0.45
Junagadh[41]	1.47	2.45	2.44	3.09	4.76	5.39	6.42	8.18	8.43	8.55	13.71
Morvi	1.66	0.98	1.17	0.82	1.39	1.84	0.85	0.54	0.89	1.28	4.63
Nawanagar	3.66	5.23	6.07	5.59	6.29	10.49	18.29	21.36	29.68	78.90	44.00
Porbandar 2.01	2.31	2.80	3.43	4.12	9.72	4.46	1.92	3.73	4.28	5.06	

Customs Receipts on Goods Re-Exported to British India, 1927/28-1933/34:

An asterisk indicates that the state collected more than two lakhs of rupees on re-exported goods.

	1927/28	1928/29	1929/30	1930/31	1931/32	1932/33	1933/34
Jafarabad	n.a.	n.a.	n.a.	n.a.	n.a.	n.a.	*
Junagadh	0.45	0.39	0.35	*	*	*	*
Morvi	0.00	0.003	0.002	0.33	*	*	*
Nawanagar	*	*	*	*	*	*	*
Porbandar 0.14	0.53	0.53	0.77	0.58	*	*	

[41] The Junagadh figures exclude the totals for Mangrol, which was ruled by a semi-autonomous Shaikh who retained the customs revenues collected at the port.

CHAPTER SIX

THE PROBLEM OF THE SMALLER STATES

Visitors, administrators and scholars often commented on the fact that the Western India States Agency did not just include the forty-two salute and non-salute states whose rulers enjoyed representation in the Chamber of Princes, but also over four hundred lesser territorial units. These areas were called talukas and estates, and they often comprised single villages. Most of them were far smaller than any polities found in pre-British days, and the only reason they existed at all was the policy of the Paramount Power: the British first inadvertently created them, and then deliberately preserved them. Until the revolt of 1857, states all over India had been regularly annexed to British India on various grounds, which raised fears among the princes that their rule was about to be terminated. In 1858, however, the Viceroy Lord Canning issued a guarantee of territorial integrity, with the objective of eliminating these fears and thus of securing the princes' support for British rule, and it was this that allowed the petty states to survive. The allegiance of the chiefs of single villages was in itself not of much consequence to the Paramount Power. But if the plea of eliminating anomalies excused the annexation of small states to their larger neighbours, it might also justify merging even the biggest states into British provinces and thus erasing from the map all of princely India. Even major princes would therefore resist any suggestion that the petty chiefs should cease to rule, and the removal of a few hundred picturesque relics of the past was not worth reawakening a major princely grievance against the Paramount Power.[1]

Then, in the 1930s, it dawned on British officialdom that in most cases, the talukas and estates lacked the resources to maintain anything beyond the most rudimentary governments, indeed that

---

[1] Copland, *Princes of India*, calls Canning's guarantees the princes' "Magna Charta" (p. 17).

they were so tiny that their independent existence was simply ludicrous. For many years, the fragmentation of princely Gujarat (the Western India States Agency and the neighbouring Gujarat States Agency) had been regarded as rather quaint, "the great social peculiarity of the country." But it now became "the problem of smaller States," in dire need of correction if it was not to hinder the Paramount Power's effort to maintain control of the situation.[2] The new perception led to one of the greatest changes in British policy towards the Indian states during the entire period of Crown rule in India. In 1932 Sir Frederick Sykes, the Governor of Bombay, suggested that the tiny artificial creations of British rule "must inevitably" be reintegrated into the larger states from which they had been separated a century earlier, and in 1940-1943–over strenuous princely objections–the Canning guarantees were abandoned and the small states in Western India and the Gujarat States Agency were merged into neighbouring states.[3] This exemplifies the changed attitude towards the states that the imperial masters adopted in the 1930s.

I

It has already been seen that during the nineteenth century, the British gave full sovereignty to hundreds of minor nobles in Saurashtra, Banas Kantha and Mahi Kantha, the bhayat of the princes of the region. It was this that created the petty states.[4] Some scholars have blamed Alexander Walker for starting this, by fragmenting Saurashtra when in 1807 he settled the tribute paid to the Marathas by its states.[5] At first glance, this charge seems justified. Before

---

[2] The quotations are from "A Run Through Kathiawar," in *Blackwood's Edinburgh Magazine*, 120 (July-Dec. 1876), pp. 191-210, 399-416, 577-600, at p. 195; and "Discussions regarding the policy of the paramount power in relation to the problem of smaller States...," 1939, IOC R/1/1/3416(1).

[3] The quotation is from Sir Frederick Sykes (Governor of Bombay) to Lord Willingdon (Viceroy), 25 Oct. 1932, IOC R/1/1/2241.

[4] See Chapter One.

[5] V.B. Kulkarni, *Princely India and the Lapse of British Paramountcy* (Bombay, 1985), p. 42; Tambs-Lyche, *op. cit.*, p. 289. Spodek, "Urban Politics," wrongly suggests (pp. 255-256) that extreme fragmentation was a longstanding

undertaking his mission, Walker outlined his objectives in a letter to the twenty-nine rulers whom he regarded as sovereign princes rather than subordinate bhayat. He presumably initially intended to deal only with these twenty-nine. But a share of each state's tribute had naturally always come from villages owned by the bhayat; and, at least since the beginning of the Marathas' tribute-collecting mulkgiri expeditions, even non-independent bhayat had often paid their share directly to the Marathas rather than through the parent state. And because he negotiated a separate settlement with every individual who paid tribute to the Gaekwad, whether independent ruler or mere bhayat, Walker eventually concluded 153 revenue engagements, rather than twenty-nine. As has been seen, simultaneously with the revenue engagements, Walker took security bonds from most of the tribute-payers in Saurashtra, guaranteeing them in possession of their lands. This was intended to end the internecine war that so disturbed the region.[6] This makes it seem that Walker's revenue engagements and security bonds abruptly replaced twenty-nine princes with 153 chieftains, which is all the more credible because it presumably made it easier to establish British supremacy over the peninsula. This, however, is incorrect. Walker was certainly aware that the bhayat remained subordinate to their parent states, and in his reports he carefully distinguished "Chieftains" from "Bhyad." Indeed, at one point, he even recommended depriving the bhayat of the judicial powers that they enjoyed over their villages:

> ... one of the principal causes of the crimes and disorders of Kattywar arises from the vast number of petty independent jurisdictions which have been established in that country. ... the condition of the

---

feature of political organization in the area.

[6] A. Walker, "Proceedings adopted in the years 1804 and 1807, by Lieutenant Colonel A. Walker, Resident at Baroda, consequent on an application from certain chiefs in the province of Kattywar, soliciting the protection of the British Government," in Thomas, *op. cit.*, 39, pp. 63-92; A. Walker, "Report on the District of Jhalawar, in the Province of Kattywar," *ibid.*, pp. 93-112.

> country can never be much improved until these inconsiderable authorities are incorporated with the larger States.[7]

When he granted the bhayat revenue engagements, Walker merely recognised that they paid tribute to the Gaekwad on their own account; and his security bonds were intended not to give the bhayat independence, but to protect them from excessive interference by their parent states. The rulers of those parent states did not want to have to maintain order in estates belonging to the bhayat, or to pay the tribute from bhayati villages, and therefore gladly acquiesced in Walker's arrangements which left responsibility for both these unpleasant tasks in the hands of the bhayat. But they certainly would not have done so if they had thought that the settlement would transform their barons into independent rulers. It seems clear that Walker, the major princes, and the bhayat all believed that the revenue engagements and security bonds would simply confirm the status quo, with the bhayat remaining autonomous landlords within the parent states; the guarantees embodied in the security bonds gave the bhayat a stronger position than they had hitherto enjoyed, but they were initially no more independent than were the bhayat of Kutch, who enjoyed similar guarantees.[8] The settlements that the East India Company subsequently mediated in Banas Kantha and in Mahi Kantha followed the same principles.

This relationship was not changed by the establishment of British paramountcy over Saurashtra, Banas Kantha and Mahi Kantha between 1816 and 1820, and the bhayat remained under the authority of their princes. Thus, in 1843, the British Political Agent in

---

[7] A. Walker, "Reports on the Resources, &c., of the ... Province of Guzerat," in Thomas, *op. cit.*, pp. 1-61, at p. 48. In an illustration of the way in which historians can inadvertently distort the historical record, Nightingale, *op. cit.*, p. 231, inaccurately paraphrases this as a desire to establish "one system of justice," which Howard Spodek, "Rulers, Merchants and Other Groups in the City-States of Saurashtra, India, around 1800," in *Comparative Studies in History and Society*, 16, 4 (Sept. 1974), pp. 448-470, at p. 454, expands to a demand for "one system of justice and rule."

[8] See memorandum, A. Walker (Resident at Baroda) to Limbdi, 1807-1808, in Aitchison, *op. cit.*, 6:23-24. Tambs-Lyche, *op. cit.*, p. 290, wrongly says that until the Walker Settlement, the petty chiefs paid the Baroda tribute through their parent states. For the Kutch bhayat, see Chapter One.

Kathiawar mediated a written agreement between the Thakor Saheb of Limbdi and his bhayat, in which the latter confirmed the Thakor Saheb's right to exercise civil and criminal jurisdiction over the people of their estates.[9] Gradually, however, the ties between parent states and bhayat were eroded. The bhayat were eager to become sovereigns in their own right by establishing their independence, and therefore gladly allowed the British rather than their parent states to resolve their disputes or confirm successions. The Paramount Power obliged them. Perhaps this was intended to increase British authority over the states. It may also show a failure to understand the diffused structure of power in a Rajput state, which led at least some Britons to believe that if a man paid tribute, administered justice, and was guaranteed in possession of his lands by the Paramount Power, he must rank as a sovereign ruler. No formal declaration of independence ever severed the bhayat from their parent states, but the tie became weaker and weaker, and disappeared altogether between 1857 and 1877, when judicial powers in western India were classified. Holding that petty states lacked the resources to try major cases fairly, the government of Bombay divided all the rulers in Saurashtra, Banas Kantha and Mahi Kantha into eight groups according to the extent of the powers that their law courts were henceforth allowed to exercise, from First Class (full civil and criminal jurisdiction), through Seventh Class (very limited criminal and no civil jurisdiction), to non-jurisdictional petty chiefs who were not placed in any class. Responsibility for serious offences and disputes in smaller units–residuary jurisdiction–was now assumed by the local British political officer, rather than either the parent state or the petty chief himself.[10] This deprived the rulers of the parent states of the last element of overlordship that many of them still exercised in their bhayat, and they protested accordingly. Not

---

[9] Limbdi to E.W. West (PA Kathiawar), 25 Oct. 1883, NAI WISA, R C-12/1884-85.

[10] See W.M.P. Wood (Agent to the Governor of Bombay in Kathiawar) to J.E.B. Hotson (Political Secretary Bombay), 19/21 Aug. 1923, IOC R/2/622/103; Aitchison, *op. cit.*, 6:1, 262-263; *Gazetteer of the Bombay Presidency*, 8:308, 318, 5:388-391. The traditional role of Rajput nobles in dispensing justice is noted in Rudolph, "Princely States of Rajputana," p. 22. The gradation of judicial authority is discussed in Chapter Eleven.

only did the classification mark a serious infringement of their sovereignty, it also caused grave administrative problems. Very often, villages belonging to the bhayat lay between districts under the direct rule of the prince of the parent state, and the independence of the bhayat meant that many states were broken into numerous fragments. This hindered travel within the state, and gravely interfered with the maintenance of order as lawbreakers could easily escape justice by fleeing into a different jurisdiction.[11] In 1883, the Thakor Saheb of Limbdi formally demanded the restoration of jurisdiction over the two dozen estates that were held by his bhayat and had been separated with the classification of judicial powers. He noted that his family's sovereignty over the estates had been fully recognised until just twenty years earlier, and that the new independence of the bhayat hindered the working of his administration. But on the advice of the Political Agent in Kathiawar, the government of Bombay turned down the proposal, primarily because "Nothing would compensate for any diminution of the trust which Native States repose in our good faith, or for the unsettling effect" which would ensue if territories were reincorporated in a larger neighbour.[12]

II

Relatively small states as Limbdi were not alone in being fragmented by the villages of chiefs who had once been their dependents. The Maharaja Gaekwad of Baroda was the third-ranking prince in all India. Despite this exalted status, however, Baroda's population placed it only seventh among the Indian states, while in area it was smaller than such nonentities as Manipur and Bastar. Moreover, the Gaekwad's dominions were broken into four widely-separated blocs

---

[11] The extent of the fragmentation is emphasized in J.S.H. Shattock, *A Report on the Future of Small States and Estates of Gujerat and Kathiawar*, IOC L/P&S/13/973. For example, Junagadh (p. 61) comprised one main bloc of territory and twenty-three "islands" within other states; Nawanagar (p. 64) was broken into nine parts; and Gondal (p. 74) consisted of twenty non-contiguous groups of villages.

[12] West to C. Gonne (Political Secretary Bombay), 22 Mar. 1884, NAI WISA, R C-12/1884-85.

of territory and numerous enclaves within British India and other states. Like the fragmentation of the states of Western India, this could be blamed on British policy, although in this case it affected tributary states rather than bhayat. When the Gaekwads established their supremacy over Gujarat in the eighteenth century,[13] they followed their Mughal predecessors in bringing some districts under their own direct rule, and leaving others in the hands of local princes. These princes paid tribute to the Gaekwad, and exercised a degree of autonomy that varied with the strength of the current Maharaja of Baroda and the size of the tributary state (major states such as Nawanagar always enjoyed considerable freedom). In 1820, however, the Gaekwad ceded to the British all his rights in Saurashtra and Mahi Kantha with the exception of that of receiving tribute, and in 1825 he did the same in his tributaries in the Rewa Kantha region of eastern Gujarat. The tributaries were thenceforth recognised by all parties as entirely independent of Baroda, save that they paid tribute. This independence often had no basis in history. For example, in northern and eastern Gujarat, many petty landlords paid revenue to the Gaekwad from the mid-eighteenth century onward. The agreement of 1820 placed under British suzerainty those estates within the boundaries of Mahi Kantha, while leaving the others under the control of the Gaekwad. The Mahi Kantha landlords executed revenue engagements and security bonds, and eventually gained the status of ruling chiefs; the others, who had hitherto enjoyed exactly the same position, remained nothing more than nobles of Baroda state.[14]

Under Maharaja Sayajirao Gaekwad III (1875-1939), Baroda had a reputation as a progressive state, with an advanced bureaucratic system, a modern tax base, and free and compulsory primary education.[15] In 1877, the Maharaja's Dewan raised a claim for the annexation of the tributaries to Baroda state, on the grounds that they had formed an integral part of the Gaekwad's dominions before the establishment of British supremacy. Despite the support of the British Resident at Baroda, however, this claim was rejected, as it

---

[13] See Chapter One.

[14] Lee-Warner, *Native States of India*, p. 35

[15] See David Hardiman, "Baroda: The Structure of a 'Progressive' State," pp. 107-135 of Jeffrey, *op. cit.*

would have necessitated overturning the Canning guarantees.[16] But Baroda was not the only major state to have claims regarding nobles who had become autonomous as a result of decisions made by the East India Company in the early nineteenth century. Around the time of the First World War, the Paramount Power restored to a number of princes jurisdiction over their nobles. For example, the Company had recognised the virtual independence of many small feudatories of the great state of Gwalior, but in 1921 forty-three feudatories were reincorporated in Gwalior. Some have said that the objective of reincorporations of this sort was to enhance the financial and administrative stability of the large states concerned, while others call it part of the British campaign to win princely good will.[17] In any case, the success of the Gwalior claim to full suzerainty over its feudatories inspired the government of Baroda to revive the old claims regarding the tributaries (even though the two cases were different–the Gwalior feudatories had never been recognised as full-fledged states, the way the Baroda tributaries were). The longstanding rivalry of the Maharajas of Baroda and of Gwalior, the two leading Maratha princes in India, may have played a role. Historically, Baroda had outranked its fellow Maratha state, but Gwalior was larger and more populous. It was at this point in 1921, when the Political Department was preparing to transfer some of the Bombay states to the control of the central government, that the Dewan of Baroda, Sir Manubhai N. Mehta, submitted a detailed scheme outlining Baroda's claims in Saurashtra, Banas Kantha, Mahi Kantha and Rewa Kantha. Mehta argued that Baroda rightfully held sovereignty over all of these territories, both by right of conquest and because the majority of their rulers paid tribute to the Gaekwad, and that the agreements of 1820 and 1825 had not affected this but had merely revised the procedure for the collection of tribute. The Dewan suggested that Baroda now resume direct collection of the tribute, and assume the judicial and administrative functions of the Paramount Power in the petty states. He did not

[16] C.J. Windham (Resident at Baroda) to Sir John Wood (Political Secretary India), 19 May 1920, IOC R/1/1/661.

[17] The opposing views are presented in Rudolph and Rudolph, "Rajputana Under British Paramountcy," p. 9, and O'Dwyer, *op. cit.*, pp. 154-157.

press Baroda's claims to the salute states, which he knew would only cause trouble.[18]

Mehta's request put the Paramount Power in an awkward position. Delhi was actively courting support for British rule from the leaders of princely opinion, who would have seen any transfer of sovereignty to Baroda as an infringement of the Canning guarantees and hence a dangerous precedent for themselves. On the other hand, Baroda was one of the greatest of all states, and the British had no desire to alienate so important a prince as the Gaekwad. To avoid what would inevitably be an unpleasant decision, Delhi stalled on Mehta's proposal for over five years. In 1927, a Political Department report concluded that the tributary states had never been under the sovereignty of the Gaekwad, and that the claim was therefore groundless. But the government of India was in the midst of negotiations with Baroda regarding the state's assertion of the right to develop salt works and ports, and its protest over the reimposition of the Viramgam Line, and Delhi had no desire to poison any chance of agreement on those questions by publicly rejecting the claim to sovereignty. Moreover, rejection would require some explanation of the Paramount Power's rights of overlordship, which would inevitably raise difficulties with other states. In 1930 and 1931, Sayajirao Gaekwad was answered in the negative when he asked two successive Viceroys whether any decision had been made on the claim that his government had laid a decade earlier.[19]

By this time, however, Mahatma Gandhi's Civil Disobedience campaign of 1930 was in full swing. The petty states included in the Baroda claim were particularly hit by the surge in political activity, both because their poverty occasionally gave rise to popular

---

[18] For Mehta's claim to sovereignty (1920-1930), see IOC L/P&S/13/1014, R/1/1/661, R/1/1/1726(1) and R/1/1/2138(1).

[19] He might have guessed the truth from the fact that when the Political Department revised its authoritative *Collection of Treaties* with the Indian states in 1929-1931, it deleted the section that in earlier editions had mentioned Baroda's sovereignty over its tributaries prior to 1820-1825; compare the 4th (1909) and 5th (1929-1933) editions of Aitchison, *op. cit.* The Political Department's practice of deleting sections of this ostensibly objective work if they became inconvenient is noted in Nicholson, *Scraps of Paper*, pp. v-vi. For the salt and ports cases, see IOC R/2/648/425 and R/2/650/450.

discontent, and because they lacked the resources to deal with agitation when it did break out. This was of direct concern to the administrations of larger jurisdictions that adjoined the petty states, whether British India or other states such as Baroda, as uncontrolled agitation in small units quickly spread to their neighbours, hampering the efforts of the latter to maintain order.[20] The result was a shift in British opinion with regard to the petty states. In 1930, the Political Agent, Eastern Kathiawar Agency, wrote of them that

> The test of the Civil Disobedience movement shows that for the most part ... these "Durbars" have not even a moral influence or prestige: it is not they but the Banias who are the real masters: and if there was any real trouble we could expect little or nothing in the way of support from these Talukdars who owe their very existence to Gov[ernmen]t. ... Their sovereignty must go.... Most of them are offshoots of bigger parent states, to which they should go back.[21]

Mehta's successor as Dewan of Baroda, Sir V.T. Krishnamachari, linked this concern with another element that entered the Indian political scene in the early 1930s, the plan for constitutional reform and federation. The 1935 Government of India Act made no provision for the inclusion in the federation of the minor states of the Western India and Gujarat States Agencies. For example, the Act listed the subjects that would be administered by the federation, and stated that acceding rulers would entrust jurisdiction over some or all of these to the federal legislature; but this made it impossible for many petty chiefs to accede, as in their territories *all* of the proposed federal subjects were exercised by the Agency rather than the ruler. Similarly, acceding princes would recognise the right of the federal court to hear appeals from their high courts; this was another barrier to the accession of lesser rulers, since many of them had

[20] Sir V.T. Krishnamachari (Dewan of Baroda), "The civil disobedience movement in British India and its repercussions in the State: policy to be followed," 11 Apr. 1932, IOC R/2/644/381.

[21] A.J. Hopkinson (PA, Eastern Kathiawar), "Handing-over notes. Eastern Kathiawar Agency," 26 Sept. 1930, IOC MSS Eur D 998/5 (Hopkinson Collection). Banias are merchants; M.K. Gandhi, like most political leaders in the Western India States Agency, was a Bania by caste, and the term is here used as a derogatory term for political agitators.

no law courts at all, much less high courts (as civil and criminal matters involving their inhabitants were handled by the Agency). And while the Act set out in detail the number of seats that each acceding state would receive in the legislature, it contained only vague provisions for the representation of the petty states, which made it clear that they were not expected ever to require it. This raised the likelihood that in the India of the future, petty territories outside the jurisdiction of the federal government would be intermingled with acceding states.[22]

In 1932, Krishnamachari unveiled a scheme that at a stroke would solve all of these problems, by placing the petty states in what he called "direct relations" with Baroda. This built on the existing concept of direct relations between the states and the government of India;[23] it would avoid any mention of Baroda's "sovereignty," and leave the petty rulers with the status of chiefs and all their existing powers and privileges. As in Mehta's scheme, however, the Gaekwad would assume the functions of paramountcy in the petty states, including the exercise of residuary jurisdiction, and provide police services and medical and educational facilities. Finally, the petty units would be represented through Baroda in the federal legislature. This scheme appeared to benefit all parties: it would solve the Paramount Power's difficulty in bringing the petty units into the federation, and eliminate the expense of overseeing their administration and judiciary; give the people of the petty states access to Baroda's public services and amenities; and both satisfy Baroda's need for enhanced dignity and enlarged territory, and ease the task of maintaining order and fostering economic development in what had been a fragmented state.[24]

Courtenay Latimer, the Agent to the Governor-General for the States of Western India, warned that "In the face of all the assurances which have been given regarding the special responsibility of the Viceroy to safeguard the rights of these States such a solution

---

[22] See the Act, 26 Geo. 5 Ch. 2.

[23] See Chapter Four.

[24] For Krishnamachari's scheme for direct relations (1932-1939), see IOC L/P&S/13/1014, L/P&S/13/1015, R/1/1/2138(1), R/1/1/2712(1), R/1/1/3025, R/2/634/284 and R/2/644/377. See also Fatesinghrao P. Gaekwad, *Sayajirao of Baroda: The Prince and the Man* (Bombay, 1989), pp. 371-372.

seems to me to be quite unthinkable."[25] But his superiors in the Political Department and the India Office were more conscious of the problems caused by the existence of the petty states, and hence more open to Krishnamachari's proposals, and encouraged the Dewan to prepare detailed plans for implementing his direct relations. The minister completed this task in 1935; as a further inducement to the petty rulers, he was prepared to relieve them of the obligation to pay what was often a heavy tribute to the Gaekwad, in return for a contribution towards administrative expenses. Delhi initially embraced the plan. In January 1936, the Viceroy Lord Willingdon visited Baroda to mark Sayajirao's Diamond Jubilee, and commented that

> I have been very greatly interested in Your Highness' reference to the scheme which you have put forward with a view to the readjustment of the relations existing between the Baroda State and certain of her tributaries. Under this scheme, while you have sought to effect an improvement in economic and administrative conditions and to provide for financial relief to the States and Estates concerned, you have wisely taken care to leave their powers and privileges unimpaired. I sincerely trust that the Feudatories to whom Your Highness has referred will give your proposals their full consideration, for they will certainly be well advised to do so.[26]

Soon after this, however, the Political Department's enthusiasm for Krishnamachari's scheme evaporated. Even such expressions as "direct relations" could not hide the fact that Baroda's objective remained the absorption of its tributaries. The chiefs' powers might not be affected, and they might nominally retain the status of rulers; but by placing them under the authority of another prince, rather than a British Political Agent, the plan really reduced them to the status of mere nobles, differing only in name from (for example) the semi-autonomous Kutch bhayat. This was made doubly clear by the fact that if the Gaekwad acceded to the federation, the federal government would treat the confederated states as integral parts of Baroda. By assenting to the proposals, Delhi would in effect break

---

[25] C. Latimer (AGG) to J.L.R. Weir (Resident at Baroda), 21 Apr. 1933, IOC R/2/634/284.

[26] Speech by Willingdon at Baroda, 5 Jan. 1936, IOC L/P&S/13/1014.

its promise to preserve all the states, which would undoubtedly raise a storm of protest across princely India. As a result, the Political Department spent two years tinkering with the Baroda proposals and trying to draft alternatives, until in 1937 the Secretary of State, Lord Zetland, who still favoured the scheme, lost patience with his subordinates in Delhi:

> The more I consider this matter the more it seems to me an anachronism that such petty units as exist in Kathiawar and Gujerat should continue to be recognised as endowed with any element of sovereignty, however attenuated. I should have thought that it might also become increasingly difficult to defend the present situation against Indian opinion.

The petty units must therefore be forced either to unite with one another or to accept merger into larger states, which would also relieve the Paramount Power of the considerable expense incurred in overseeing their affairs:

> I am conscious of the political difficulties with States as a whole which would be likely to arise if it became necessary to implement such a threat, but these do not seem to me to outweigh the disadvantages of maintaining the estate-holders in their present position at an appreciable cost to Indian revenues.[27]

Baroda and Delhi hoped that the petty states would voluntarily accept "direct relations," which would provoke less discontent than a forced merger would do. At the beginning of 1938, Krishnamachari's scheme was accordingly presented to the Gaekwad's 157 petty tributaries in the Western India and Gujarat States Agencies. Unfortunately, only ten tributaries accepted the proposal without reservations, and a further twenty-nine on condition of modifications; forty-three were non-committal, and sixty-five entirely rejected any change in the current political arrangements. A year later, W.Le B. Egerton of the Political Department met with the rulers of most of the tributaries, and reported that "I am impressed with the hatred and distrust which the policy of the late Maharaja [Sayajirao

---

[27] Lord Zetland (Secretary of State) to Lord Linlithgow (Viceroy), 29 Dec. 1937, IOC L/P&S/13/1014.

had died shortly before] inspired in the girassia and jagirdar [land-holding] class. ... Whether Sir Krishnamachari by personal contact with the Thakors [petty chiefs] can eliminate their deep-seated distrust of Baroda remains to be seen. While it remains undisturbed, it is a fatal obstacle to any settlement by agreement."[28] Egerton felt that the "direct relations" ought to be introduced regardless of this, but he warned that there would be great resistance.[29] Furthermore, several major princes in Western India criticized the Baroda scheme on the grounds that if the petty states were to be eliminated, it ought to be through reunification with their own parent states, rather than through incorporation into Baroda, and the rulers of Nawanagar, Bhavnagar, Limbdi and Lathi all countered with schemes for establishing "direct relations" with their own respective bhayat.[30] By this time, moreover, one of the assumptions underlying Krishnamachari's plan had become irrelevant. By 1936, legal opinion had swung around to the view that the lesser units could accede to the federation even if they did not exercise any judicial powers to cede; and by 1939, efforts at establishing the federation were moribund. A few years earlier, this combination of fierce resistance to "direct relations" and changed political circumstances would have saved the petty states. But as the Viceroy commented in the spring of 1939, it had become necessary to undertake "the merger of such entities [petty states] for administrative purposes in the larger States. To secure even this considerable pressure would be necessary. But in my judgment we should not hesitate to apply such pressure...."[31] This was because even with the end of the question of federation, the petty states threatened the Paramount Power's control over the political situation in India: after 1937, the suggestion that the states' people were being politicized caused the British to take a new interest both in law and order, and in the conditions of life for the princes' subjects, and the Baroda scheme seemed to address both concerns. As Linlithgow

---

[28] For example, Sayajirao's administration had made it very easy to confiscate the lands of nobles for the slightest offence.

[29] W.Le B. Egerton (Officer on Special Duty) to E.W. Fletcher (Secretary to Resident), 3 Apr. 1939, IOC L/P&S/13/1015.

[30] See IOC R/1/1/2847(1), R/1/1/3025 and R/2/644/377.

[31] Linlithgow to Zetland, 5 Apr. 1939, IOC L/P&S/13/971.

noted only a few weeks after the Mahatma inaugurated Congress's new policy of taking part in state politics, the small states gave special cause for concern, as their tiny revenues rendered them unable to meet popular demands for changes in their methods of administration. During 1939, the Political Department urged neighbouring petty states to pool their resources and establish joint social and administrative services such as police or high courts, but the chiefs concerned opposed such "grouping" on the grounds that it infringed on their individual sovereignty.[32]

With grouping unacceptable to the rulers, the Paramount Power took a fresh look at Krishnamachari's scheme. The chief of the small state of Pethapur in Mahi Kantha paid a crippling tribute of thirty-five percent of his annual revenues to the Gaekwad, and as long ago as 1936 he had declared his readiness to accept Krishnamachari's scheme in return for the removal of this burden. By 1939, there were also fears that political agitation was about to spread to Pethapur, and E.C. Gibson, the Resident for the States of Western India, recommended forestalling this with an immediate transfer of the state to the control of Baroda. Delhi agreed to use Pethapur as a model to show other petty chiefs the benefits of Krishnamachari's scheme, and in 1940 the state was therefore placed in direct relations with Baroda.[33] The same year, the petty estates in the Katosan *thana*, which lay entirely within Baroda territory, were also placed under the Gaekwad.[34]

III

The Resident, Gibson, had however now changed his mind about eliminating the petty states a few at a time:

---

[32] For British concern over the smaller states, and the question of grouping, see IOC L/P&S/13/971 and R/1/1/3416(1).

[33] For the attachment of Pethapur, see IOC L/P&S/13/1015; NAI WISA, C-37-51/1947, and WISA, Office of the PA, Sabar Kantha Agency, C/Fed-16/1936.

[34] Shattock, *Report*, p. 9. For judicial purposes, most of the non-jurisdictional talukas and estates of the Western India States Agency were grouped into units known as thanas.

> Personally, ... after careful consideration I do not recommend this course. It seems to me that a question of such importance, involving so radical a change and such complicated re-arrangements and adjustments, and affecting generally the whole body of semi-jurisdictional and non-jurisdictional talukdars, should not be tackled piecemeal, but should be dealt with as a whole in one comprehensive settlement.[35]

And

> In my opinion the important thing at the present moment is to concentrate on the Baroda scheme and similar schemes put forward by other states. The best solution of the difficulties attending the present anomalous situation seems to lie in amalgamation of the petty semi-jurisdictional and non-jurisdictional talukas with larger States.

Gibson therefore proposed a thorough study detailing exactly how such amalgamations might be accomplished, and then disposing of all the remaining petty states at a stroke.[36] The Political Department accepted this idea, and appointed a young political officer, J.S.H. Shattock, to study the claims to petty units put forth by Baroda and other large states, and to decide on how to dispose of every petty state in the Western India and Gujarat States Agencies. After extensive travels in the two Agencies, Shattock submitted his report in October 1940. He retained the basic principle of Krishnamachari's plan, but extended it to benefit other large states beside Baroda: a number of major rulers would assume the Agency's functions (minority administration, residuary jurisdiction, and the like), and supply police and other services, in neighbouring petty states, subject to a guarantee of the existing powers of the petty chiefs. In the hope that a euphemism would limit princely opposition to his proposal, Shattock suggested calling these mergers "attachment," with the large states being attaching states, and the petty ones attached states. He recommended implementing his attachment scheme in two stages. All states with annual revenues below about one lakh of rupees should be attached as soon as possible; the remaining petty states would follow in the near future,

---

[35] E.C. Gibson (Resident) to Sir Bertrand Glancy (Political Adviser), 3 July 1939, IOC L/P&S/13/1015.

[36] Gibson to Glancy, 14 June 1939, IOC L/P&S/13/971.

and in the end the Western India States Agency would comprise just twenty-one states and the units that had been attached to Baroda. Shattock anticipated that attachment would permit development, social services, improved law and order, and opportunities for employment, by reducing the territorial, economic, and administrative fragmentation of Gujarat, and he warned the petty chiefs that "Government are of opinion that fundamental changes in the present system are necessary for your future well-being. ... if the smaller States and estates are to survive at all under modern conditions the only course for them is to attach themselves to neighbouring units of sufficient importance."[37] His chief concern was creating contiguous units that would be self-supporting (which provided a good excuse for not giving any one large state all the bhayat and tributaries that it wanted):

> The recommendations for the smaller units are based on the three considerations of geography, tribute and parentage. Though almost every recommendation has been made on grounds of geography and administrative convenience, I have not overlooked Baroda's special position in regard to its tributaries. Where however geography and tribute clash, I have invariably given preference to the former. ... where two bigger States have equally strong claims to attach particular smaller units, I have generally given preference to the bigger of the two.[38]

Shattock's report represented much hard work, and closely followed the instructions that he had received. Nevertheless, it was poorly received in Delhi, for two contradictory reasons. On the one hand, Sir Francis Wylie, who took over as Political Adviser to Lord Linlithgow in December 1940, felt that the attachment scheme was inadequate in that it preserved the existing powers of the petty rulers, whose territories he believed ought to be completely merged into the attaching states as soon as possible. On the other hand, Linlithgow held that any tampering with the Indian states would be unwise for the duration of the Second World War, which had made

[37] For Shattock's own account of his work, and his recommendations, see Shattock, *Report*, *passim*. The quotation is *ibid.*, p. 21.

[38] Shattock, *Report*, p. 32.

Britain's position precarious enough without a crew of angry princes.[39] As a result, Shattock's proposals were put "in cold storage."[40] But even Linlithgow gradually came around to Wylie's view, and in October 1942 the new Political Adviser Sir Henry Craik commented that

> The impact of the war has converted what was in millions of men a more or less doctrinaire admiration for liberal institutions into an active hatred of any form of autocracy. It is now, I suppose, generally accepted by thoughtful opinion that no form of personal rule can hope to survive unless it can justify itself as benevolent, progressive and in harmony with popular feeling.[41]

As the petty states could never enjoy this justification, Craik concluded that they must be attached as quickly as possible. He persuaded Lord Linlithgow and the India Office to begin acting on the Shattock report immediately, but with two important modifications of the original scheme: first, if the Political Department considered that an attached chief had "abused" his powers of administration in any way, he would lose all his rights of sovereignty, and his state would be completely merged into its attaching state and cease to exist as a separate unit altogether; and secondly, after seven years the Political Department would review its guarantee of the existing powers of the attached rulers, and reduce or extinguish them altogether. Both revisions were intended to provide for the complete disappearance of the petty units in the future. On 16 April 1943, the Political Department formally announced that the first stage of the attachment scheme was about to be implemented, covering states with revenues of less than about one lakh; the "second-stage" states, with revenues above one lakh but nevertheless insufficient resources to survive indefinitely, were left for the time being. In June 1943, the rulers of the attaching states signed Instruments of Attachment drafted by Shattock, and the 435-odd units that had existed in the

---

[39] For these reactions, see IOC L/P&S/13/973. Wylie's hostility to the rulers' sovereignty is noted in Copland, *Princes of India*, pp. 196-198.

[40] Letter from John S.H. Shattock to the author, 12 Mar. 1989.

[41] Sir Henry Craik, "Note on Mr. Shattock's Report on the Future of the Smaller States and Estates of Gujarat and Kathiawar," 21 Oct. 1942, IOC L/P&S/13/973, p. 20.

Agency were reduced to just thirty-six, of which fourteen were listed by Shattock as candidates for attachment in the second stage.[42]

Most of the chiefs affected by the first stage of attachment sullenly accepted their fate with token protests. This suggested that the scheme was workable. In the first week of December 1943, the Political Department therefore implemented the second stage, which was extended to include four non-salute states in Western India (Jasdan, Manavadar, Malpur and Muli) that Shattock had considered large enough to remain separate. The Western India States Agency now consisted merely of Baroda and sixteen salute states.[43] A similar reduction took place in the neighbouring Gujarat States Agency. This ended the independent existence of well over half the states in India, including the great majority of the petty units.[44]

IV

After the attachment scheme was implemented, one petty chief commented that the changes "have created widespread discontent and deep resentment and have resulted in acute embitterness (*sic*) amongst us who have been traditionally loyal to the Crown and who

---

[42] See Table Three. For the implementation of the Attachment Scheme, see IOC L/P&S/13/971 and L/P&S/13/973. For the notifications implementing the first stage of attachment, see NAI WISA, A-5-101/1943; the instruments are in IOC R/2/580-R/2/584.

[43] See Table Three. The non-salute state of Vijaynagar could not be attached mainly because its ruler enjoyed high standing and outranked at least one salute prince; instead Vijaynagar, and its neighbour the salute state of Idar, were transferred from the Western India States Agency to the control of the Rajputana Agency. There also remained seven tiny estates that Shattock had earmarked for attachment to the Bombay Presidency. The Bombay Legislative Assembly, however, refused to accept charge of them until 1947, and they therefore stayed under Agency control.

[44] For the implementation of the second stage of attachment, see IOC L/P&S/13/973.

have been wholeheartedly supporting the war efforts."[45] The Political Department's decision to ignore this sentiment is yet another illustration of the great change that took place in the relationship between the Paramount Power and the Indian states in the late 1930s. Nevertheless, the reasons for the elimination of the petty states are a mystery. The Agency communiqué announcing the scheme stated that attachment was being implemented mainly because "without some drastic simplification of existing arrangements any kind of co-ordinated development of the countryside or any form of real progress is impossible."[46] There is no question but that the petty states needed schools, hospitals, roads and so on, and that a lack of resources made it impossible for either their chiefs or the Agency to provide their people with the amenities that were deemed necessary in the mid-twentieth century. In 1944, the India Office noted of the petty states that

> While in some places the police were under the control of the Agency, in others police powers were exercised by the Chiefs. The small police forces of the latter had no means for the investigation of crime; and it was easy for offenders to escape beyond their control. In consequence robbery with violence, kidnapping and other crimes were rampant. Owing to the long distances between different parts of the same unit and to the bad communications, the bulk of the population found that access to the only court open to them was difficult or impossible. Except for primary schools, which were under the supervision of the Political authorities, there were no social services, educational, medical, agricultural or veterinary. Roads were deplorably undeveloped and any large scale plans of irrigation or afforestation were unknown. Lastly, there were in Kathiawar innumerable internal customs lines, which became even more numerous owing to the scattered territories of the larger states.[47]

Many of these amenities did, however, exist in the larger states, and the surviving correspondence leaves no doubt that many British

---

[45] Ghodasar to L.M.S. Amery (Secretary of State), 12 July 1943, IOC L/P&S/13/973.

[46] *The Western India States Agency Gazette*, 16 Apr. 1943, IOC L/P&S/13/973.

[47] IO, background notes on the India (Attachment of States) Bill, undated [Feb. 1944], IOC L/P&S/13/974.

officials sincerely believed that attachment would better the lot of the people of the petty states. Scholars have accepted the Paramount Power's word that this improvement was the principal objective of attachment.[48] But several considerations stand in the way of accepting this claim. First, the original Instruments of Attachment did not oblige the rulers of attaching units to undertake any improvements in the petty states, beyond giving their people access to "secondary and technical education, and medical treatment in the hospitals and dispensaries of my State, on the same terms as the subjects of my State." It is true that most princes did begin to develop their new dependencies, and the Gaekwad's modernisation fund of a lakh of rupees a year was only the most impressive of many projects. For two years, however, the wealthy state of Gondal spent no money whatsoever in its attached areas; the Paramount Power finally forced its Maharaja to institute some token reforms, but only because his behaviour was discrediting the whole idea of attachment.[49] Indeed, there were persistent claims that the attaching states economically exploited attached units, for example establishing monopolies to buy or sell vital commodities.[50] When, as will be seen, the instruments were revised in 1945, the rewritten versions addressed such criticisms with provisions requiring the attaching states to implement reforms in the attached areas. But even this did not solve the problem. Attaching states that wished to institute necessary changes often found that the instruments debarred them from what was considered interference in the internal affairs of attached units. For example, attaching states could do nothing to help exploited tenants in attached units beyond trying to persuade their rulers to pass tenancy legislation.[51]

In any case, while the Western India and Gujarat States Agencies did contain most of the very small Indian states, such units were found across India. To ensure that all state subjects enjoyed the basic amenities of modern life, Delhi should have attached every small state. Instead, the scheme only affected the two Agencies in

---

[48] See Coen, *op. cit.*, p. 113; Phadnis, *op. cit.*, pp. 140-144; Hari Sharma, *Princes and Paramountcy* (New Delhi, 1978), pp. 122-124.

[49] See IOC R/2/578/3 and R/2/579/16.

[50] See Bhadwa to C.P. Hancock (Resident), 7 May 1945, IOC R/2/579/14.

[51] See IOC R/2/579/11.

Gujarat, even though (for example) the attached state of Jetpur was more populous than units that survived untouched in ten of the thirteen other Agencies in India.[52] And as the political officer Sir Terence Creagh Coen admitted, the attached units were not "necessarily unhappy or badly ruled."[53] Why, then, were the petty states of Western India tackled so vigorously, even though this raised a storm of anger across princely India? The India Office hinted at the real reason in 1945:

> Even though the professed object of the administrative improvements which he [Linlithgow] planned was to benefit the Rulers' subjects, it is the Rulers' dynasties and territories that the Crown is pledged to maintain, and its ameliorative policy cannot be divorced from that obligation.[54]

By this time, the British no longer sought to use the states as counterweights to the nationalist movement in an effort to maintain their rule in India, and accepted that independence was inevitable in the near future. But there was still a feeling that Britain was responsible for ensuring the survival of the states (it must be borne in mind that the Cripps Offer of 1942 allowed not merely Muslim-majority provinces, but also states to opt not to accede to an independent India), or at least for giving them a fighting chance of survival. And it was felt that the survival of the states depended on a favourable image. Creagh Coen said that attachment was "a conscious effort ... to bring the States into a position where they could present a more respectable front to the post-war world."[55] The problem was that of all the Indian states, the mass of petty territories in Gujarat most undermined the effort to project this "more respectable front." At the Ludhiana session of the All-India States' People's Conference in February 1939 which installed Jawaharlal Nehru as its president, the AISPC announced a new plank in its platform:

---

[52] This point was raised by Fatehsinhji Ratansinhji Dabhi [chief of Ghodasar], *The Indian States and Paramountcy* (Bombay, 1945), IOC R/2/579/25.
[53] Coen, *op. cit.*, p. 115.
[54] P.J. Patrick (IO) to Sir Francis Wylie (Political Adviser), 7 Jan. 1944, IOC L
[55] Coen, *op. cit.*, p. 113.

> It is the considered opinion of the Conference that only those states which have a population exceeding 20 lakhs souls or Revenue exceeding 50 lakhs rupees can maintain the standard of administration necessary and suitable for being workable units for the purpose of uniting with the provinces in a scheme of a Free and Federated India and, therefore, all States not coming within the above category should be amalgamated, either singly or by groups, with the neighbouring provinces....[56]

These high standards of population and revenue would have left only twenty-one states in all of India. In the succeeding months, the people's movements conducted a concerted propaganda campaign against the petty states. Local political organizations voiced their support for the Ludhiana Resolution; the Conference launched its series of information pamphlets with *What are the Indian States?*, which simply listed 584 states arranged alphabetically, by population, by revenue and by area, with appropriate figures that were clearly intended to show how few of the states were really worthy of preservation (the pamphlet also included a helpful appendix, the text of the Ludhiana Resolution, for any readers who had not yet grasped the purpose of the publication); and plans were discussed of issuing another pamphlet, even more bluntly "showing the feasibility of a federation of Kathiawar States, which are mostly tiny, and hopelessly numerous."[57] And the petty states of Gujarat were the most vulnerable of all to charges that the Indian states were too small; of the AISPC's 584 states, 354 had populations below 10,000–and 306 of these were in either the Western India States Agency or the Gujarat States Agency.[58] The very existence of these

---

[56] Resolution No. 6, All-India States' People's Conference, eighth session, Ludhiana, February 1939; printed in *What are the Indian States?*, p. 111.

[57] Support for the Ludhiana Resolution is expressed in "Resolutions passed in the meeting of the Himalayan States' Peoples Conference held at Delhi on the 2nd. April 1939...," NL SPC, file 181 (i), and G.K. Godbole (Secretary, State People's Society, Sangli) to Diwans of the Patwardhan States, 4 May 1939, NL SPC, file 181 (ii). The plans for future pamphlets are discussed in Balwantray Mehta (Secretary, AISPC) to Shanti Swaroop Dhawan (Director, Research Bureau, AISPC), 27 June 1939, NL Nehru Papers, subject file 103.

[58] In 1946, the Conference's Gwalior session raised the demand still higher, to a minimum population of fifty lakhs or five million and a minimum revenue of eight crores or eighty million rupees; Mathur, *States' People's Conference*, p. 41.

small states threw all of the Indian states into disrepute. They were therefore perhaps the weakest element in the Paramount Power's effort to portray the Indian states as viable political entities that would form part of the Indian political scene with or without the British. This is why in 1944 the Viceroy Lord Wavell was "so impressed with the necessity–in the interests of all the Indian States–of finding a solution for this problem [the existence of the petty states] that he is inclined to regard this subject as perhaps the most important of the issues now confronting the British Crown in its relations with the Indian States."[59] As the same Viceroy commented to the Secretary of State L.M.S. Amery, "It is hardly any longer a secret that we regard the petty Indian States as an embarrassment."[60]

The approach of India's independence made the British more rather than less eager to safeguard the position of the states. It has been said that by citing its obligations to the states, the Paramount Power was able for many years to justify its failure to give independence to India.[61] Actually, by the 1940s, the British saw these wide-ranging obligations as nothing but a burden:

> the Instrument of Attachment ... does constitute not only a departure from previous policy in regard to the Indian States but by implication a breach of numerous pledges which we have given in the past. I am, however, in full sympathy with the purpose underlying the attachment scheme in so far as it is directed to the removal of the intolerable administrative anomalies which exist in these tracts. ... I realise too that we can only rid ourselves of the incubus of our well meaning if somewhat nearsighted undertakings to these petty people by jettisoning the greater part, if not the whole, of these promises.[62]

And by reducing some 435 states in Western India to sixteen, all governed by salute rulers who enjoyed full membership in the Chamber of Princes, the attachment scheme eliminated the majority of the indefensibly small states in India. This, the Paramount Power

---

[59] L.C.L. Griffin (Secretary to Crown Representative) to Bhopal, 2 Dec. 1944, IOC R/1/1/4168.

[60] Lord Wavell (Viceroy) to Amery, 28 Nov. 1944, IOC L/P&S/13/981.

[61] Fisher, *Indirect Rule*, pp. 450-451.

[62] Wavell to Amery, 28 Aug. 1944, IOC L/P&S/13/976.

hoped, would render more tenable the position of its remaining princely allies. As a political officer told the Raja of Lunawada, a salute state in the Gujarat States Agency,

> Though the Attachment Scheme has been unpopular and much misunderstood, I think you will appreciate that its object was to perpetuate the princely system of government in the areas in which it existed, and to continue the present dynasties in the States whose resources were insufficient to maintain the standard of administration which modern conditions demand.[63]

Indian political leaders knew exactly why the Paramount Power had decided to merge the petty states, and reacted accordingly. The cartoonist Shankar's comment on the announcement of the scheme was entitled "Pickling and Preserving."[64] And from the beginning, the AISPC

> viewed with concern the attempts being made to transfer certain minor States and estates to either parent, contiguous or tribute States without any reference to the wishes of the people concerned. The suggested conditions of such transfer were such as to perpetuate existing evils and to add to them. As a general rule no State area could be enlarged and amalgamation of the smaller States could take place with the neighbouring provinces, and, in any event, the wishes of the people concerned could be the deciding factor.[65]

By eliminating the small units, and creating larger ones in which it was intended that monarchical government could survive even after the departure of the British, the attachment scheme directly chal-

---

[63] E.W.M. Magor (Secretary to Resident) to Lunawada, 2 Aug. 1947, NAI WISA, file of the PA, Gujarat States Agency, C-63-47 volume II/1947.

[64] *The Hindustan Times*, 17 Apr. 1943.

[65] Resolution of the Standing Committee of the AISPC, Oct. 1939, reported in "States People during the Second World War," NL Vyas Papers, file 10. The same sentiments are expressed in "Representation from the people of those parts of the Province of Kathiawar which is now being attached to bigger States," 1940, and R.U. Parikh (Kathiawar Political Conference) to E.W.R. Lumby (IO), 17 Feb. 1944, both IOC L/P&S/13/975. But one Political Agent in Saurashtra suggested that a local politician, Chimanlal Shah, was fervently against attachment because he had been bribed by petty chiefs; P.C. Hailey (PA Western Kathiawar) to J.R. Cotton (Officer on Special Duty, Rajkot), 26 May 1945, IOC R/2/578/3.

lenged one aspect of the movement's drive for power. Indeed, a general consensus arose among the British that even the attachment scheme did not go far enough, and that it had eliminated only part of the problem. In 1945, the Thakor of Ghodasar, one of the principal opponents of attachment among the petty chiefs, warned his fellow rulers that the logical end result of attachment was the elimination of all but some fifteen truly large states across India, perhaps those that the Ludhiana resolution was prepared to accept.[66] This warning was not as far-fetched as British official pronouncements claimed. Around the same time, Wavell told Bhopal that

> the aim of His Majesty's Government was a united and self-governing India.... In such an arrangement the Princes would obviously have a place but some re-grouping, such as small States joining a larger State, or of other States into Unions, would have to be considered. It was His Majesty's Government's desire that the Princes should find their rightful place within an Indian Union and they would give them every assistance to do so.[67]

And how this might be brought about was the subject of private discussions in the upper ranks of British officialdom. In November 1943-January 1944, two top political officers, Sir Arthur Lothian (the Resident at Hyderabad) and Sir Francis Wylie (the Political Adviser), corresponded on the question of the smaller states. They agreed that all but twenty or twenty-one of the very largest states must disappear into other states or into British India in the near future, since the overwhelming majority of states lacked the minimum revenue of fifty lakhs of rupees which they, like the AISPC, considered necessary to function in the modern world. Lothian and Wylie disagreed only as to who should carry out this unpalatable task, Lothian suggesting the authorities of independent India and Wylie urging it as a British responsibility, which at least would make the largest states viable in independent India. As Wylie was Political Adviser, his views held the field, and were accepted

---

[66] Dabhi, *Indian States and Paramountcy*.

[67] Wavell, journal entry, 12 Mar. 1946, in Penderel Moon, editor, *Wavell: The Viceroy's Journal* (London, 1973), p. 223.

by Lord Wavell.[68] And at least some leaders of princely India shared this view; in April 1946, Sir C.P. Ramaswami Aiyar, the Diwan of Travancore in South India, delivered what Wavell called "quite a brilliant lecture" to the Cabinet Mission, in which he stated that in the run-up to independence "the States should group themselves into viable units...; they should have some sort of popular government...." Aiyar's standards were high: he envisaged a population of three million and a revenue of two crores of rupees for viable units.[69]

V

However, the implementation of attachment did not go as smoothly as the British had hoped. From the beginning, two petty chiefs had determined not to join the other first stage rulers in accepting the attachment of their states. These were Chandrasinhji of Bhadwa in Saurashtra (area, 7 square miles; population, 1,644) and Fatehsinhji of Ghodasar in Mahi Kantha (16 square miles and 6,708 people). Both men were intelligent and well-educated, far-seeing enough to realise that the ultimate goal of the scheme was the disappearance of their states, and sufficiently perceptive to recognise just how great a break with the past attachment really was. Bhadwa and Ghodasar refused to accept their Instruments of Attachment (from Gondal and Baroda, respectively), and sent protests against the scheme to the Secretary of State and the King. When this failed, they drummed up support among other chiefs who had previously cooperated in attachment, and by the time the second stage was implemented in December, twenty-nine first-stage units were

---

[68] See IOC L/P&S/13/980. In a review of Menon's *The Story of the Integration of the Indian States* some years later, Lothian made a blistering attack on the way that independent India had eliminated the states, in *Journal of the Royal Central Asian Society*, 44, 1 (1957), pp. 58-62.

[69] Wavell, journal entry, 9 Apr. 1946, in Moon, *Wavell*, p. 241.

refusing to recognise the authority of the attaching states.[70] Meanwhile, Bhadwa and Ghodasar had taken a new line of attack. They hired the great lawyer Sir Chimanlal Setalvad, who had represented the Maharaja Jam Saheb of Nawanagar at the Mount Abu ports conference of 1927, and asked him to unearth legal grounds for challenging the attachment scheme. Setalvad soon found a section of the 1935 Government of India Act that had been drafted to reassure the princes that in the federal India of the future, the British would not transfer control over the states to politicians from British India:

> any powers connected with the exercise of the functions of the Crown in its relations with Indian States shall in India, if not exercised by His Majesty, be exercised only by, or by persons acting under the authority of, His Majesty's Representative for the exercise of the functions of the Crown[71]

–the Crown Representative, a post held by the Viceroy. Now, before the attachment scheme, political officers exercised various "powers connected with the exercise of the functions of the Crown" in the petty states. These included judicial powers in the form of the exercise of residuary jurisdiction by the Agency, which meant that civil and criminal cases lying beyond the competence of semi-jurisdictional and non-jurisdictional chiefs were decided by the local Political Agent or his deputy. As a consequence of attachment, however, residuary jurisdiction in the attached units was transferred from the Agency to the attaching states.[72] Setalvad realised that this

---

[70] For the beginnings of Bhadwa and Ghodasar's campaign against attachment, see IOC L/P&S/13/973. The other malcontents were Dedhrota attached to Baroda, Sathamba and Vadagam to Idar, and Ankewalia, Bhalala, Bhalgamda, Bhathan, Bhoika, Chachana, Chhalala, Darod, Devalia, Gedi, Jakhan, Kamalpur, Kantharia, Karol, Khambhlav, Khandia, Laliad, Palali, Sahuka, Samla, Talsana, Tavi, Untdi and Vanala to Limbdi.

[71] 26 Geo. 5 c. 2, section 2(1).

[72] PD notification, 25 Aug. 1943, IOC L/P&S/13/973. For the transfer of cases, see NAI WISA, A-11-1(1)/1943-47, A-11-1/1943 Part II, and A-11-1(a)/1943.

transfer violated the 1935 Act. All that he needed was a test case from which to argue the point, and one shortly presented itself.[73]

Some time earlier, Bai Jivi, a woman from Bhadwa, had attempted suicide. This was a criminal offence, carrying a sentence of up to one year. As the powers of the chief of Bhadwa were limited to criminal cases in which the maximum sentence did not exceed three months, Bai Jivi was committed for trial before the local Deputy Political Agent. Following the attachment of Bhadwa to Gondal, the residuary jurisdiction in Bhadwa passed from the Agency to the Gondal state court, and the attempted suicide was accordingly transferred to a Gondal judge. On Setalvad's instructions, Chandrasinhji of Bhadwa now went to the Judicial Commissioner for Western India, the Agency's court of appeal, and filed a challenge to the right of the Gondal judge to hear the case. The grounds were that the latter was not competent to exercise the Crown's power of residuary jurisdiction in Bhadwa, since he was not under the authority of the Crown Representative. The Judicial Commissioner, R.W.H. Davies, knew that Bhadwa's challenge was potentially explosive, and supplemented his tribunal with two other judges. They began hearing arguments on 29 November, the day that the second stage of the Attachment Scheme was announced. The Political Department's lawyers claimed that the Crown's undefined powers of paramountcy gave it the right to do as it pleased with regard to the Indian states. Setalvad conceded that this was normally true, but that in this instance an Act of Parliament had explicitly restricted the Crown's freedom of action. The court rendered its decision one week later, and upheld Setalvad's contention that the attachment scheme was unconstitutional:

> these orders ... are a startling reversal of the purpose and policy clearly set out in the Government of India Act. They ... are ..., not only according to the strict letter of the law but also in essence, ultra vires of the powers of the Crown Representative, until the necessary further parliamentary sanction has been obtained.[74]

---

[73] For Setalvad's judicial challenge to attachment, see Setalvad, *op. cit.*, pp. 515-516; IOC L/P&S/13/974; NAI WISA A-11-1/1943 Part II.

[74] Judgement of R.W.H. Davies (Judicial Commissioner, Western India States Agency), 6 Dec. 1943, IOC L/P&S/13/974.

Until this point, most chiefs had cooperated in attachment in the belief that there was no alternative. But after the court's decision, many rulers joined Bhadwa and Ghodasar in refusing to accept the merger of their states. On 21 December 1943, the rulers of the second-stage states voted unanimously to return their Instruments of Attachment. Moreover, Davies followed his judgement with orders that only Agency courts could hear cases that originated in the attached units, and petty chiefs now flocked to Agency courts where they filed both fresh cases, and appeals against decisions rendered by the courts of attaching states during the previous few months. The problem was that the Agency judicial officials had already been withdrawn, leaving no one to handle the cases, which raised the threat of a complete breakdown of law and order. And the collapse of attachment had more than merely legal ramifications. Commodities subject to wartime rationing (such as sugar, kerosene and petrol) were supplied to the attached units through the attaching states. As part of their repudiation of attachment, the petty chiefs refused to draw their people's allotted rations from the attaching states, which led to shortages of essential goods. Meanwhile, the attaching states insisted that the scheme was still functioning. They tried to enforce their rights in the attached areas, and by mid-January 1944 the Resident reported that he expected this to end in violent confrontations.[75]

But while the judgement had found that attachment violated the constitution, the court had also noted that the scheme would only remain illegal "until the necessary further parliamentary sanction has been obtained." The British notion of parliamentary supremacy meant that any measure could be rendered constitutional if it were embodied in a properly-drafted piece of legislation. As the Indian constitution was an act of the British Parliament, Westminster could easily take the necessary steps. The legal advisers to the Political Department immediately drafted a parliamentary bill to overcome the decision, by declaring that the 1935 Act did not prevent the Paramount Power from attaching one state to another; and on 8 February 1944, the India (Attachment of States) Bill was introduced

---

[75] For the immediate effects of the ruling, see IOC L/P&S/13/973 and L/P&S/13/974.

in the House of Lords. The bill provided that the Crown Representative might bring about the attachment of any petty state,[76] and explicitly permitted "the exercise by, or transfer to, courts and officers of the [attaching] last-mentioned Indian State ... of any powers or jurisdiction in or in relation to the [attached] first mentioned Indian State which were or could have been exercised by or on behalf of the Crown ... notwithstanding anything in ... the Government of India Act, 1935...."[77] With the wartime coalition government in power in the United Kingdom, the success of the Bill was a foregone conclusion. Nevertheless, the opponents of attachment lobbied hard against it, seeking the support not only of "Conservative members ... who are upholders of long established institutions like the Order of Indian Princes," but also of "Liberals, Radicals, extremists."[78] And indeed, the strongest opposition to the Bill came from several members of the left wing of the Labour Party in both houses, who had been bombarded with telegrams from the petty chiefs and what claimed to be associations of their subjects. The main speakers were Lords Faringdon and Strabolgi in the Lords, and James Maxton and Reginald Sorensen in the Com-

---

[76] The phrasing was "any Indian State not mentioned in Divisions I to XVI of the Table of Seats appended to Part II of the First Schedule of the Government of India Act, 1935," which enumerated those states large enough to be entitled to representation in the planned federal legislature while omitting the petty units.

[77] For the drafting of the bill, see IOC L/P&S/13/974. For its course through Parliament, see the following pages of *Hansard*: motion for leave to introduce and First Reading in the Lords, 8 Feb. 1944, cxxx H.L.Deb. 5s, col. 689; Second Reading in the Lords, 16 Feb. 1944, *ibid.*, cols. 803-813; Committee Stage in the Lords, 22 Feb. 1944, *ibid.*, cols. 882-890; Committee report to the Lords, 22 Feb. 1944, *ibid.*, col. 890; Third Reading in the Lords, 23 Feb. 1944, *ibid.*, col. 956; message from the Lords that they had passed the Bill and First Reading in the Commons, 23 Feb. 1944, 397 H.C.Deb. 5s, col. 837; Second Reading in the Commons, 1 Mar. 1944, *ibid.*, cols. 1498-1533; Committee Stage in the Commons, 14 Mar. 1944, 398 H.C.Deb. 5s, cols. 177-199; Committee report to the Commons, 14 Mar. 1944, *ibid.*, col. 199; Third Reading in the Commons, 14 Mar. 1944, *ibid.*, cols. 199-202; Bill returned to the Lords with an amendment, 15 Mar. 1944, cxxxi H.L.Deb. 5s, col. 29; consideration of the Commons amendment in the Lords, 16 Mar. 1944, *ibid.*, cols. 69-70; message from the Lords that they had agreed to the amendment, 16 Mar. 1944, 398 H.C.Deb. 5s, col. 411; Royal Assent, 21 Mar. 1944, cxxxi H.L.Deb. 5s, col. 117, and 398 H.C.Deb., 5s, col. 722.

[78] Telegram Lakhtar to Douglas Grant and Dold (Solicitors), 19 Mar. 1944, IOC L/P&S/13/975.

mons, who–on the advice of the petty chiefs–adopted a suitably left-leaning line of attack: that attachment meant that without their consent, the people of the attached units were being removed from British administration and placed under "the officials of an absolute monarchy."[79] This was a misstatement of the effects of attachment, and from the critics' own party F.W. Pethick Lawrence (a future Secretary of State for India) explained that concern for their sovereignty underlay the petty chiefs' opposition to attachment:

> We all know that people in this country are willing to spend money on the purchase of land and estates not for the economic advantages that they obtain from them but for the prestige which being a landlord gives to persons in this country. Now I rather gather that these Taluqdars [chiefs of talukas] fear the loss of prestige which will result if the powers which have been exercised by the British are handed over to the large Indian States. They are afraid they will cut a smaller figure as the smaller part of a large State, even if theoretically their rights are preserved, than they do at the present time.[80]

The India (Attachment of States) Act, making the attachment scheme retroactively constitutional, became law on 21 March 1944. One amendment was made to the original bill, which had permitted the attachment of any petty state in India: on the motion of the Conservative member Godfrey Nicholson, the scope of the Act was explicitly confined to the Western India and Gujarat States Agencies.[81]

---

[79] Lord Faringdon, 16 Feb. 1944, cxxx H.L. Deb. 5s, col. 808. For examples of lobbying against the bill, see the telegrams in IOC L/P&S/13/975, and Fatehsinhji Ratansinhji Dabhi [chief of Ghodasar], *Attachment of States and its Implications: A plea to the Chamber of Princes to oppose the Scheme of Attachment* (Bombay, 1944), IOC R/2/579/25.

[80] F.W. Pethick-Lawrence, 1 Mar. 1944, 397 H.C. Deb. 5s, col. 1509.

[81] 7&8 Geo. 6 c. 14.

VI

The legalisation of attachment did not defuse the opposition of the petty chiefs. Some bombarded Delhi and London with petitions against the Act. In Limbdi, the rulers of the attached units held a Gandhian unarmed protest, until they were dispersed by a police charge (negotiations followed, and in August 1944 the twenty-four recalcitrant units attached to Limbdi agreed to cooperate in attachment). More ominously, there were reports that some chiefs "have even shown their readiness to rise in rebellion, if the occasion so demands, by becoming outlaws."[82] Meanwhile, two leading princes who had initially supported the attachment scheme had now turned against it. These were the Maharaja Jam Saheb of Nawanagar and the Maharaja Rana Saheb of Porbandar. It was alleged in some quarters that the former was upset with the scheme because Baroda had secured the attachment of many petty states that he wished for himself. Porbandar had received no attached states, and was said to be influenced by his friendship with Fatehsinhji, a member of the ruling family of Limbdi; Fatehsinhji had quarrelled with the British administrator of his home state and was seeking revenge by fomenting trouble among Limbdi's attached states. Whatever the reason, by the end of 1943 Nawanagar and Porbandar were reported to be actively encouraging the second stage rulers in their rejection of attachment.[83] And early in 1944, the malcontents secured the support of the Chamber of Princes. Ghodasar published a pamphlet demonstrating that by violating the Canning guarantees, the attachment scheme had set a precedent that could eventually lead to the extinction of all the states. The second stage of attachment gave added force to Ghodasar's arguments; for while the states affected by the first stage in June 1943 were so small that their existence was

---

[82] "Copy of a source report received from the Central Intelligence Officer, Bombay," 22 June 1944, IOC R/1/1/4140. For the petitions, see NAI WISA, A-11-1/1944 volumes II and II(a); and for the situation in Limbdi, see IOC L/P&S/13/977 and R/2/579/15. For the traditional habit among discontented Rajputs of going into outlawry, see *Gazetteer of the Bombay Presidency*, 8:317.

[83] Letter from John S.H. Shattock to the author, 12 Mar. 1989; IOC L/P&S/13/977; NAI WISA, A-11-1/1943 Part II.

an embarrassment even to many princes, the eighteen second stage units were as large as states found anywhere else in India, and moreover controlled two seats in the Chamber.[84]

Two days after the India (Attachment of States) Act became law, the Standing Committee of the Chamber met to discuss the attachment scheme. Porbandar was named chairman of a committee to study the Chamber's position on the question of the smaller states. The Porbandar Committee submitted its first report in mid-April. It criticized attachment in general, and instructed the Chancellor of the Chamber of Princes to obtain a guarantee from the Paramount Power that no further states would be attached (this reflected Ghodasar's warning); to secure reversal of the attachment of the second stage units; and to negotiate revision of the Instruments of Attachment, in particular removing the provision that after seven years the powers of the attached rulers would be reviewed, and inserting a requirement that the attaching states take measures to benefit the people of the attached units.[85] The new Chancellor, to whom this assignment fell, was Hamidullah Khan, the Nawab of Bhopal. Bhopal, son of the last of the great female rulers who governed Bhopal in the nineteenth and early twentieth centuries, was an excellent champion. Fluent in English, dynamic, and with a thorough understanding of constitutional issues, he had long been a thorn in the side of the Political Department; in 1943, Lord Linlithgow warned his successor Lord Wavell that Bhopal had undoubted "ability, but said that he was sometimes like a mischievous boy with a catapult."[86] Bhopal understood that the small states had to go, and that the attachment scheme provided a means of eliminating them while safeguarding the existence of the larger states. Publicly, however, he felt compelled to oppose attachment. As Chancellor, he was responsible for arguing the claims of his constituents. More

---

[84] The twenty-six principal non-salute states of Gujarat, which included all eighteen second stage units, elected two of their number to represent them in the Chamber; *A Handbook of the Chamber of Princes (Narendra Mandal)* (Simla, 1942), pp. 32-34. This representation was not affected by attachment. Ghodasar's pamphlet is Dabhi, *Attachment of States*.

[85] "Summary of the proceedings of the Standing Committee of the Chamber of Princes held in New Delhi on 23rd March 1944," IOC L/P&S/13/981; Porbandar to Bhopal (Chancellor of the Chamber of Princes), 11 Apr. 1944, IOC R/1/1/4168.

[86] Wavell, journal entry, 19 Oct. 1943, in Moon, *Wavell*, p. 34.

importantly, whatever his views on the principle of attachment, he saw that the India (Attachment of States) Act was particularly dangerous. It unilaterally amended a section of the Indian constitution that had been drafted to protect the princes, and set a precedent that could easily be abused by the anti-monarchical Congress government that would assume charge when the British departed.[87] Fortunately, British opinion seemed to be moving in the direction of the Porbandar report: an India Office official commented that "One is tempted to think now that we were all rather rash in applying the scheme to the Second Stage units so soon after it had been launched;" a conference of Residents and Political Department officials in Delhi agreed that no further states would be attached, unless events made it absolutely imperative; and during the parliamentary debates on the Bill, the government promised to preserve the rights of the petty rulers in perpetuity.[88]

In September 1944, Wavell met with Bhopal and other representatives of the Chamber of Princes to discuss a range of issues: joint administrative services for groups of neighbouring states; protection of states against attacks from British India; industrial policy; treaty rights, the question of whether the agreements by which Britain had promised to protect the states would be honoured after the independence of India; arbitration of disputes between the states and the government of India; postwar reconstruction; and the attachment scheme.[89] But these discussions between the Viceroy and the Chamber delegation were a precursor to the most serious crisis in relations between the rulers and the British during the twentieth century. Matters were immediately precipitated by two issues. First, Wavell agreed to send Bhopal a written reply to the questions that the Chamber delegation had raised at the discussions. The document, representing the Paramount Power's official position, was

---

[87] Note by Wylie on talks with Bhopal, 1 Aug. 1944, IOC R/1/1/4148; C.G. Herbert (Resident, Central India Agency) to Griffin, 26 Jan. 1945, IOC L/P&S/13/982.

[88] Patrick to Wylie, 19 Apr. 1944, IOC L/P&S/13/974; Wavell to Amery, 11 Dec. 1943, IOC L/P&S/13/981; R.A. Butler, 1 Mar. 1944, 397 H.C. Deb. 5s, cols. 1531-1533.

[89] See IOC R/1/1/4168; Wavell, journal entry, 16 Sept. 1944, in Moon, *Wavell*, p. 90. For the rulers' attitude to industrial development, see Copland, *Princes of India*, pp. 184-185, 201-203.

presented to Bhopal on 2 December. The Chancellor was particularly incensed by one section of the reply. In 1920, it had been decided that at his discretion, the Viceroy might appoint a judicial tribunal to rule on disputes between Indian states and the government of India; again if he so wished, he might wholly or partially adopt the tribunal's recommendations. The Chamber asked that the rules governing these tribunals be changed, making their appointment compulsory if requested by a state, and their decisions binding on both parties. This demand was intended to safeguard the position of the princes in independent India, as the rulers were fearful of what would happen if the tribunals were under the control of a Congress-appointed head of state; but it was rejected in Wavell's reply.[90] But the real cause of the crisis was the question of treaty rights. A full session of the Chamber of Princes was due to open on 5 December. Bhopal decided that at this session, he would put forward a resolution demanding that no state should be removed from British paramountcy without the consent of its ruler. This linked treaty rights with the attachment scheme: if the British could hand over the functions of paramountcy to the large states, as they had already done, they could just as easily transfer suzerainty over all the states to an independent India, and this was something that the rulers wished to avoid at all costs. Bhopal's resolution would place Wavell in a very awkward position. The Viceroy knew that it was very likely that when independence came, the British government would indeed allow the new authorities in New Delhi to inherit paramountcy. For political reasons, however, a Chamber resolution on the question would require from him an assurance that this would never happen; and Wavell did not want to have to make a promise that he did not believe in. He therefore made it clear that he did not want to see the resolution presented, although he did not actually forbid Bhopal's raising it. On 3 December, Bhopal, Nawanagar (the Pro-Chancellor of the Chamber), and nineteen of the thirty-five members of the Standing Committee met to discuss the agenda of the forthcoming session. Bhopal informed the Standing Committee of Wavell's reply to the September delegation, and of the Viceroy's

---

[90] Griffin to Bhopal, 2 Dec. 1944, IOC R/1/1/4168. For many years, the princes had sought revision of the arbitration procedure; see Copland, *Princes of India*, pp. 101-102, 121.

opposition to the proposed resolution; and after a long meeting behind closed doors, Bhopal emerged with the resignations from Chamber office of himself and all those present. The immediate reason was the question of the resolution. More broadly, the Standing Committee was angry over a general deterioration in the Paramount Power's treatment of the states in recent years, as exemplified by both attachment and the rejection of the demand for courts of arbitration. During the following weeks, seven further members of the Standing Committee who had not been present in Delhi on 3 December also resigned.[91]

Delhi sought comfort in suggestions that Bhopal and a few other princes had engineered the crisis for personal reasons: Bhopal was a megalomaniac; Nawanagar was angry that the British had learned of his involvement in a smuggling ring; the Maharaja of Indore wanted revenge on the Paramount Power that had refused to give official recognition to his American wife; and so on.[92] But actually, the resignations showed that the princes fully recognised the trend of recent events. Delhi had convinced itself that in the hopes of postponing for as long as possible the advent of a Congress government, the princes would acquiesce in any policy that might be imposed on them. The resignations showed that this belief was mistaken; some major princes held aloof from the Chamber, but on the whole Bhopal and the Standing Committee represented the opinions of princely India. The attachment scheme in particular showed the extent of the change in the relationship between the Paramount Power and the Indian states in the last years of British rule. The "Canning guarantees" were a series of policy decisions of the government of India; none of them had any legislative basis, and only the renunciation of the Doctrine of Lapse had any moral force (as it was embodied in a proclamation of the queen). Breaking them was ungentlemanly, and gave the princes genuine grounds for

---

[91] For the resignation of the Standing Committee, see IOC L/P&S/13/982; Wavell, journal entries, 3-6 Dec. 1944, in Moon, *Wavell*, pp. 103-104. Alone of the active members of the Committee, the Nawab of Junagadh refused to resign, perhaps because he supported the attachment scheme which had greatly enlarged his dominions.

[92] Sir Evan Jenkins (Private Secretary to Viceroy) to Residents, Dec. 1944, IOC R/1/1/4169.

alarm, but did not exceed the recognised limits of paramountcy. But the promises in the Government of India Act had been negotiated by British and state representatives, and had been included in the constitution as a sign that they would always be honoured by the Paramount Power. The fact that the British government could so easily change the Act was a sign that the days of careful attention to princely interests were definitely over: Delhi would now do anything it deemed necessary to further its current political aims. As Wavell explained to Amery, "In effect the attitude of the group responsible for this incident is 'we have tolerated your interference in our affairs because you upheld our status and privileges; now we do not believe you intend to defend us to the last, but you are increasing your interference, and we don't like it.'"[93] The resignations showed Delhi that it could not take the princes' support for granted, and that it would occasionally have to heed their concerns if it wished to retain their cooperation.

The Viceroy claimed that the princes had only hurt themselves with the resignations, which had put out of action the machinery for joint discussions between the rulers as a body and the Paramount Power, and he repeatedly used the word "blunder" to describe the action.[94] But the crisis was also bad publicity for the British in their struggle to retain control of the situation in India; Sir Francis Wylie, a fierce opponent of princely rule who resumed the post of Political Adviser to the Crown Representative in August 1943, commented that "however worthless the Princes may be it is not a good thing that we should be openly at quarrel with them. It gives too much joy in other even more unholy quarters."[95] For six months, Wavell and Bhopal met repeatedly to resolve the dispute and reestablish the Standing Committee. They finally reached a compromise in June 1945. Wavell presented it as a victory on his part, requiring nothing more than a "face-saving letter" to the Chancellor. This was not entirely true. The Viceroy agreed to further discussions on his reply to the Chamber delegation, which he had hitherto insisted

[93] Telegram Wavell to Amery, 7 Dec. 1944, IOC L/P&S/13/982.

[94] Telegram Wavell to Amery, 7 Dec. 1943, IOC L/P&S/13/982; Wavell, journal entries, 5 and 6 Dec. 1944 and 28 Jan. 1945, in Moon, *Wavell*, pp. 103, 104, 111.

[95] Wylie to Patrick, 20 Feb. 1945, IOC R/1/1/4169.

represented the Paramount Power's final word on the points at issue; and he informed Bhopal that the Political Department had drawn up revised instruments of attachment that addressed most of the Chamber's concerns. The Chancellor, Pro-Chancellor, and Standing Committee thereupon withdrew their resignations.[96]

VII

The Political Department had begun revising the instruments over a year earlier, since it recognised that at least some of the objections to the attachment scheme were well grounded. Thus, the original instruments had provided that if an attaching state acceded to the planned federation, all of its attached units would also automatically accede; but as the constitution said that all Indian states would accede individually, and the India (Attachment of States) Act confirmed that the attached units were Indian states, this provision was plainly illegal. The Department therefore removed all references to federation from the instruments (this was made easier by the fact that the creation of the federation had become most unlikely). And the British government's promise during the debate on the bill, that the petty chiefs would retain all of their existing powers under attachment, necessitated eliminating the section of the instrument regarding the review of powers after seven years. As the Porbandar Committee had noted, one of the biggest flaws in the scheme was that, despite the supposed reasons for attachment, the instruments did nothing to provide for improvements in the attached units. The Political Department now made it compulsory for attaching states to bring judicial and administrative services in the attached units up to the same standard as prevailed in their own territories. Unfortunately, in October 1944, the India Office informed Delhi that the revisions were unacceptable, as they undermined the whole purpose of attachment. For example, the provision regarding the eventual extinction of powers was essential, given that (whatever promises

---

[96] See IOC L/P&S/13/982 and R/1/1/4169; the reference to a face-saving letter is in Wavell, journal entry, 20 June 1945, in Moon, *Wavell*, p. 143.

might have been made) the ultimate objective *was* the disappearance of the petty states.[97] Work on the revisions accordingly stalled

The resignation of the Standing Committee changed Whitehall's view of the situation. Just five days after Bhopal presented the resignations, the Secretary of State Amery informed Wavell that revision was necessary after all. The Political Department refined the revised instruments, and in May 1945 unveiled them to the second-stage rulers. The attachment scheme was functioning smoothly in three second-stage states, Malia, Jetpur, and Bilkha, and a fourth, Malpur, now accepted the revised instrument. But the remaining fourteen second-stage states (in order of precedence, these were Lakhtar, Sayla, Chuda, Vala, Jasdan, Manavadar, Thana Devli, Vadia, Mansa, Lathi, Muli, Bajana, Virpur and Kotda Sangani) remained firm in their rejection of attachment in any form, refusing to cooperate with the attaching states in the administration of justice or the distribution of rationed commodities.[98] Meanwhile, Wavell and Bhopal concluded the agreement that rescinded the resignation of the Standing Committee. This made acceptance of the revised instruments particularly pressing, and (on the day the agreement was reached) the Political Department ordered C.P. Hancock, the Resident at Baroda and for the States of Western India and Gujarat, to do whatever was necessary to bring the recalcitrant chiefs to heel. Hancock first tackled the chief of Vadia, and by means of threats and bullying secured his assent to the instrument on 7 July. This example was sufficient to persuade the chiefs of Thana Devli and Dedhrota (one of the handful of non-cooperating first stage units) to give in. Next on Hancock's list was the chief of Bajana; when he remained obdurate, a party of Agency police went to Bajana on 21 July and forcibly made over the administration to an official from Baroda (the attaching state). The same day, however, the Political Department telegraphed Hancock to suspend further action, as Lord Wavell was considering fresh proposals

[97] For the revision of the Instruments of Attachment, see IOC L/P&S/13/974 and L/P&S/13/976.

[98] For the reactions of the second-stage rulers to the revised instruments, see IOC R/2/578/1 and R/2/578/2.

made by the Nawab of Bhopal.[99] These proposals had originated in a suggestion made some months earlier by the chief of Jasdan, one of the second-stage chiefs. Jasdan had expressed himself willing to accept the principles of attachment if they were implemented through a bilateral agreement between himself and the Maharaja of Bhavnagar (his attaching state) rather than a unilateral Instrument of Attachment. This idea found favour with the other second-stage rulers, who soon brought it to the notice of the Chancellor of the Chamber of Princes. Bhopal himself had recently concluded an agreement with his neighbour the Nawab of the petty state of Kurwai, under which the two states had agreed to cooperate in the administration of justice and the police; and he now suggested to Wavell that similar agreements might replace the instruments of attachment, at least as far as the second-stage rulers were concerned. Bhopal promised he would try to ensure the acceptance of these bilateral agreements.[100]

The Political Department set to work, and released its "bilateral agreements" for the second stage states in December 1945. These were not, however, what Bhopal had in mind. Far from being the result of negotiation between the parties concerned, they were identical to the revised instruments that had already been rejected by most second-stage rulers. The only change was that they were phrased as an agreement between attaching and attached rulers rather than a declarative instrument given by the former to the latter. As a result, only one noncooperating second stage ruler, the chief of Chuda, accepted the bilateral agreement (which also went into effect in Thana Devli, Vadia, Malpur, Malia, Jetpur and Bilkha, all already cooperating in attachment). In January 1946, an exasperated Hancock informed the eleven recalcitrants that they had ten days to sign the bilateral agreements. Otherwise, they would be removed from power. One by one the holdouts assented. The last of them, the chief of Lathi, gave in on 21 March, after the arrival of armed police at his capital.[101] All of the second stage units were

---

[99] For the action against Vadia and Bajana, see IOC L/P&S/13/976, R/2/ 578/3 and R/2/578/4.

[100] See IOC L/P&S/13/976, R/2/578/2, R/2/578/3 and R/2/578/4.

[101] For the implementation of the bilateral agreements, see IOC R/2/578/5 and R/2/578/6.

therefore now cooperating in attachment, and it was time to settle relations with the four first stage chiefs who still refused to cooperate in attachment, Ghodasar, Vadagam, Sathamba and Bhadwa. They were given one month to accept the revised instrument or face removal. All but one agreed to cooperate; Bhadwa, defiant to the end, was removed from power in May 1946.[102]

The attachment scheme was at last functioning across the Agency. But one week before Bhadwa's removal, attachment became irrelevant. On 12 May, the British Cabinet Mission declared that on the independence of India, British paramountcy over the Indian states would lapse, and with it the legal basis of all arrangements that had been made under its authority–including attachment.[103] In July 1947, Lord Mountbatten, the last Viceroy, expressed the hope that "in the case of all attached States, the present arrangements on a Standstill basis will be continued by agreement until a permanent constitutional solution is found."[104] But such agreement was not forthcoming. The incoming government of India had already decided that the attachment scheme would come to end with the lapse of British paramountcy, and that it would assume the functions that until 1943 had been exercised in the petty states by the Crown Representative. In August 1947, the new Ministry of States (successor to the British Political Department) accordingly presented the attached units with Instruments of Accession ceding residuary jurisdiction and supervisory functions to the Dominion of India; and at the moment of independence on 15 August 1947, the attaching states lost all their powers over the attached units, which were placed under the jurisdiction of the incoming government's Regional Commissioner at Rajkot.[105] The secretary of the Ministry of States claimed attachment was undone to meet the wishes of the rulers of

---

[102] For the recalcitrant first-stage rulers, and the final attachment of their states, see IOC L/P&S/13/975, R/1/1/4140, R/2/578/6, R/2/578/7, R/2/579/14, R/2/579/25 and R/2/579/28.

[103] Cabinet Mission, "Memorandum in regard to States Treaties and Paramountcy," 12 May 1946, in Government of India. Ministry of States, *White Paper on Indian States* (2nd edition, Delhi, 1950), pp. 152-153.

[104] Agency note on Vanod to L.G. Coke Wallis (Resident), 10 July 1947, IOC R/2/579/26.

[105] For this Instrument of Accession, see *White Paper on Indian States*, pp. 169-172.

the attached states. British intelligence, on the other hand, suggested that Delhi wished "to obtain a vantage ground from which to observe the activities of the Maritime States of Western India whose sea borne trade with the interior might escape Indian customs duties." There are also suggestions that the goal was to fragment Gujarat anew, giving the new authorities greater ammunition in their campaign to present the Indian states as inherently unviable entities.[106] It is impossible to say which of these explanations is nearest the truth. But the end of attachment was criticized almost as much as the implementation of the scheme had been. A month after independence, a member of the Limbdi government protested to Delhi over his state's loss of its newly-regained jurisdiction over the bhayat.[107] A politician in the areas formerly attached to Baroda pleaded for the help of the AISPC, as now

> the protection of these big States is withdrawn and the people of the at-tached area are left to their own fates. The Talukdars of the attached Units are absolutely not able to give any protection to their subjects as a result of which disorder and chaos is bound to ensue.[108]

But the unification of Saurashtra in January-February 1948, and the merger of most of the remaining states of Gujarat into the province of Bombay in June, brought to an end the whole problem of the smaller states.

---

[106] In order, these suggestions are offered by Menon, *op. cit.*, p. 110; Intelligence Branch Report, 12 Sept. 1947, IOC L/P&S/13/973; and H.H. of Dhrangadhara.

[107] V.K. Trivedi (Finance Member, Executive Council, Limbdi) to V.P. Menon (Secretary, Ministry of States), 16 Sept. 1947, NAI WISA, E-13-33/1947.

[108] President, Mehsana Patan Attached Areas Praja Sangh, to Pattabhi Sitaramayya (acting President, AISPC), 9 July 1947, NL SPC Papers, file 8.

TABLE THREE

THE ATTACHMENT SCHEME IN WESTERN INDIA

ATTACHED TO BOMBAY

1 Apr. 1947:

Bawishi Thana: Ged, Morwad, Polajpur
Vatrak Kantha Thana: Dana, Kaprupur, Mahisa, Porda

ATTACHED TO BARODA

Total area of attached units: 5,690 square miles; total population: 488,467.

PRELIMINARY STAGES

1 Feb. 1940:

State: Pethapur

June 1940:

Katosan Thana: Deloli, Ijpura Barotna, Ijpura Jethajina, Kasalpura, Maguna, Memadpura, Rampura, Ranipura, Tejpura, Virsoda

July 1940:

Jurisdictional Taluka: Palaj

FIRST STAGE

10 July 1943:

States: Ambaliara, Ghodasar, Ilol, Katosan, Khadal, Patdi, Punadra, Ranasan, Sudasna, Tharad, Varsoda, Wao
Jurisdictional Talukas: Bagasra Majmu, Barwala, Bhalusna, Bilkha Majmu, Champrajpur, Dabha, Dedhrota, Deodar Virampur, Deodar Himmatsinhji's, Derol, Hadala-Bagasra, Hadol, Hapa, Kadoli, Khari-Bagasra, Khedawada, Kotda Pitha, Natwarnagar, Prempur, Ramas, Satlasna, Tajpuri, Thara, Thumbala, Vaktapur, Valasna, Vanod, Vasna, Vithalgadh and Pipalwa, Zainabad
Non-Jurisdictional Talukas and Estates: Dangavadar, Harsurpur, Pipalia

Babra Thana: Ankadia, Babra, Bhadli, Bildi, Itaria, Janbai-ni-Derdi, Kamadhia, Kariana, Khambhala, Khijadia, Nilvala, Noghanvadar, Randhia

Dasada Thana

Dedan Thana

Jhinjhuwada Thana: Jhinjhuwada, Rozwa

Lakhapadar Thana: Charkha, Dahida, Dhasa, Dholerva, Gadhia, Garamli Moti, Garamli Nani, Gigasaran, Halaria, Jhamka, Kaner, Kathrota, Khijadia-Nayani, Lakhapadar, Manavav, Monvel, Padargadh, Silana, Vaghavdi, Vekaria

24 July 1943:

Bawishi Thana: Sachodar

Deodar Thana: Bhatvar, Chalva, Chibhda, Delwada, Dhanakwada, Dhunsal, Duchakwada, Forna, Golvi, Jhalodha, Kapdi Dev, Makdala, Malukpur, Mithi Paldi, Mojru, Niladar, Sanadar, Surana, Vajapur, Vasarda, Vatam Juna Vas, Vatam Nava Vas

Gadhwada Thana: Ambavada, Dedasan, Mota Kothasna, Nana Kothasna, Nedardi, Timba, Umbri, Thakor of Undani's Estate in Hadol Taluka, Vinchhi

Kankrej Thana: Akoli, Anganwada, Arnivada, Balochpur, Bhadramali, Bhalgam, Bukoli, Chemla, Dasana Vas, Dev Darbar, Dugrasan, Indermana, Kakar, Kamboi, Kevalpuri Thali, Kharia, Khengarpur, Khimana, Lunpur, Madkol, Manpur, Ranawada, Ranekpur, Raner, Runi, Ruppura, Sadarpur, Samau Mota Vas, Samau Nana Vas, Shirwada, Sihori, Thara Saduji Vas, Umri, Un, Vada, Zabadia

Suigam Sub-Thana: Asara, Golap, Jelana, Kanothi, Koreti, Mamana, Nalodar, Nesda, Radosan, Suigam

Vatrak Kantha Thana: Telnob

SECOND STAGE

7 Dec. 1943:

States: Bajana, Bilkha, Malpur, Mansa, Vadia

10 Sept. 1945:

Jurisdictional Taluka: Magodi (previously attached to Malpur)

ATTACHED TO IDAR

Area: about 240 square miles; population: about 40,000.

FIRST STAGE:

28 June 1943:

States: Mohanpur, Ranasan

Jurisdictional Talukas: Bolundra, Dadhalia, Gabat, Likhi, Rupal, Sathamba, Vadagam

Bawishi Thana: Bhaderdi

Gadhwada Thana: Mohor

ATTACHED TO JUNAGADH

Area: 560 square miles; population: 144,816.

FIRST STAGE:

14 June 1943:

Jurisdictional Talukas: Alidhra, Anida, Bantwa Bara Majmu, Bantwa Chhota Majmu, Bhayavadar, Jetpur Majmu, Khijadia, Manpur, Mayapadar, Nadala, Sanala, Sardargadh, Suryapratapgadh

Non-Jurisdictional Talukas and Estates: Akala, Sardarpur

Dhrafa Thana: Amrapur, Lunagiri

Lakhapadar Thana: Kuba, Vinchhavad

SECOND STAGE:

7 Dec. 1943:

States: Amarnagar (Thana Devli), Jetpur, Manavadar

ATTACHED TO NAWANAGAR

Area: 1,069 square miles; population: 97,177.

FIRST STAGE:

14 June 1943:

State: Khirasra

Jurisdictional Talukas: Anandpur Senior, Anandpur Junior, Gadhka, Gavridad, Jalia Devani, Kotharia, Lodhika Senior, Lodhika Junior, Pal, Vasavad

Chotila Thana: Anandpur, Bamanbore, Bhimora, Chobari, Chotila, Mewasa, Sanosra
Dhrafa Thana: Dhrafa, Satudad-Vavdi
Lodhika Thana: Baldhoi, Kankashiali, Kanpur-Ishvaria, Mulila Deri, Nana Mahuva, Sisang-Chandli, Vadali, Virva
Paliad Thana: Sejakpur, Sudamda-Dhandalpur

1 Oct. 1943:

Jurisdictional Taluka: Lodhika Majmu

SECOND STAGE:

7 Dec. 1943:

State: Virpur

ATTACHED TO BHAVNAGAR

Total area: 779 square miles; total population: 94,811.

FIRST STAGE:

28 June 1943:

Chok-Datha Thana: Aiyavej, Bhandaria, Boda-no-nes, Chiroda, Chok, Datha, Dedarda, Gandhol, Jalia-Amraji, Jalia-Manaji, Junapadar, Kanjarda, Morchupna, Pah, Rahishala, Rajpara, Ranigam, Samadhiala, Sanala, Sata-no-nes, Shevdivadar, Vadal, Vija-no-nes
Paliad Thana: Paliad
Songadh Thana: Alampur, Bhojavadar, Chamardi, Chitravav, Dhola-Godadji, Gadhali, Gadhula, Katodia, Khijadia-Dosaji, Limbda, Pachhegam, Panchvada, Ramanka, Ratanpur-Dhamanka, Samadhiala-Charan, Samadhiala-Chhabhadia, Songadh, Toda-Todi, Vadod, Vangadhra, Vavdi-Dharwala, Vavdi-Vachhani

SECOND STAGE:

7 Dec. 1943:

States: Jasdan, Lathi, Vala

1 Dec. 1946:

Paliad Thana: Matra (previously attached to Jasdan)

ATTACHED TO DHRANGADHARA

Area: 686 square miles; population: 76,146.

FIRST STAGE:

10 June 1943:

Chotila Thana: Ramparda

SECOND STAGE:

7 Dec. 1943:

States: Chuda, Lakhtar, Muli, Sayla

1 Dec. 1946:

Wadhwan-Bhoika Thana: Kesharia (previously attached to Lakhtar), Munjpur (previously attached to Muli)

ATTACHED TO RADHANPUR

Area: 866 square miles; population: 32,953.

FIRST STAGE:

31 July 1943:

State: Warahi–Husseinyavarkhanji's State

Jurisdictional Talukas: Adesar, Terwada, Warahi–Rawaji's

Deodar Thana: Bhabhar Juna Vas, Bhabhar Nava Vas, Chatra, Gangun, Ganjesar, Kaprupur, Kareli, Oghadpura, Panvi, Ujanwada

Santalpur Thana: Adesar, Anternes (Jadeja and Rahumas), Babra, Bakutra, Barada, Boru, Chalanda, Charanka, Chhanasara, Dadhia Padar, Dhokawada, Dhrechana, Eval, Garamdi, Jakhotra, Kilana, Limbuni, Madhutra, Masali, Mora Pati, Nanda Pati, Par, Piprala, Rajusara, Sanva, Soneth, Vahuva, Varnisari, Zazam

Warahi Thana: Bamnoli, Chichodra, Daigamda, Daisar, Daldi, Gadha, Gokhantar, Inderva Juna Vas, Inderva Nava Vas, Jhekda, Koliwada, Korda, Lodra and Unadi, Sedav, Saiyadpur, Sidhada, Tanvad, Uchosan, Unrot, Warahi, Zundada

ATTACHED TO MORVI

Area: 120 square miles; population: 12,454.

FIRST STAGE:
20 June 1943:

Jurisdictional Taluka: Hadala
Lodhika Thana: Kotda-Nayani

SECOND STAGE:
7 Dec. 1943:

State: Malia

ATTACHED TO GONDAL

Area: 156 square miles; population: 22,534.

FIRST STAGE:
10 June 1943:

Jurisdictional Talukas: Bhadwa, Mengni, Rajpara, Shahpur

SECOND STAGE:
7 Dec. 1943:

State: Kotda Sangani

ATTACHED TO LIMBDI

Area: 248 square miles; population: 31,004.

FIRST STAGE:
25 June 1943:

Jurisdictional Taluka: Rai and Sankli
Wadhwan-Bhoika Thana: Ankewalia, Bhalala, Bhalgamda, Bhathan, Bhoika, Chachana, Chhalala, Darod, Devalia, Gedi, Jakhan, Kamalpur, Kantharia, Karol, Khambhlav, Khandia, Laliad, Palali, Sahuka, Samla, Talsana, Tavi, Untdi, Vanala

ATTACHED TO WADHWAN

Area: 222 square miles; population: 18,350.

FIRST STAGE:

16 June 1943:

Jurisdictional Taluka: Rajpur
Chotila Thana: Morwad
Paliad Thana: Bharejda
Wadhwan-Bhoika Thana: Bhadvana, Dudhrej, Gundiala, Jhamar, Jhampodad, Karmad, Kherali, Vadod, Vana

ATTACHED TO LAKHTAR

Area: 3 square miles; population (1931): 216

FIRST STAGE:

14 June 1943:

Wadhwan-Bhoika Thana: Kesharia (later detached from Lakhtar and attached to Dhrangadhara)

ATTACHED TO JASDAN

Area: 6 square miles; population (1931): 352

FIRST STAGE:

7 June 1943:

Paliad Thana: Matra (later detached from Jasdan and attached to Bhavnagar)

ATTACHED TO MALPUR

Area: 23 square miles; population (1931) 3,953

FIRST STAGE:

18 June 1943:

Jurisdictional Taluka: Magodi (later detached from Malpur and attached to Baroda)

ATTACHED TO MULI

Area: 3 square miles; population (1931): 587

FIRST STAGE:

7 June 1943:

Wadhwan-Bhoika Thana: Munjpur (later detached from Muli and attached to Dhrangadhara)

PART THREE: THE LIMITS OF SOVEREIGNTY

CHAPTER SEVEN

BRITISH INTERFERENCE IN STATE AFFAIRS

The princes' subordination to the Paramount Power was most clearly demonstrated when the latter intervened in the internal affairs of the states, particularly by taking charge when a minor succeeded as ruler, by stepping in when it was alleged that a state was misgoverned, and by asserting the right to approve the succession of new rulers.[1] The princes naturally disliked these severe limitations on their sovereignty; but, in the interests of control, the British asserted that paramountcy gave them the right to intervene in minorities, cases of maladministration, and succession disputes. This was confirmed even in the charter of princely freedom, the Montagu-Chelmsford Report of 1918.[2] The princes found the Paramount Power's intervention all the more objectionable because it was capricious in nature. There were no set rules governing British behaviour here, and even the extent to which the Paramount Power exercised its right to intervene varied with the shifts in British policy towards the princes. In 1930, the Chamber of Princes passed a resolution in favour of "defining by joint consultation between nominees of H[is]. E[xcellency]. the Viceroy and those of this Chamber the bases of intervention in the internal affairs of the States." The Viceroy, Lord Irwin, however, refused even to discuss the matter, on rather specious technical grounds.[3] The third partici-pant in the triangular dialogue, the Indian politicians, objected to British intervention in state affairs just as much as the rulers did, although for different reasons–Jawaharlal Nehru claimed that it worsened the conditions of life for the states' people:

---

[1] C.L. Tupper, *Indian Political Practice: A Collection of the Decisions of the Government of India in Political Cases* (4 volumes, Calcutta, 1895), 1:44-48.

[2] *Report on Indian Constitutional Reforms*, pp. 242-243.

[3] Panikkar, *Indian Princes*, pp. 30-32.

> The semi-feudal conditions are retained, autocracy is kept, ... but one change is made which alters the whole background. The executive becomes stronger and a measure of efficiency is introduced, and this leads to a tightening-up of all the feudal and autocratic bonds. ... a combination of feudalism and the modern bureaucratic machine with the disadvantages of both and the advantages of neither.[4]

I

On rare occasions, the Mughals took charge of young princes and raised them to be loyal vassals, but only when they came from powerful and hitherto rebellious states; the most notable example is Shahu, grandson of the seventeenth-century Maratha king Shivaji, who was brought up at Aurangzeb's camp during that emperor's long wars in the Deccan. But normally when minors succeeded, the Mughals and their successors as overlords of the states of Western India, the Marathas, let their families or the state officials make their own arrangements for the administration. The result was usually a regency headed by the widow or brother of the deceased ruler.[5] Two examples of minority arrangements in the Jhala family of Halvad (later Dhrangadhara) will illustrate this norm. On the death of Rajodharji of Halvad in 1500, his father-in-law Thakor Lakhdhirji of Muli installed his own grandson Ranoji as ruler, in preference to Rajodharji's two elder sons by another wife. For some time, Lakhdhirji administered the state on behalf of the minor, but he was then eased out by his daughter Ashade, who assumed the regency for her young son. Ashade, who did not observe seclusion, administered the state with the assistance of a council comprising herself and her husband's four brothers, and established a reputation as a good ruler. When Ranoji himself died in 1523, his widow

---

[4] Nehru, *Autobiography*, p. 114.

[5] In Muslim dynasties, the succession generally passed to the eldest surviving male, which often excluded children from inheriting the throne. Certain Rajputs, including the Jadejas of Western India, followed this–and many other–Muslim customs until at least the nineteenth century. But in most other ruling families, the accession of minors was by no means infrequent in pre-British times, and the sense of legitimacy inherent in Indian kingship generally safeguarded the position of minor rulers from usurpers.

Kalyande assumed the regency on behalf of her son Mansinhji I, and ruled well until the boy reached adulthood.[6]

The British initially followed these precedents and did not intervene in state affairs during minorities. The result was that during the first half of the nineteenth century, most minority administrations were headed by the widows of deceased rulers, despite British suggestions that East India Company officials were more likely to see to the interests of the people of the state.[7] Gradually, however, the new Paramount Power began to take charge of minors, rather than allowing ruling families to make whatever arrangements they deemed fit, and minority administrations were increasingly placed under loyal Indian or British superintendents. Ostensibly this was because being in seclusion, a queen mother was supposedly open to manipulation by sinister court factions, or because her male relatives, usually themselves rulers, would interfere in the minority administration, but the real reason was that the British found dowager queens almost impossible to control, as political officers were by and large excluded from any direct contact with them. If, however, it placed minority administrations in the charge of its own appointees, the Paramount Power could exert enormous influence over the administration of the states and the upbringing of minors. This helped the British to implement "reform" in the states, which during the latter part of the nineteenth century they came to see as one of the bases of the legitimacy of their rule in India. Adult rulers usually thought that the preservation of their sovereignty debarred them from submitting to British pressure to change the way they governed, which meant that British-initiated reforms could not easily be implemented in their states. But control over minorities removed this stumbling block: the Paramount Power could appoint committed

---

[6] H.H. of Dhrangadhara.

[7] For examples of regencies headed by widows in the first half of the nineteenth century, see Stern, *op. cit.*, pp. 68-79 (Jaipur 1818-1835), and Ramesh Chandra Munje, "Succession issue and the conflicts between Jankoji Rao Sindhia and Baiza Bai (A.D. 1827-33)," in S.K. Bhatt, editor, *Studies in Maratha History: Proceedings of the 4th All India Maratha History Seminar* (Indore, 1979), pp. 54-64 (Gwalior 1827-1833); Rudolph and Rudolph, "Oligopolistic Competition," p. 152. The suggestion that state government ought to remain in Indian hands, even if Britons would do more for the people, was made by a senior political officer in 1825, and is noted in Fisher, *Indirect Rule*, pp. 34-35.

reformers to govern states until young rulers reached adulthood; educate young rulers so that they too would be reformers; and, by deciding when and under what conditions minorities ended, give those reformers enough time to do their work. The supposed result was proudly stated by one officer of the Indian Civil Service: "whenever an Indian State is found to be well organised and well administered, the foundations have been well and truly laid by some capable British administrator," usually during a minority.[8]

The first notable occasion on which the Paramount Power stepped in in this fashion came in 1869, on the accession of a two-year-old as Nizam of Hyderabad, the greatest state in all India, when the Resident assumed control of all aspects of the minority administration and of the upbringing of the new ruler. This set a precedent that was followed for half a century, as having asserted a right to take charge of a minor in the premier state, the British considered that they could thereafter do the same in every minority.[9] The assumption of control over the education of minor princes was an important element of the new policy. In the Hyderabad minority of 1869, the British sought to give the new Nizam "a sound education on English principles," to "emancipate him from the dominion of those around him, and fit him at once to command and adorn his future position."[10] This became the normal education for minors, probably because the British sincerely believed that

---

[8] O'Dwyer, *op. cit.*, p. 90. For the British assumption of control over minorities, see Tupper, *op. cit.*, 1:26-28 and 2:172, 180-191; Copland, *British Raj*, pp. 137-139 and 168-169, and *Princes of India*, pp. 18-20.

[9] See Tupper, *op. cit.*, 2:170-201. For the Hyderabad minority, see Bharati Ray, *Hyderabad and British Paramountcy 1858-1883* (Delhi, 1988), pp. 58-62. The official view that these arrangements constituted a precedent for all other minorities is stated by Tupper, *op. cit.*, 2:170-179. The elimination of the princes' participation in minority arrangements is illustrated by a study of minority policy in the Sikh states of Patiala, Jind and Nabha between 1858 and 1905; A.C. Arora, "British Rule and Minority Arrangements in the Phulkian States, 1858-1905," in *Bengal Past and Present*, 92, 1 (1973), pp. 89-103.

[10] Tupper, *op. cit.*, 2:173. In the twentieth century, the education of a future ruler was normally overseen by his father; the British only took charge in minorities because the father was dead.–Bayly, *op. cit.*, p. 111, notes that British control over the upbringing of young rulers went back to the very beginning of the nineteenth century; but until the 1860s, such instances were the exception rather than the rule.

English schooling was an ideal preparation for rulers of men, but also because it ensured that rulers spoke fluent English, and perhaps shared at least some values with their overlords, including loyalty to British rule. Minors were either placed in the charge of British tutors, or sent to one of the princes' colleges modelled on English public schools (Rajkumar College at Rajkot in Western India was opened in 1870), and some went on to schools and universities in Great Britain. Indeed, it has been suggested that because of their fears of the pernicious influence of royal women, the British adopted a "two-pronged strategy" of sending young rulers to chiefs' colleges, and building them new palaces in the suburbs of their capitals; here, they could be protected from possible assassination as a result of palace intrigue, while simultaneously indoctrinated with suitable ideas.[11] The British also held that once his schooling was finished, a minor had to acquire practical experience of ruling, and therefore sent him for training in administration in his own state, another state, or British India. It was felt that a ruler should undergo at least some training in his state, so that he would be familiar with its administrative methods and the problems he would encounter once he took charge, but some experience of the administration elsewhere was also desirable; most rulers were sent to states that were larger and more westernised than their own, probably in the hope that they would adapt what they had learned to the needs of their states. The ideal result was someone like Madhavrao Scindia II of Gwalior (1886-1925), "a bridge between the twain [India and Britain], who, rooted in the arcane orthodoxy of inherited beliefs, was yet fully at ease among the miracles of steam and electricity."[12] Often, however, all of this so westernised young rulers that they lost touch with their people and became unwilling or

---

[11] Michael Sugich, *Palaces of India: A Traveller's Companion Featuring the Palace Hotels* (London, 1992), pp. 21, 60, 84. Diwan Jarmani Dass's scurrilous *Maharaja* claims that a major objective of the Paramount Power in assuming charge of the education of young rulers was to impart strong communal sentiments in them. This claim is based solely on the fact that at the chiefs' colleges, students received teaching in the principles of their respective religions, and it seems to have no basis in fact. Dass, *op. cit.*, p. 142.

[12] Scindia, *op. cit.*, p. 109.

unable to rule their states. As the head of one old princely line comments,

> At Mayo and other Chiefs' Colleges, the boys were made as different from their people as possible–they spoke English; wore ties and trousers; and played cricket. They were educated up to the Senior Cambridge Level, which was the level at which they were prepared to take orders but not to think for themselves. This suited British policy perfectly.[13]

The princes protested so strongly against this deracination that at the beginning of the twentieth century, the Viceroy Lord Curzon (a fervent British imperialist, but also a defender of Indian culture) instituted measures to ensure that an English education did not destroy an Indian identity.[14] Even this did not apparently work, and one of the resolutions proposed at the first session of the Indian States People's Conference in 1927 was that "the system of education that is now imparted to Kumars [young princes] in the Rajkumar Colleges is both ill-conceived and ill-suited and has the effect of denationalising them."[15] By then, the British campaign for princely support had, as will be seen, led to major changes in the system of minority administration.

II

In the same way as they originated the notion of systematic control over minorities in the Indian states, the British introduced the concept of "maladministration" to princely India. This does not

---

[13] H.H. of Danta. The transformation is noted in Copland, *Princes of India*, p. 26, who comments that it meant that by the beginning of the twentieth century, many rulers belonged to a completely new breed. Bayly, *op. cit.*, p. 197, comments that "A succession of English-educated rajas and diwans in Travancore [in South India] ... more effectively promoted British interests ... than any number of interfering early-nineteenth-century residents."

[14] See Copland, *British Raj*, pp. 185-186 and 191; Dirks, *op. cit.*, pp. 390-393; Lionel Knight, "British Paramountcy and the Education of the Mysore Prince," in *Bengal Past and Present*, 92, 1 (1973), pp. 37-57, at pp. 37-38.

[15] Mathur, *States' People's Conference*, p. 166.

imply that traditional Indian government was bad, or that British ways were good. It simply means that the British were the first overlords who believed that maladministration, however defined, rather than disloyalty or failure to pay tribute, was grounds for intervening in the states' internal affairs. They acted on this belief almost from the beginning of their dominance. Early in the nineteenth century, the East India Company forced many states to stamp out what it considered barbarous practices–for example, several princes in Western India were ordered to prohibit female infanticide in their territories, and the British later took measures to check such problems as rulers' interference in justice or allegedly oppressive taxation.[16] Such activity may have ended genuine abuses, but a consideration of the Paramount Power's changing explanations of when and why intervention against misrule was justified shows that the definition of "abuses" changed over time. This was because maladministration is a much more subjective concept than minority. Although the age of majority might change, it was usually easy to determine whether a new ruler was a child and minority arrangements were consequently needed. But there was no objective definition of maladministration, which could include anything from heavy expenditure on traditional state rituals, to a capable ruler's resistance to British designs.[17] For "maladministration" was really a term for anything that interfered with a state's performance of its role as currently designated by the Paramount Power, and not simply a flawed government. Prevailing British preconceptions and policy towards the states therefore determined not merely what the Paramount Power did to end misrule, but whether it considered that maladministration existed in a state at all.

In some cases, the Paramount Power had abjured all interference by its treaties with the states, but it was prepared to break these on the grounds that the changes brought about by British rule had made non-interference unviable: by crushing rebellions against tyrannical

---

[16] Tupper, *op. cit.*, 1:74-84, 88-89.

[17] Traditional expenditure as a form of maladministration is noted by Fisher, *Indirect Rule*, p. 410, and Waghorne, *op. cit.*, pp. 45-53; the case of recalcitrant rulers is cited in Jawaharlal Nehru (President, All-India States' People's Conference), "A Note on Rewa Affairs," 7 Mar. 1942, NL, Nehru Papers, Notes, serial no. 185.

rulers, the new Paramount Power had deprived the states' people of their traditional remedy for misrule, and thus had acquired responsibility for preventing maladministration by means of direct intervention. A textbook case occurred in 1933, when the Paramount Power first suppressed an uprising in the state of Alwar in Rajasthan, and then deported the Maharaja and placed his state under a British officer.[18] But this tidy explanation was more an excuse than anything else, and other considerations better explain why the British began to intervene to end maladministration fairly early in their dealings with the Indian states. All of them are in one way or another manifestations of the desire for control. The British sincerely believed that they had a duty to bring what they considered good government to the people of India; in 1939, the Political Department removed one ruler in the Western India States Agency from power because his state suffered from a "complete absence of any ordered system of administration and of all the facilities which every government is under an obligation to provide."[19] Moreover, unchecked maladministration could easily spread: if one ruler were allowed to misgovern his state, others might well follow suit. Many Britons justified their domination of India by claiming that they had introduced "good government" to the subcontinent; if they allowed misrule, even in a minor state, they would undermine the legitimacy of their control. Then, there was the danger that the oppressed people of a badly maladministered state might rise up against their ruler. Even a local rebellion would be difficult to suppress without much bloodshed, which would alienate many Indians who might otherwise have supported British rule. And an uprising could easily spread to neighbouring states or even to British India, which would both destroy another base of British legitimacy (peace and order) and perhaps grow into a serious threat against British paramountcy. This was a matter of particular concern in the Western India States

---

[18] For the principle, see Tupper, *op. cit.*, 1:74, and Fisher, *Indirect Rule*, pp. 260-262. Interference is abjured in twenty of the thirty-nine formal treaties that the Company concluded with states; Ashton, *op. cit.*, p. 5. For the Alwar case, see Ramusack, *Princes of India*, pp. 179-180.

[19] Minute on the Thakor of Tharad by J.S.H. Shattock (PD), 26 Oct. 1946, IOC R/1/1/4492. For the Tharad case, see IOC R/1/1/3685, R/1/1/4492 and R/2/599/32.

Agency where state and British territories were closely interwoven, as became clear in 1873 when oppressed peasants in Baroda state raided into neighbouring British districts.[20]

The Paramount Power had several remedies for this ailment called maladministration; which of them it used depended on the seriousness of the situation at hand, on current British policy towards the states, and on the personal attitude of those British officials who were responsible for dealing with the matter at the time. During the nineteenth century, a bad ruler might suffer a reduction of his artillery salute, a fine, the annexation of his territories to British India, even death. It was difficult to justify such punishments, however, since they humiliated rulers without guaranteeing that misrule would cease (a heavy fine, in fact, might encourage a prince to exploit his people in order to raise the money to pay it). None of these personal punishments was therefore employed during the period of the existence of the Western India States Agency, although the British never renounced the right to use any of them if it became necessary. Instead, in the twentieth century, four measures were employed to correct (rather than punish) maladministration. The local representative of the Paramount Power often privately told an offending ruler to mend his ways, which served several purposes: it hid the fact that the ruler had misgoverned his state or had yielded to dictation, and thus avoided publicly embarrassing him; it disguised the full extent of paramountcy, so that rulers who were constantly watching for British intrusion in the states were not angered; it made it harder for nationalist politicians to prove their claim that the rulers were mere British puppets; and it perhaps meant that when maladministration *did* occur, the Paramount Power could avoid direct responsibility for it (open and frequent intervention might be interpreted as admission of a duty to end all misrule, however minor). If advice did not work, a ruler's powers might be restricted. He was nominally left in charge of the administration of his state, but was required to give real control to a minister nominated by the Paramount Power. This spared princes the humiliation of being declared unfit to rule, and avoided direct Agency manage-

[20] Hardiman, *op. cit.*, p. 113. For British fears regarding maladministration, see Fisher, *Indirect Rule*, p. 248, and Tupper, *op. cit.*, 1:48.

ment over their states, but effectively placed states under British control. Such veiled management was retained only for short periods, and if the ruler cooperated and seemed prepared to change his standards of government, his powers were restored. But if he resisted mild measures to end maladministration, or if his misrule were serious, Agency management might be imposed on his state. Although he would retain the title of ruler and his personal freedom, he was in effect treated as a minor. Sometimes he was eventually restored to the administration; but if he was thought incapable of ruling properly, he would remain excluded from power until his death. The most extreme remedy was deposition, in which a ruler ceased to reign in both name and fact, and generally was imprisoned; he had no hope of restoration, and his heir immediately succeeded to the throne.[21] Deposition was reserved for extremely serious cases, especially where rulers were guilty of what were normally criminal offences (sovereigns cannot be convicted of crimes). It was rarely used, and was only once employed in the history of the Western India States Agency (when the chief of Sardargadh was deposed in 1933).[22] Whatever the punishment, however, it was likely to meet with strong opposition from both the affected ruler and other princes, who deeply resented such an infringement of their sovereignty.

---

[21] "Deposition" is often loosely applied to the imposition of British management over a state. This, however, is a misuse of the term, which properly refers only to cases in which a prince or chief was deprived of his status as a ruler and succeeded by someone else.

[22] For the possible remedies, see Tupper, *op. cit.*, 1:48-73, 87-90, and 2:44-47. For the rarity of deposition, see John McLeod, "Towards the Analysis of Hindu Princely Genealogy in the British Period, 1850-1950," in *South Asia Research*, 6, 2 (Nov. 1986), pp. 181-193, at pp. 185-186.–According to Lee-Warner, *Native States*, pp. 170-171, the East India Company's only remedy for misrule was annexation; in 1858, however, the Crown renounced the acquisition of territory from the states, and it therefore had to find other ways to end maladministration. This is wrong; Tupper, *op. cit.*, 2:44-47, notes that in 1875 the Paramount Power could have annexed Baroda after deposing its Maharaja for misrule, but for political reasons allowed a new ruler to succeed.

III

Rulers did not object merely to the principles of British intervention in state affairs, but also to its objectionable results. They frequently complained that in states under British administration on account of a minority or of maladministration, the appointees of the Paramount Power would introduce unnecessary western institutions or make concessions that adult princes would never yield, such as giving up sources of wealth that challenged the revenues of the government of India. For example, between 1897 and 1904 the British-led administration of Radhanpur banned the cultivation of poppy and hemp, and closed the state mint.[23] The use of British administrators as agents of what the Paramount Power considered to be reform outraged the princes, who were made even more angry by what seemed to be excessively frequent interference against maladministration; of the eighteen salute states and twenty-four major non-salute states that were later included in the Western India States Agency, no fewer than three salute and five non-salute states were placed under management on account of alleged misrule between 1858 and 1918.[24] All of this constituted a clear limitation on the states' sovereignty, as no foreign government can legally force a fully sovereign monarch to change the way he rules his people.[25] The princes detested anything that detracted from their sovereignty, and interpreted it as a slur on their honour, and it was a further slur to suggest that the British knew better how to rule a state than a man whose family had often been governing for centuries. Moreover, a prince's authority was undermined if his subjects knew that the British would redress their grievances against his administration; and by intervening in state affairs, the British gave credence to the claims of mismanagement in the states put forward by rulers' opponents. When the British decided early in the twentieth century

---

[23] Framroz Sorabji Master, *The Palanpur Agency Directory*, volume 1 (Ahmedabad, 1908), p. 73.

[24] The salute states are Kutch (1859), Porbandar (1886) and Radhanpur (1909); and the non-salute states are Kotda Sangani (*ca* 1870), Maliya (1892), Wao (1901), Mohanpur (1905) and Chuda (1911). The frequency of such action across princely India during this period is noted in Copland, *Princes of India*, pp. 18-19.

[25] Tupper, *op. cit.*, 1:48.

to enlist the princes as allies against nationalism, they therefore revised their policy towards minorities and maladministration. In 1909, Lord Minto's speech at Udaipur renounced the Paramount Power's right to intervene in all but the most serious cases of misrule.[26] And in August 1917, after discussions with the princes, the government of India issued a resolution outlining a similar policy to be followed during future minorities, freely admitting that

> In framing this Resolution the Government of India have been guided mainly by the valuable advice of the Princes who attended the Conference [of princes and chiefs at Delhi], whose views, it will be observed, have been accepted with a few slight modifications. ... Except in the case of obvious and unmistakable abuses, radical changes (such as important constitutional reforms, alteration of the Court language or of the postal, taxation or currency systems, etc.) should, as a general rule, be avoided.[27]

While the following year the Montagu-Chelmsford Report confirmed the right of intervention in minorities, the abandonment of the drive to reform meant that British control over minority administrations could be greatly relaxed. In their quest to limit British intervention, the princes had demanded a return to the traditional institution of queen-regent. The 1917 rules accordingly ordered that whenever possible, minority administration would be conducted by a regency under the widow of the late ruler; and the following year, the first queen-regent in Saurashtra in the twentieth century took office, when the widowed Begum of Manavadar began a very successful regency on behalf of her young son.[28] Again, in 1920 the widow of the chief of Lathi in Saurashtra was appointed regent

---

[26] See Chapter Three.

[27] Kharita of Lord Willingdon (Governor of Bombay) to Bhavnagar, Dhrangadhara, Gondal, Morvi and Nawanagar, 22 Sept. 1917, NAI WISA, C-48/1917. For the origins of the new minorities policy, see Ashton, *op. cit.*, pp. 48-51; Copland, *British Raj*, pp. 263-265.

[28] See IOC L/P&S/10/1299 and R/2/620/76.

during the minority of her son.[29] Where a widow could not serve as regent (for example, if she had predeceased her husband), a council of administration was to be established, preferably composed of state officials such as the chief minister. Thus, on the death of the Thakor Saheb of Rajkot in 1930, a council composed of Indian officials took charge, mainly because the mother of the new ruler was dead.[30] Only if "local conditions appear to render it impossible for a Council to administer the state successfully" was an Agency or Political Department officer to take charge.[31] Minority administrations were now granted considerable autonomy even when they were headed by Britons. In 1932 C.P. Hancock, a political officer (and later Resident at Rajkot), became head of the minority administration in the Rajasthan state of Bharatpur; he was told "that I was first and foremost a servant of Bharatpur and that I must not hesitate, whenever necessary, to protect the rights of the local people against claims from British India." Indeed, far from collaborating with the local Political Agent, Hancock instructed him not to leave the Agency buildings without his (Hancock's) consent.[32]

The new rules also provided that minors would be given their powers as soon as they reached adulthood. Since the beginning of British rule, the minimum age at which minors were given charge of their states had been eighteen, and the normal maximum twenty-one;[33] but the Paramount Power had always decided exactly when a young ruler received his powers according to the circumstances of

---

[29] See IOC R/1/1/1564, R/2/621/89 and R/2/628/171. Complaints from other rulers about her unchaste widowhood led to her removal from the regency in 1923; she was restored in 1926 when she promised to mend her ways, but was again deposed in 1927 when she continued as before.

[30] See IOC R/1/1/1910(2), R/1/1/1925, R/1/1/2080 and R/2/626/138.

[31] See E.H. Kealy (AGG) to PD India, 10 Feb. 1930, and minute by G.F. Squire (Secretary to AGG), 3 Feb. 1930, both IOC R/2/626/138.

[32] Sir Cyril Hancock, "Bharatpur 1932-38," in the newsletter of the Mahratta Light Infantry Regimental Association, 1988 (sent to me by Lieutenant-Colonel P.M.W. Doyle, MC, editor of the newsletter). Several scholars have suggested that even in the 1920s Delhi used minority administrations to intervene in the states' internal affairs, which seems to be wrong. Stern, *op. cit.*, pp. 230-231; Dirks, *op. cit.*, p. 396.

[33] The extremes may have been determined by English law–the age of majority for a British monarch is eighteen, while under Common Law it was twenty-one.

his case, usually on the basis of whether its purposes were best served by a long or a short minority.[34] With the beginning of reformism in the nineteenth century, the age had begun to rise; in Rajkot, a minority in 1862-1876 ended when the young prince was nineteen, while one in 1890-1907 lasted until his successor was almost twenty-two. This was naturally disliked by the princes, and the 1917 resolution included a report on the education and training of minor rulers, drawn up by a committee that included the Political Secretary and eight rulers.[35] The report advised that "ruling powers will ordinarily be assumed by the Minor Ruler at the age of 18 years." This recommendation was not, however, binding on the government of India, and the Viceroy Lord Irwin (1926-1931) favoured withholding powers until rulers were at least twenty. In 1928, after intense lobbying by the princes for investiture immediately after the eighteenth birthday, Irwin agreed to consider an age of majority of about nineteen or nineteen and a half, but only if in his opinion the young ruler was ready.[36] In 1931, for example, the young chief of Lathi was given full powers a month before his nineteenth birthday, while the same year, the Khan of Manavadar had to wait until he was almost twenty to receive his powers, as the Agency believed that he lacked sufficient knowledge of the administration.[37] Moreover, from the 1870s, the Paramount Power had in effect prolonged minority administrations well beyond a young ruler's twenty-first birthday by requiring him to rule in consultation with a British nominee, sometimes for as long as ten years, on the pretext that he was not yet ready to exercise full powers on his own.[38] After 1917, however, restrictions were imposed only when

[34] Tupper, *op. cit.*, 2:191-196.

[35] Report of the Committee convened to consider the question of the education and training of minor Rulers, 1917, NAI WISA, C-48/1917. The Committee comprised the rulers of Baroda, Kutch, Nawanagar, Dewas Senior, Cooch Behar, Kapurthala, Bikaner and Jhalawar; J.B. Wood (Political Secretary India); C.J. Windham (Resident, Western Rajputana States); and B. Egerton (Sadr-ul-Maham of the Paigah Estates in Hyderabad).

[36] See the correspondence in IOC R/1/1/1762.

[37] For Lathi, see IOC R/2/628/171; for Manavadar, IOC R/2/620/76.

[38] Tupper, *op. cit.*, 2:191-199; Copland, *British Raj*, pp. 169-172; Stern, *op. cit.*, pp. 174-175. A.C. Arora, "British Government and Minorities of Native Chiefs (1858-1905): A Case Study of Bahawalpur State," in *The Panjab Past and*

there were well-founded fears that a young ruler was truly incapable of ruling.

All of these changes were in accordance with the wishes of the princes, and were granted in order to secure their support. Delhi henceforth retained control only over the education and administrative training of young rulers. This was because the British still considered it essential for a new ruler to know how the government of his state worked. If he could not rule he would be useless to the Paramount Power, which therefore always kept control of this aspect of a minority. Thus, when in 1930 the Begum of Manavadar tried to hire a guardian for her young son, the Agent to the Governor-General angrily wrote that "the Government are entirely responsible for the training and upbringing of minors and we cannot allow such an important question as the selection of a suitable European guardian in a case like this to be taken out of our hands."[39] Nevertheless, by and large the recommendations of the 1917 committee on education and training were followed: that young rulers be made fluent in English and the language of their state, and acquire a good knowledge of colloquial Hindi and Urdu; and that from about the age of sixteen, they undergo administrative training on such matters as law and administration.

At the same time, the policy regarding maladministration was changed. In 1918, the princes' representatives asked Montagu and Chelmsford that all charges that could end in deposition be investigated by commissions of enquiry on which other rulers would sit. This request was duly adopted as a recommendation of the Montagu-Chelmsford Report.[40] In 1920, the procedure for conducting enquiries was codified. If a ruler came under grave suspicion of wrongdoing, he would be allowed to choose to have the case against him heard either by a public Commission of Enquiry or privately by the Political Department. If he selected the former, he

---

Present, 10, 1 (Apr. 1976), pp. 108-119, at pp. 113-114, 118, notes that in 1879 the Secretary of State declared that such restrictions violated the Paramount Power's treaties with the states; but he approved them at the insistence of the government of India.

[39] Kealy to J.C. Tate (PA, Western Kathiawar), 13 Sept. 1930, IOC R/2/620/76. See also Lee-Warner, *Native States*, p. 334.

[40] Ramusack, *Princes of India*, pp. 76-83; *Report on Indian Constitutional Reforms*, p. 246.

would be put on trial before other rulers, jurists, and political officers; the prosecution would be conducted by a lawyer, and he could have his own counsel. If the Commission found him guilty, it could recommend an appropriate penalty to the Viceroy, who reserved the right to make his own final decision. If, however, he asked for an enquiry by the Political Department (or in petty states, by its local representative), he would avoid public humiliation but would not be allowed to defend himself.[41] So that the threat of a Commission would remain an effective deterrent, the Paramount Power sought to ensure that "there is almost certain to be justification for deposition" before it even offered to institute a commission of enquiry.[42] Most rulers knew this, and some preferred to abdicate when they were told to choose between a Commission and a private investigation.[43] As a result, no Commission of Enquiry was set up anywhere in India until 1933, when the Talukdar of Sardargadh in Western India asked for one to hear charges against him.[44] Thanks to the new policy of non-intervention, the Western India States Agency did not deprive a single salute or non-salute ruler of his powers of administration between 1924 and 1939, and the Sardargadh case was the only significant instance where it intervened against misrule. In 1932-1933, there were repeated charges of maladministration against Mansinhji, the Dewan of Dhrangadhara. Latimer, the Agent to the Governor-General, ruled that "the allegations against the State are grossly exaggerated," and refrained from action. A year later, however, the Maharaja Raj Saheb of Dhrangadhara dismissed Mansinhji and took personal charge of his state, and all complaints against the administration promptly

---

[41] For the institution of the new rules, see Ashton, *op. cit.*, pp. 54, 90, 100-102 (notes). The working of Commissions in petty states was modified in 1922 and 1939; see the correspondence in IOC L/P&S/13/985.

[42] Note by A.F. Morley (IO), 28 Sept. 1933, IOC L/P&S/13/1571. This did not always happen; in 1942, a Commission exonerated the Maharaja of Rewa in Madhya Pradesh of crimes of which he was almost certainly guilty. Copland, *Princes of India*, pp. 187-188.

[43] The most notorious case is that of the Maharaja of Indore in Madhya Pradesh, who in 1926 abdicated rather than face an enquiry into charges of murder. See Dass, *op. cit.*, pp. 142-146.

[44] For the Sardargadh case, see Chapter Nine. For other cases of suspected misrule, see Ashton, *op. cit.*, pp. 100-102.

ceased.[45] This suggests that the Dewan really had misgoverned Dhrangadhara, but Latimer had ignored this in the interests of non-interference. Indeed, this policy dovetailed with the wishes of the AISPC, which in 1933 passed a resolution to the effect that the people of a state alone had the right to determine whether their ruler was guilty of misrule, and "demanded that no ruling prince should be removed from his '*Gaddi*' for alleged misrule unless there was a clearly expressed demand from his subjects or the All-India States' People's Conference to that effect."[46]

IV

The policies set down in 1917-1920 governed minority administrations and alleged cases of maladministration for twenty years, even though in 1926 Lord Reading reaffirmed the Paramount Power's right to intervene to maintain "the general welfare of the people of a State."[47] Then, as the Paramount Power changed its policy in the late 1930s, intervention resumed. As in the nineteenth century, minorities presented ideal conditions for carrying out the reforms that were now considered necessary for forestalling popular complaint and ensuring the survival of the states.[48] Delhi once more imposed its own nominees to head minority administrations. In 1941, the sentence of the 1917 resolution eschewing major changes during a minority was formally deleted and replaced with a provision that "reforms may be carried out in a minority State to bring the administration up to the level required under modern conditions,

---

[45] See IOC R/1/1/2372 and R/1/1/2586; NL Vyas Papers, file 13. The quotation is from C. Latimer (AGG) to Watson, 9 Mar. 1933, IOC R/1/1/2372.

[46] Mathur, *States' People's Conference*, p. 36.

[47] Lord Reading (Viceroy) to Hyderabad, 27 Mar. 1926, in *White Paper on Indian States*, pp. 149-151. Copland, *Princes of India*, pp. 51-53, notes a brief resurgence of British intervention against supposed misbehaviour by rulers under Reading's administration (1921-1926).

[48] See also Chapters Three and Four.

provided the reform does not go beyond the administrative standard obtaining in the best administered State in the Agency" (the odd qualification was intended to forestall princely complaints that reforms unsuitable for a state were being implemented); and in August 1946, the Political Department also authorised minority administrations to carry out constitutional reforms, which in effect meant democratizing the state government.[49] The age of majority again rose, and minors were not granted their powers until they were over twenty; and Lord Linlithgow revived the old policy of restricting the authority of new rulers even after the end of their minorities. Ostensibly, this was because the young Nawab of Cambay in Gujarat had quickly spent his state's savings when he received full powers in 1930 after a long minority, and on taking charge of their states the new Maharajas of Alwar (1937) and Bharatpur (1939) had both had to agree to continued British supervision. But the new policy was really intended to assist the Paramount Power now that it was taking every possible opportunity for intervention in state affairs. Thus, Mayurdhwajsinhji (Meghrajji III) succeeded as Maharaja Raj Saheb of Dhrangadhara in 1942, a month before his nineteenth birthday. In earlier days, he would probably have received full powers immediately. Now, however, he was kept in subordination to a council of administration for over a year and a half, and even after receiving his powers he was ordered to follow the resident's advice in his administration for two years.[50] From 1939 until almost the end of British rule in 1947, the Paramount Power used minorities "for the cleansing of certain Augean stables," especially "The orderly liquidation of debts and the replacement of corrupt officials...."[51] This might go to lengths that only a few years earlier would have been unheard of, extending even to political reforms as well as administrative ones. At the end

[49] E.F. Lydall (Secretary to Resident) to R.K.M. Saker (PA, Gujarat States), 19 Nov. 1946, NAI WISA, C-36-10/1946.

[50] See IOC R/1/1/3989, R/1/1/4012, R/1/1/4015 and R/1/1/4350. This was in keeping with what Copland, *Princes of India*, p. 198, calls the Wylie Scheme (for Sir Francis Wylie, the Political Adviser who implemented it).

[51] Sir Kenneth Fitze, *Twilight of the Maharajas* (London, 1956), p. 173. Fitze was second in command at the Political Department from 1940 to 1944. The same sentiments are expressed in Wylie to Patrick, 25 Mar. 1944, IOC L/P&S/13/981.

of 1946, for example, the Political Agent impressed on Nicholson, the British head of the minority administration in Limbdi, "the necessity for introducing representative institutions as soon as possible, since whatever we may think of such a move the future independent existence of any State probably depends on it."[52] For the same reasons, a much stricter policy on maladministration was also implemented. In 1939, the petty states of Pethapur, Tharad and Vasavad were placed under Agency management. In 1940 it was the turn of Ilol; and Ambaliara, Jetpur, Bhayavadar, Champrajpur and the Bantwa Bara Majmu Taluka followed over the next five years. In 1941 the Maharao of Kutch, the highest-ranking prince in all Western India, was forced to appoint an Englishman as his minister. The change from the practice of the 1920s and 1930s is obvious.[53] Nevertheless, it seems that bad government alone was not grounds for removing rulers from power, either before or after 1939: it had to be compounded by something else that interfered with British control–a ruler might be defying the Paramount Power's authority; or Delhi might be seeking to prevent the politicians from gaining adherents, or maintaining security. The main change brought by the abandonment of non-interference was that after 1939, the "other factors" that warranted intervention were not necessarily the serious offences that they had been before. It was for this reason, rather than because of greater vigilance against simple misrule, that so many states and talukas were placed under Agency management in the last eight years of British rule. "Maladministration" was therefore not merely misgovernment, but a set of circumstances (including misrule) that made the Paramount Power decide that a ruler had to be removed.

---

[52] A.E. Drake (PA, Eastern Kathiawar), "Tour Notes, Limbdi," Dec. 1946, NAI WISA, C-36-8/1945.

[53] The Ambaliara and Kutch cases are examined in Chapter Nine. The files on some of the other cases are as follows: Tharad IOC R/1/1/3685, R/1/1/4492 and R/2/599/32; Ilol IOC R/1/1/3617; Jetpur IOC R/2/597/20 and NAI WISA, C-44-13/1947; Bantwa Bara Majmu Taluka IOC R/1/1/4265; Bhayavadar IOC L/P&S/13/1509; Champrajpur IOC L/P&S/13/1611, R/1/1/2939, R/1/1/4362 and R/1/1/4582; Vasavad IOC R/1/1/3382. Copland, *Princes of India*, p. 276, suggests that even during this period, British intervention was not sufficiently far-reaching to accomplish the Paramount Power's goal of making the states viable entities in an independent India.

The Paramount Power changed its policy again in the last months of British rule. In February 1947, the British government announced that India would become independent by June 1948, and in April 1947 the various Residents met with officials of the Political Department to decide what arrangements would be made in connection with the lapse of paramountcy. The conference decided that all Political Agents would be withdrawn in September 1947; skeleton staffs would wind up the Agency work for several months after that, and by the end of December the Residencies would be shut down. As in most Agencies (including Western India) minority administrations were supervised by Political Agents, a new means of governing states under minor rulers was necessary. The Residents accordingly

> decided to terminate minorities wherever possible at an earlier age than had been customary, without the usual elaborate period of training. In cases where the ruler was too young, a regency preferably in the form of a regency council should be set up. ... From the members of a ruling family a committee could be selected, who would exercise strictly limited functions of sovereignty under constitutional safeguards, just as an adult ruler would if a constitution were in force.

At the same time, the Political Department resolved that "restrictions imposed on account of recently-ended minorities should be allowed to lapse on the introduction of constitutional government." And "Rulers under restriction owing to incompetence could have their restrictions removed on joining a composite unit or establishing such constitutional rule as furnished the necessary internal check."[54] Thus, the chief of Jetpur, who had been removed from power in 1945 for selling his subjects' rationed sugar supplies for personal gain, was restored when he undertook to rule under the advice of the Joint Central Organisation, Kathiawar States, an association of rulers.[55] As a result, during the last months of British paramountcy, many minorities were abruptly terminated, and rulers

---

[54] T. Creagh Coen (PD) to Sir Cyril Hancock (Resident), 22 Apr. 1947, NAI WISA C-44-14/1947.

[55] See NAI WISA, C-44-13/1947.

who had earlier been considered delinquent were restored to full powers.

The successive minority policies were only outlines, however, and their application was worked out individually at the start of each minority. At worst, this lack of set procedure might cause unsuitable persons to be included in minority administrations. At best, it led to long delays in the establishment of administrations, while the Political Agent, the Agent to the Governor-General or Resident, and Delhi exchanged opinions and selected a course of action; when in 1930 Rajkot presented the first minority in a salute state since the creation of the Western India States Agency, the Agent to the Governor-General had to ascertain from his counterparts elsewhere how they had handled such a situation.[56] In Limbdi in 1941, a permanent minority administration was not established until over ten months after a child had come to the throne. These delays must have had deleterious effects on the state administrations.

V

British policy towards succession in the Indian states differed somewhat from that in minorities or in cases of alleged maladministration, although the paramount power's control over succession was another limitation on the rulers' sovereignty. Succession signifies a critical junction in any political system, but particularly one in which (as in the Indian states) the ruler is a personal, autocratic monarch. The British, like their Mughal and Maratha predecessors, insisted that no new ruler could take charge until they had confirmed his accession. Although it often gave rise to complaint among the rulers (who felt that a monarch who had duly succeeded according to the rules of his own family did not need the approval of anyone), this confirmation was usually a mere formality, and the late ruler's eldest son (or whoever else was heir according to custom) was

[56] See IOC R/2/626/138.

quickly installed by the local political officer.[57] But it was not always clear who the heir was, especially if a ruler died without any sons at all. On a few occasions, the daughter of a sonless ruler was allowed to inherit the throne.[58] Normally, however, neither custom nor the British permitted the accession of a woman. The East India Company occasionally sought to avoid disputed successions by urging rulers without sons to adopt.[59] But under Lord Dalhousie (1848-1856), the Doctrine of Lapse annexed to British India the territories of seven sonless rulers. The doctrine was only applied to states that had been either created by the East India Company or reestablished after a military defeat by the British, and did not affect the many states that did not fall into either category (including all of Western India).[60] Nevertheless, it was loathed by the princes, and after 1858 the government of India repudiated lapse in its quest for princely support for British rule. Between 1862 and 1914, most of the principal Hindu and Sikh rulers were granted deeds guaranteeing that sonless princes would be allowed to adopt heirs; since formal adoption is not a Muslim custom, Muslim rulers were promised that if they died without a son, the throne would pass to the next heir under Islamic law.[61] All of the salute princes of Western India received such deeds, or Adoption Sanads. Besides assuaging the

---

[57] Tupper, *op. cit.*, 2:117; for examples, see *ibid.*, 2:143-146. For the Mughal and Maratha precedents, see Lee-Warner, *Native States*, p. 323. The importance of succession in the Indian states is suggested by Fisher, *Indirect Rule*, pp. 65-66; and the princes' view of British policy is noted in Ramusack, *Princes of India*, p. 69.

[58] As in the Muslim state of Bhopal several times between 1819 and 1901, and in the Hindu state of Bastar in 1921 (both Bhopal and Bastar are now in Madhya Pradesh). In British as in earlier times, exceptions are rare, and often governed by particular circumstances; for example, it may be relevant that the bulk of the population of Bastar was tribal.

[59] In 1826 and again in 1835, sonless Maharajas of Gwalior were unsuccessfully advised to choose heirs. Hira Lal Gupta, "Gwalior Succession, 1826-1827," in *Journal of Indian History*, 34, 3 (1956), pp. 249-262, and *idem*, "Gwalior Succession 1836-1843," *ibid.*, 34, 1 (1956), pp. 59-65.

[60] Sir William Lee-Warner, *The Life of the Marquis of Dalhousie K.T.* (2 volumes, London, 1904), 2:145-157.

[61] Tupper, *op. cit.*, 2:i-vii, 35-36 and 81-116; Thomas R. Metcalf, *The Aftermath of Revolt: India, 1857-1870* (Princeton, 1964), pp. 224-226. See the deeds granted to the Muslim Nawab of Junagadh and the Hindu Jam Saheb of Nawanagar, in Aitchison, *op. cit.*, 6:151 and 167-168.

princes' fears that their states would lapse, the Adoption Sanads were intended to end succession disputes, by ensuring that every ruler left an indisputable heir in a real or adopted son. The Paramount Power therefore once more encouraged sonless rulers to exercise their right of adoption.[62] Many princes did so; between 1850 and 1950, the 327 rulers of the major Hindu states of India included no fewer than seventy-six adoptees.[63]

But many sonless rulers did not adopt an heir; some hoped eventually to father a son, others feared that an adoption would provoke jealousy within the ruling family, still others felt that by adopting they would acknowledge that their own death was near. And if a ruler died without a real or adopted son, several of his kinsmen might claim the throne. In such cases, the British asserted that their right to confirm new rulers also made them the arbiters in disputed successions.[64] This was a new element in the relationship between the Indian states and their overlords. Although the Mughals and Marathas had ratified accessions, they normally allowed rival would-be rulers to settle their claims, and then recognised the victor as ruler (although they occasionally intervened if the disputants requested their help, or if a succession dispute provided an opportunity for increased tribute or control in a particular state).[65] The British, however, made such intervention a practice from the beginning of their relations with the Indian states; indeed, succession disputes were the occasion for some of the Company's earliest interference in the states' internal affairs.[66] The British also assumed the right to find the heir in several other circumstances. When a ruler was deposed, they decided whether to entrust the chiefship to his eldest son, or to exclude all members of his immediate family from the succession and install a more distant relative.

---

[62] Tupper, *op. cit.*, 2:81-87.

[63] McLeod, "Towards the Analysis," pp. 184-185.

[64] Lee-Warner, *Native States*, p. 327; Tupper, *op. cit.*, 2:88.

[65] Fisher, *Indirect Rule*, p. 187. Tupper, *op. cit.*, 2:132, notes that in 1793, the Maratha Peshwa adjudicated a disputed succession in Savanur state in Karnataka.

[66] See Bayly, *op. cit.*, pp. 103, 110-111 and 171, and Fisher, *Indirect Rule*, pp. 139-144, 186-188, 224, 255-260.

Occasionally, too, the Paramount Power had to intervene if a ruler's sons could not agree which of them was the heir.[67]

The British claimed that they preferred not to intervene in succession disputes. They knew that it was often difficult for an outsider to determine which of several rivals was entitled to the throne, and moreover feared the criticism that would result if they recognised a candidate who subsequently misgoverned.[68] Nevertheless, they insisted that they alone could select a new ruler when a throne fell vacant. There were several reasons for this.[69] Probably the most important was to avoid disorder, which raised the spectre of widespread revolt and hence posed a threat to British rule; it has already been noted that this consideration often guided the Paramount Power's policy in the Indian states. By the mid-nineteenth century, the British had virtually ended armed succession struggles by insisting that their recognition was the sole means by which a claimant could win the throne. Again, by arbitrating in a disputed succession, the Paramount Power could strengthen its control over the state concerned; in choosing a new Maharaja of Baroda in 1875, the British were guided by "the moral obligation to do what seemed best for the interests of the Baroda State and the Empire."[70] In practice, this meant that a staunch supporter of British rule might be rewarded with the throne (indeed, any successful claimant would tend to express his gratitude with loyalty, if not more concrete signs of gratitude such as territory or money, which in fact might be extracted from reluctant new rulers), or the claims of a child might be preferred over those of an adult, as the Paramount Power could then establish a minority administration. British arbitration also had a symbolic role; by depriving the states of the right to resolve

---

[67] Tupper, *op. cit.*, 2:48. For example, in 1862 the throne of Tripura was claimed by three brothers: the eldest illegitimate son of their father, the eldest legitimate son, and the son of the principal wife; John McLeod, "Indian States and British Courts: The Tripura Succession Dispute of 1862-1869," in *Indo-British Review*, 15, 2 (Dec. 1988), pp. 31-46.

[68] Tupper, *op. cit.*, 2:81-87. For the same fears regarding the appointment of British nominees as ministers in states, see Fisher, *Indirect Rule*, p. 217.

[69] The authorities of the Political Department never seem to have thought it necessary to explain why they adjudicated all succession disputes; see Tupper, *op. cit.*, 2:35-138, and Lee-Warner, *Native States*, p. 127.

[70] Tupper, *op. cit.*, 2:42.

disputed successions on their own, the new Paramount Power showed that it enjoyed greater authority over the subordinate rulers of India than any of its predecessors had ever done.[71]

The British said that in the adjudication of succession disputes, "The questions for consideration were questions of policy or political expediency...."[72] In other words, they were not consistent in how they selected heirs; perhaps this was because their intervention was motivated by several concerns, and the final decision was determined by whichever of these was dominant in the case at hand. The policy adopted in one state might therefore conflict with that employed in another.[73] Nevertheless, the Paramount Power normally settled disputed successions in one of five ways. A ruler's widow might be permitted to adopt an heir, but this kind of adoption was disliked by the British who feared that it invited palace cliques to secure the adoption of their own candidates by pliant queens. In some states, the nobility enjoyed the right to choose the successor to a sonless ruler, but again this might allow a powerful

---

[71] H.L. Gupta, "Banswara Successions, 1838 and 1844," in *Journal of Indian History*, 42, 3 (1964), pp. 763-770, at p. 770, and *idem*, "Orchha Succession, 1837-1842," *ibid.*, 36, 3 (1958), pp. 397-411. See also Fisher, *Indirect Rule*, pp. 65-66, 140.

[72] Tupper, *op. cit.*, 2:42.

[73] See Gupta's studies of succession disputes under the East India Company. Besides the articles already cited, these are Hira Lal Gupta, "Bhopal Succession 1819-20," in *Indian Historical Records Commission. Proceedings*, 32, 2 (1956), pp. 13-19; "Dhar Succession, 1834," *ibid.*, 34, 2 (1958), pp. 134-139; "Udaipur Succession, 1841-42," *ibid.*, 35, 2 (1960), pp. 96-102; "Holkar Succession, 1844," *ibid.*, 33, 2 (1958), pp. 85-93; "Kotah Succession Affairs, 1820-1838," in *Journal of Indian History*, 37, 3 (1959), pp. 375-384; "Datia Succession 1839-40," *ibid.*, 36, 2 (1958), pp. 163-170; "Dungarpur Succession, 1846," *ibid.*, 37, 1 (1959), pp. 85-95; "Martin's interference to control succession in Hyderabad," in *Indian History Congress. Proceedings of the Sixteenth Session* (1953), pp. 326-332; "Indore Successions, 1833-34 & 1843," *ibid., Eighteenth Session* (1955), pp. 243-251; "Kishangarh Succession, 1841," *ibid., Twenty-First Session* (1958), pp. 453-462. See also Ramesh Chandra Munje, "Succession issue and the conflicts between Maina Bai and Annapurna Bai of Dhar State (1834-37)," in S.K. Bhatt, editor, *Studies in Maratha History: Proceedings of the 4th All India Maratha History Seminar* (Indore, 1979), pp. 69-74. The wide range of policies that were followed throughout the 1820s, 1830s and 1840s argues against Fisher's generalisation that the 1830s saw a reduction in British intervention in, among other things, succession disputes; Fisher, *Indirect Rule*, pp. 224-227.

baron to install a puppet chief. Because of the perceived dangers, the Paramount Power never felt bound to recognise an heir chosen by queens or nobles, which in any case does not appear to have been the custom among the ruling families of Western India. Three other considerations seem to have guided the Paramount Power in all succession disputes in Western India, although in a given case one of them usually predominated. It sometimes happened that a sonless ruler chose a successor but for some reason did not adopt him; the British considered themselves compelled to recognise only heirs who had been formally adopted, but they might take into account a deceased chief's wishes in making their own selection. A second principle was "personal fitness," which Tupper's handbook for political officers called "The primary requisite for a candidate." The meaning of this term was deliberately left vague; it might refer to intelligence and dedication, or a westernised education and outlook, or support of British rule. During the nineteenth century the Paramount Power rarely used the third consideration, the rules of inheritance of the family in question, although these often clearly identified the heir to a man who had died without sons.[74] The reason was probably that the British wanted to remain unfettered in their choice of an heir. But by the 1920s, political officers frequently appointed the nearest relative of a sonless ruler to the throne. In most Hindu families, and many Muslim ones, this nearest relative was found by the laws of primogeniture: in the absence of a son, a man's heir was the brother nearest him in age; if the brother was dead, it was the latter's eldest son; in default of any brothers, it was the uncle next in age to the father of the deceased, and so on through first cousins and more distant relatives.

There were several reasons for this increasing reliance on primogeniture to resolve succession disputes. First, primogeniture was the norm in Rajput states, and governed uncontested successions in most

---

[74] Tupper, *op. cit.*, 2:43-44, 48, 128, 136. For the classical Hindu laws of inheritance in the absence of a son, see Pandurang Vaman Kane, *History of Dharmaśāstra (Ancient and Mediaeval Civil Law)*, Volume 3 (Poona, 1946), pp. 700-769.

states, where rulers were succeeded by their eldest sons.[75] It was therefore logical to use it to find the heirs to sonless rulers. Secondly, primogeniture provided an easy way to decide between two candidates whose qualifications were otherwise equal. Thirdly, and most importantly, the adoption of primogeniture in disputed successions removed yet another of the princes' grievances against Delhi's policies that affected their sovereignty: if the Paramount Power merely recognised the nearest relative of a deceased ruler, it could avoid the charge that it used succession disputes to force its own nominees on states.[76] Given that the British considered themselves free to choose whomever they pleased to fill a vacant throne, one might have expected that succession disputes would always be resolved in favour of whichever candidate was most willing to obey the dictates of the Paramount Power. In fact, this was not generally the case. The Western India States Agency would not enthrone rulers who it knew were unreliable, but beyond that, its primary considerations were primogeniture and the wishes of the late ruler, rather than the servility of a particular claimant. As always, succession disputes were resolved on the basis of "political policy," but by the time of the First World War that policy no longer called for the imposition of rulers whose sole qualification was that they would make good puppets. The reason was probably that Delhi had voluntarily renounced its freedom of action in succession disputes, and tried to find new rulers by means that were acceptable to the princes as a body. The dangers were more apparent than real, since so long as an openly disloyal ruler did not succeed, the usual sanctions (for example, the threat of intervention

---

[75] Tupper, *op. cit.*, 2:52, 130, 131-133. The prevalence of succession by primogeniture is noted in McLeod, "Towards the Analysis," p. 183, and in Susanne Hoeber Rudolph and Lloyd I. Rudolph, "Rajput Adulthood: Reflections on the Amar Singh Diary," in Rudolph and Rudolph, *op. cit.*, pp. 177-210, at p. 207. A notable exception to the spread of primogeniture came in 1926, when the Begum of Bhopal abdicated. By primogeniture, her heir was the son of her deceased eldest son; but at her insistence, she was instead succeeded by a younger son, Hamidullah Khan.

[76] Indeed, this manipulation of succession disputes by the Paramount Power was one of the oldest and keenest of the rulers' grievances; as early as 1814, the Governor-General Lord Hastings commented on the animosity caused by the Company's intervention in successions. Fisher, *Indirect Rule*, pp. 187-188.

against maladministration) sufficed to ensure that the successful candidate was a more or less faithful ally of the Paramount Power. The question of primogeniture occasionally affected not only the choice of a new ruler, but the future of the state itself. In some families, it was the custom for a deceased ruler's state to be partitioned among his sons; if he had no sons, the territory was divided among his surviving male relatives. After several generations, this practice produced states too small to function or to serve as allies of the British. The Paramount Power therefore encouraged rulers whose families had employed partition to institute succession by primogeniture, so that on a chief's death his territory would pass undivided to his eldest son; if he had no sons, an heir would be found by the usual means. But the Kathi caste of Western India was particularly attached to partition, and by the late 1920s only a few Kathi rulers had given in to Delhi's pressure to adopt primogeniture. If one of the many chiefs whose families practised division died, the Paramount Power, as the arbiter of disputed successions, had to determine whether it should allow the territory to be partitioned, or institute primogeniture so that the state would pass undivided to a single heir.[77] It will be seen that this question, like practice in minorities, maladministration, and succession disputes in general, was determined by current policy in Delhi.

---

[77] For families that practised partition and the British imposition of primogeniture, see Tupper, *op. cit.*, 2:48-49, and Bayly, *op. cit.*, p. 109. For the Kathis, see Aitchison, *op. cit.*, 6:4, and Tambs-Lyche, *op. cit.*, p. 116. In the early 1930s, there were proposals to abolish regulations that prevented moneylenders from foreclosing on the estates of petty chiefs in Gujarat, who would now only be protected if they agreed to institute primogeniture; see IOC L/P&S/18/D272, R/1/1/1493 and R/1/1/2371(1).

CHAPTER EIGHT

MINORITY ADMINISTRATION

The British might set the age at which minorities ended, but normally it was providence rather than the Paramount Power that determined whether a child succeeded as ruler of an Indian state. Even in the twentieth century, many Indian princes and chiefs died at a relatively young age, before their heirs had reached adulthood. As a result, minorities were surprisingly common in the Indian states. When the Western India States Agency was established in 1924, eight of its forty-two principal states were under minority administration: Lathi (where the minority lasted from 1918 to 1931), Manavadar (1918-1931), Jasdan (1919-1924), Bhavnagar (1919-1931), Bajana (1920-1926), Chuda (1920-1929), Jafarabad (1922-1933) and Malpur (1923-1935). Between 1924 and 1947, eight more minority administrations were established, in Patdi (1928-1940), Rajkot (1930-1931), Kotda Sangani (1930-1940), Wadhwan (1934-1942), Jetpur (1936-1943), Malia (1939-1947), Limbdi (1941-1947) and Dhrangadhara (1942-1943). Many of these minorities illustrate the rulers' quest for sovereignty and the Paramount Power's for control. This chapter examines three of them. The Bhavnagar minority is an example of a minority that ended in the age of non-intervention; the Wadhwan minority began in the age of non-intervention and ended after its renunciation; and the Limbdi minority administration was established during the period of renewed British interference in state affairs.[1]

[1] The files on most of the minorities that are not studied in this chapter are: Lathi, IOC R/1/1/1564, R/2/621/89 and R/2/628/171; Manavadar, IOC L/P&S/10/1299 and R/2/620/76; Jasdan, IOC L/P&S/11/290; Bajana, IOC R/2/619/33; Patdi, IOC L/P&S/13/1719, R/2/626/134, R/2/629/191, R/2/632/232, R/2/638/314; Rajkot, IOC R/1/1/1910(2), R/1/1/1925, R/1/1/2080 and R/2/626/138; Kotda Sangani, IOC L/P&S/13/1711; Jetpur, IOC R/2/599/33 and R/2/648/326; Malia, IOC L/P&S/13/1542 and R/2/626/137; Dhrangadhara, IOC R/1/1/3989, R/1/1/4012, R/1/1/4015, R/1/1/4034, R/1/1/4350 and R/1/1/4596.

I

The large Rajput state of Bhavnagar was the most important Western Indian state to be under minority administration during the period under study.[2] When seven-year-old Krishnakumarsinhji became Maharaja of Bhavnagar in 1919, his mother was dead; in accordance with the rules set down in 1917, a council of administration was accordingly instituted under the presidency of the state's elder statesman, the former Dewan Sir Prabhashankar Pattani, who after twenty-five years in the Bhavnagar government had served on the Bombay Executive and Legislative Councils and in the central legislature, and on the Secretary of State's Council of India.[3] Pattani evoked mixed reactions among Britons: to some, he was "the most delightful person–humorous, learned, speaks perfect English and has met all the most distinguished people of the last 3 generations," and "a very wise old man."[4] But to others, Pattani was nothing but a "a warm admirer of Gandhi, and is approaching senility, though few realise it," who during his time as head of the minority administration neglected public works and wasted money on projects of no benefit; indeed,

> The difficulties one encounters here may be summed up in one word, "Pattani." I mean nothing unkind. It is simply human nature. ... Everything in the Bhavnagar garden is [according to Pattani] lovely. Nothing needs improving or amending. ... Add to this, what I consider the key note to Pattani's character, his colossal vanity, and the picture is complete.[5]

---

[2] For Bhavnagar, see *The Ruling Princes, Chiefs and Leading Personages in the Western India States Agency* (2nd edition) (Delhi, 1935), pp. 185-196. This account of the Bhavnagar minority is based on IOC R/1/1/1569, R/1/1/1762, R/1/1/1961, R/2/621/94 and R/2/626/136.

[3] See the notice on Pattani in *Who Was Who*, 3:1053.

[4] The first quotation is from H.A.N. Barlow (Under-Secretary to AGG), private letter, 18 Mar. 1934, SAS Barlow Papers, II.31; the second is from Lord Birkenhead (Secretary of State) to Lord Irwin (Viceroy), 19 July 1928, IOC R/1/1/1762.

[5] The description of a senile Gandhiite appears in A.J. Hopkinson (PA, Eastern Kathiawar), "Handing-over notes. Eastern Kathiawar Agency," 26 Sept. 1930, IOC MSS Eur D 998 (Hopkinson Collection). The longer quotation is from R.J.C. Burke

When Pattani took charge of Bhavnagar, the state was still under the control of the government of Bombay. Sir George Lloyd, the Governor of Bombay, was among those who disliked the new president of the council, and the two men often clashed during the early years of the minority. The government of Bombay seems to have attached much less importance to securing the goodwill of the Indian states than did the Political Department in Delhi, and Lloyd apparently tried to provoke Pattani's resignation by overruling "Sir Prabhashanker somewhat ruthlessly on every point of difference that has arisen between them."[6] But the Political Department at Delhi sided with Pattani in these disputes, and it allowed him more or less a free hand after it took over the supervision of Saurashtra from the Bombay authorities on the creation of the Western India States Agency in 1924. Pattani enhanced this free hand with a remarkable skill at playing off the Agent to the Governor-General against his superiors in Delhi. Indeed, only once was he defeated in his plans for the young Maharaja's future. This was over Krishnakumarsinhji's education: the boy's father had wanted him to go to a public school in England after a few years at Rajkumar College in Rajkot, but Pattani vetoed this on the grounds that an education abroad would isolate Krishnakumarsinhji from his people and culture and expose him to the temptations of western life. The Political Department sided with Pattani, but in the spring of 1925, the Viceroy Lord Reading intervened and sent the boy to England for three years. This was partly in fulfilment of the late ruler's wishes, but also in unexplained "interests of the young Maharaja."[7] The three years ended in 1928, when Pattani proposed that Krishnakumarsinhji should attend college and simultaneously study administration at Bhavnagar, and then assume charge of the state at the end of two years, in May 1930. That would be one month after the Maharaja's eighteenth birthday. But the new Viceroy, Lord Irwin, was against granting young rulers their powers until they had reached the age of twenty, and insisted on *four* years of training. The Political Depart-

---

(Vice-President of the Council of Administration, Bhavnagar) to C.C. Watson (AGG), 24 June 1925, IOC R/2/621/94.

[6] Watson to Sir John Thompson (Political Secretary India), 27 Nov. 1924, IOC R/1/1/1569.

[7] S.B.A. Patterson (PD India) to Watson, 5 Jan. 1925, IOC R/1/1/1569.

ment added that Krishnakumarsinhji should spend the four years outside of Bhavnagar, since at home he might be caught up in court intrigues (presumably meaning Pattani's schemes), and ordered Pattani to draw up a course of study with this in mind. But the president of the council simply ignored Delhi. He launched the Maharaja on a course of administrative training in Bhavnagar, and refused to make any plans to extend the programme beyond 1930. The Paramount Power yielded for the time being, but at the end of the two years demanded that Krishnakumarsinhji spend a further eighteen months studying the administration in British India or a "model state" such as Mysore, and travelling abroad. This would take the Maharaja to the autumn of 1931, when he would be nineteen and a half, the age at which Irwin now favoured investiture. Political Department minutes make it clear that the main concern was to separate the Maharaja from Pattani; the president's defiance of orders was not a good model for a young ruler, and Pattani made no secret of his support the Civil Disobedience movement (he had visited Gandhi the day before the beginning of the Dandi Salt March a few months earlier). Pattani realised that an immediate investiture was impossible, but he did not want to lose charge of Krishnakumarsinhji. He therefore announced that outside training and foreign travel were out of the question, as the people of Bhavnagar would not let their Maharaja leave them again. A few weeks later, however, Pattani was selected to attend the Round Table Conference in London in October 1930. Pattani and Irwin now changed their positions rather abruptly, since both wanted charge of the Maharaja. Pattani declared that a visit to England was just what Krishnakumarsinhji needed, while the Viceroy forgot his plans for foreign travel and insisted that the Maharaja remain in India until his investiture. Irwin eventually gave in, partly because Pattani was strongly supported by E.H. Kealy, the Agent to the Governor-General (who pointed out that the conference would be an excellent education for a young prince), more because it would not do for a prominent state delegate to arrive at the conference full of resentment against the Viceroy. But Irwin did order that Krishnakumarsinhji return to India no later than the end of December, and promptly resume his training.

But after participating in the conference, Pattani took Krishnakumarsinhji to Geneva to observe the workings of the League of

Nations, and they did not return to India until February 1931. Pattani now advised that, in the interests of economy, the investiture should be combined with the Maharaja's wedding, which was set for April. The Political Department insisted that Krishnakumarsinhji would not receive his powers until autumn, and told Pattani "not to attempt to pursue the point any further, but to accept His Excellency's decision, expressed for the 4th time, with a good grace."[8] But Pattani had already won over Kealy, who agreed on the merits of a speedy investiture, and he now set to work on Sir Charles Watson, the Political Secretary, and Lord Irwin. He pointed out that Krishnakumarsinhji had a thorough command of administration, and reiterated that a combined wedding and investiture would greatly reduce expenses. Watson objected that an early investiture in Bhavnagar would lead other minor rulers to demand their powers, but caved in when he found that only two other princes were approaching the end of their minorities. Finally, on 27 March Pattani scored his greatest victory when the Viceroy agreed to end the minority. The ostensible reason was that by autumn, Pattani would be back in London for the Round Table Conference, although the deciding factor was again probably the British need for Pattani's support at the conference. Krishnakumarsinhji took charge of Bhavnagar on 18 April 1931, four days before his wedding and a full month before his nineteenth birthday. He ruled well, and seventeen years later Nehru appointed him Governor of Madras, the first prince to hold such a post.[9]

II

The first minority in Western India to end after the abandonment of the policy of non-intervention was the Wadhwan minority of 1934-

---

[8] E.H. Kealy (AGG) to Sir Prabhashankar Pattani (President of the Council of Administration, Bhavnagar), 28 Feb. 1931, IOC R/2/626/136.

[9] It may be noted that Pattani's continued lobbying for an early investiture provides a contrast to the situation in Gwalior, where for two years the dominant member of the Council of Regency, Sir Kailas Narain Haksar, blocked the young Maharaja's assumption of powers so that he (Haksar) could continue to govern the state. Scindia, *op. cit.*, pp. 139-140.

1942. Wadhwan lay in eastern Saurashtra, and was the seat of a Jhala Rajput family that had separated from the parent stock (the Dhrangadhara dynasty) in the seventeenth century.[10] The extent of the change that took place in 1939 may be seen in a comparison of the termination of the Bhavnagar and Wadhwan minority administrations. In 1934, Jorawarsinhji of Wadhwan was succeeded by his twelve-year-old son Surendrasinhji. Because of suspected financial problems, the Agent to the Governor-General wanted a minority administration under a political officer, who could implement whatever reforms were needed, but this became unnecessary when the Political Agent, Gordon, found the finances to be "quite satisfactory."[11] Gordon, however, rejected the Wadhwan family's request for a regency under the late prince's mother, mostly because the old lady's past history suggested that her main goal would be to further the interests of her surviving sons. Instead he proposed to appoint Jorawarsinhji's widow Rajendrakunverba as regent, but after talks with the rulers of Shahpura, Dhrangadhara and Wankaner (all related to the family) he opted for a three-man council of administration: Rajendrakunverba was only nineteen years old (Jorawarsinhji's children were by a previous wife) and quite inexperienced in the tasks of government, and her bad relations with her mother-in-law would hinder the functioning of a regency. Bhimji V. Joshi, the Chief Karbhari of Wadhwan, would normally have been president of the council, but he wished to retire and at his suggestion his place was taken by Harilal Raval, a Deputy Political Agent. The second seat on the council was given to Pravinsinhji of the ruling family of Lathi state, a Deputy Superintendent of Police in Bombay; he had been recommended by Dhrangadhara and Wankaner and approved by Latimer, the Agent to the Governor-General, because "the administration has stagnated for some years and not least in the Police Department, Wadhwan having been notorious for non-cooperation activities during the agitation in

[10] For Wadhwan, see *The Ruling Princes, Chiefs and Leading Personages*, pp. 244-250. This account of the Wadhwan minority is based on IOC R/1/1/2588, R/1/1/3713, R/1/1/4280, R/2/642/340, R/2/642/342 and R/2/642/343, and NAI WISA, C-45-16/1944 Part II.

[11] J. de la H. Gordon (PA, Eastern Kathiawar) to W.F. Campbell (Secretary to AGG), 29 July 1934, IOC R/2/642/340.

Kathiawar a few years ago, and some fresh blood and a younger man than the present staff includes in a position of responsibility is desirable."[12]

Surendrasinhji attended Mayo College at Ajmer in Rajasthan rather than the nearby Rajkumar College, apparently because Mayo was close to his uncle's state of Shahpura. In 1933, he and his younger brother Virendrasinhji entered the Palace School at Dhrangadhara, where the sons of the Maharaja Raj Saheb of Dhrangadhara and of his nobles were educated; two years later, this school was moved to Millfield in Somerset in England, where it still exists. The council and the Political Department both approved the transfer of Surendrasinhji to England (there was no Pattani to cite the evil results of education abroad). He returned to India in 1940 and for two years studied administration at Wankaner and in his own state. He was now ready to receive his powers, but, in keeping with the post-1939 policy, the Resident and the Political Department agreed that this would be on terms that denied the Thakor Saheb any real authority: for three more years, he was to rule with the "aid" of a Dewan and a two-man council, all chosen with the approval of the Resident. Moreover, the council was to control the appointment of all state officials. As one of its new restrictions on their powers, the Political Department began to demand that young rulers secretly undertake to make reforms, which they would then seem to have implemented voluntarily. Surendrasinhji was informed of this, and protested that all this was "an infringement of Sovereignty ... hardly in keeping with the solemn declarations ... of the British Government for the maintenance intact of the rights, dignities, prerogatives and Izzat of Ruling Princes," and refused to accept his powers at all unless Delhi removed the provision that his council would appoint state officials.[13] This was a shrewd move on his part: all the princes of India would be outraged if one of them were denied his powers for not agreeing to limits on his authority, and the offending clause was dropped as soon as the Thakor Saheb promised to let the Resident make the final selection if he and the council

[12] C. Latimer (AGG) to Sir Bertrand Glancy (Political Secretary India), 16 Aug. 1934, IOC R/2/642/340.

[13] Wadhwan to V.M.H. Cox (Secretary to Resident), 27 Jan. 1942, IOC R/1/1/3713.

disagreed over appointments. Surendrasinhji consented to the other conditions, and was invested in June 1942. In June 1945, the Viceroy Lord Wavell granted him full powers, but made it clear that it was an act of kindness to lift the restrictions as soon as the minimum three years had expired.

III

With the abandonment of non-interference in 1939, minority administrations acquired free license to resume the old policy of reformism. Delhi preferred to exercise its new power indirectly, as in Wadhwan, but if necessary would act openly. This was particularly evident in the Limbdi minority of 1941-1947, which also illustrates the final shift in British policy during minorities in the last months before the independence of India. Like Wadhwan, Limbdi was ruled by Jhala Rajputs. It was of very ancient origin, tracing its establishment to a younger son of the first Jhala to enter Saurashtra in the eleventh century.[14] Daulatsinhji of Limbdi, who succeeded in 1908, was the kind of prince many Britons liked, "a sort of exemplar of 'the old type of benevolent autocrat.'"[15] More important, he was a firm supporter of British rule, and in 1930-1931 he played a prominent part in helping the Paramount Power to crush the Civil Disobedience movement, leading the Agent to the Governor-General to comment that "there are few Rulers in India and certainly none in this Agency more completely and whole-heartedly loyal to the

---

[14] For Limbdi, see *The Ruling Princes, Chiefs and Leading Personages*, pp. 237-243. This account of the Limbdi minority is based on IOC L/P&S/13/1478, R/1/1/3663(1), R/1/1/4035, R/1/1/4346, R/1/1/4347, R/1/1/4428, R/1/1/4599, R/2/599/30, R/2/599/34 and R/2/599/35; NAI WISA, B-12-2-C/1946, B-12-4/1944, B-12-4/1946, B-12-4/1947, C-36-3/1942 Part II, C-36-8/1945, C-44-14/1947, C-45-16/1944 Part II, D-12-12/1943, D-22-1/1941 and E-8-7/1946; NAI WISA, Eastern Kathiawar B-66-1(b)/1947.

[15] Note by Sir Francis Wylie (Political Adviser), 8 Mar. 1941, IOC R/1/1/3663(1). For a hagiographical biography by the prince's British personal secretary, see Elizabeth Sharpe, *Thakore Sahib Shri Sir Daulat Singh of Limbdi, Kathiawar: a biography* (London, 1931).

British connection."[16] In reward, he was allowed to rule more or less as he pleased, with no checks to ensure that his autocracy really was benevolent. A vocal element among his subjects felt that it was not. In December 1938, as disturbances spread across many Indian states, widespread popular agitation began among members of the Limbdi merchant community against claimed abuses by Daulatsinhji and his family, which ranged from the conduct of the state administration to exorbitant personal expenditures. A Limbdi State Praja Mandal was established the same month to demand responsible government. In February 1939, the wife of K.M. Munshi, the Congress Home Minister of Bombay, presided over a praja mandal conference at Limbdi. The meeting was attacked by cultivators loyal to Daulatsinhji, and disturbances to intimidate participants continued afterwards. Finally, thousands of Daulatsinhji's subjects (comprising virtually all of the Banias in the state and several hundred artisans) fled into British India to escape the threats to person and property in Limbdi. The exodus was called the Hijrat; widely varying estimates of the number of people involved were given, but the Agency suggested a figure of about 3000, in a total state population of around 44,000. The states' people's movement took up the cause of the Limbdi merchants. Pattabhi Sitaramayya, outgoing president of the AISPC, commented that "Limbdi has outamritsared Amritsar...;"[17] the Conference detailed Daulatsinhji's misdeeds in an angry pamphlet,[18] and Sardar Vallabhbhai Patel organized a widely-observed boycott of Limbdi cotton, the state's main export. The state administration did make some changes, including giving Daulatsinhji's appointed Advisory Committee a voice in the administration of Limbdi town, and promising to establish village councils, and by the end of July the majority of the émigrés had returned. But the Paramount Power remained unconcerned by what might have been taken as indicative of a serious problem, and the Resident reported that the agitators had singled out

---

[16] Kealy to G. Cunningham (Private Secretary to Viceroy), 27 Aug. 1930, IOC R/1/4/465. See also Hopkinson, "Handing-Over Notes."

[17] "A Year in the Indian States Struggle: Periodical Survey of the Year 1939," NL SPC, file 186.

[18] *Lawless Limbdi* (n.p., n.d. [*ca* 1939]).

Limbdi to punish Daulatsinhji's role in suppressing the disturbances of 1930-1931 rather than because they had real grievances.[19]

Daulatsinhji died in 1940. The throne passed to his son Digvijaysinhji, who with his younger brothers had dominated Limbdi for some time, and the popular leaders therefore saw no prospect of any change in the administration of the state. But Digvijaysinhji in turn died three months later in January 1941, and was succeeded by his ten-month-old son Chhatrasalji. The Agency Secretary, Worth, was deputed to ascertain whether there were any financial problems that would need attention during the minority. His preliminary report found no evidence of any, and he therefore left the administration in the hands of the infant prince's uncle Fatehsinhji, the most able member of the Limbdi family and Dewan for several years. The political leaders knew that a minority administration offered a possible resolution of their grievances, and they now demanded that an Agency manager be appointed to end the domination of Fatehsinhji and his brothers. The Political Department was not prepared to go this far. Still, since 1939 Delhi had been leery of minority administrations composed exclusively of members of ruling families: an Agency official, even in a subordinate role, made it easier to exercise the control demanded by the new policy of reformism. Moreover, it was at least possible that there was some justification to the complaints against the Limbdi administration; Fatehsinhji was not universally liked, and the Maharaja of Jammu and Kashmir once commented that he "ought to be locked up."[20] Delhi therefore refused to give Fatehsinhji sole control of the minority administration. This also made it impossible to follow the directions of the late ruler Digvijaysinhji, who had asked that the Maharaja Rana Saheb of Porbandar, his brother-in-law, be appointed regent for Chhatrasalji. As Porbandar was at the opposite end of Saurashtra from Limbdi, such a regency would have left Limbdi entirely in the hands of the Fatehsinhji. Instead, Delhi decided to appoint Fatehsinhji to a council of administration, in which he would have to share power with an Indian official of the

---

[19] For the Hijrat, see IOC L/P&S/13/1478 and R/1/1/3337, and NL AICC, G-35 1939. This sort of exodus by Banias was common in history; see Tambs-Lyche, *op. cit.*, p. 234.

[20] Minute by P.J. Patrick (?) (IO), 18 July 1944, IOC L/P&S/13/977.

Western India States Agency. As a concession to Digvijaysinhji's wishes, Porbandar would be associated with the Resident in supervising the council. Meanwhile, Worth had completed his investigations into the state finances. He found that Daulatsinhji's loyalty to British rule had blinded the Paramount Power to the fact that the complaints of mismanagement and extreme wastefulness by the old Thakor Saheb and his sons were fully justified. Indeed, there was virtually no modern infrastructure in Limbdi whatsoever: as the head of the minority administration commented a few years later,

> the State has neglected its roads, Village schools, dispensaries, uttaras [lodges], granaries and other buildings and done very little to develop the land by bunds [embankments] or save it from being inundated for a very long time. The only public works of note (other than the Guest House and palaces for the Raj family in Limbdi and Abu) during the 30 years before the minority are the bridge over the river at Limbdi the hospital (mainly from subscriptions) and the High School in Limbdi. Pacca roads do not exist in the rural areas of the State.[21]

Only swift action could avert renewed agitation against this situation. Moreover, Worth had proved that, at least in Limbdi, Congress was right to denounce the Indian states as tyrannies where the British ignored oppression by backward rulers. Delhi could not afford to give Indian nationalism such ammunition for propaganda, and Linlithgow told the Political Department "to make use of the long minority which now confronts the Limbdi State to create an ordered administration practically *de novo*."[22] The Viceroy felt that reconstruction should start in the land revenue system of the state's villages. He also wanted to reduce the family's expenditure, beginning with the huge cash allowances enjoyed by Digvijaysinhji's brothers. A council headed by Fatehsinhji and supervised by Porbandar would never implement such reforms; Linlithgow therefore ordered that a senior member of the Indian Civil Service head the council, with Fatehsinhji as his junior colleague, and that Porbandar be limited to advising on "matters affecting the traditions and

[21] J.P. Nicholson (Administrator, Limbdi) to Cox (now PA Eastern Kathiawar), 30 July 1946, NAI WISA, B-12-4/1946.

[22] K.S. Fitze (Secretary to Crown Representative) to E.C. Gibson (Resident), 6 June 1941, IOC R/2/599/30.

customs of the Limbdi State."[23] For two months Fatehsinhji stalled by insisting that Digvijaysinhji's wishes be followed, but, rather than be excluded altogether from the administration, he finally agreed to serve on the council under M.S. Jayakar, a retired Collector whom the Political Department had appointed to head the council, and the two men took office in November 1941. The council, however, did not function as planned, mostly because Jayakar proved utterly unable to assert himself in the face of Fatehsinhji's forceful personality, and he allowed the young Thakor Saheb's uncle to obstruct the reforms that Linlithgow had ordered. It can have come as little surprise when in February 1942 Jayakar announced his resignation.

This episode highlighted the problems that might arise in the establishment of a minority administration. The Paramount Power had already ruled out any suggestion that Fatehsinhji be given sole charge of Limbdi. But if an experienced officer of the Indian Civil Service had been unable to counterbalance the uncle's influence, it seemed unlikely that anyone could. The only solution, the Resident Gibson felt, would be to remove Fatehsinhji from all connection with the administration. At the same time, his importance within the ruling family made it impossible to exclude him from any regency council that might be established, and Gibson therefore concluded "that we should abandon the experiment of having a State Council and that a capable Administration should be appointed." Presumably because he connected Jayakar's weakness with the fact that he was an Indian, Gibson added that "It would be preferable to have a European" as administrator.[24] The difficulty, however, was finding a suitable Briton for the post. The needs of the war only compounded the usual shortage of British officers in India, and the Agency repeatedly delayed accepting Jayakar's resignation. A suitable candidate was finally found in J.P. Nicholson, the Collector of the Budaun district in the United Provinces (now Uttar Pradesh) and a close relative of the British hero of 1857, John Nicholson. Nicholson was not a member of the élite Indian Civil Service, as Jayakar had been, but belonged to the less prestigious Provincial Executive

---

[23] Fitze to Gibson, 6 June 1941, IOC R/2/599/30.

[24] Gibson to Fitze, 26 Feb. 1942, NAI WISA, C-36-3/1942 Part II.

Service of the United Provinces. His Governor, however, considered him "definitely a strong officer, possibly a bit old-fashioned in his ideas...,"[25] and this, and his race, was all the qualification Nicholson needed. The need to deal with Congress's Quit India disturbances in his own district during the summer of 1942 somewhat delayed Nicholson's transfer to Limbdi, but in October he assumed charge as administrator with "the full powers of the state, subject to the administrative control of the Resident...."[26] The Council of Administration was abolished, and Jayakar's resignation was at last accepted. Nicholson set to work carrying out Linlithgow's orders. The land revenue system was complicated: some villages paid rents in cash, others with a share of the produce, and the peasants in a third of Limbdi's villages, alone in all of Western India, enjoyed security of tenure and could not be arbitrarily evicted. Nicholson and the Resident, Gaisford, agreed that rents in kind and occupancy rights should be made general, but they considered that such drastic reforms should not be forced through by a minority administration, and proposed to leave them for Chhatrasalji to implement when he received his powers. Lord Wavell's Political Adviser, Sir Francis Wylie, retorted that occupancy rights, "one of the most insistent reforms required at present in Kathiawar," could not be put off for twenty years until Chhatrasalji's minority ended, and in 1946 Limbdi peasants were duly granted security of tenure and the right to sell their tenancies (with regulations to prevent the acquisition of land by moneylenders). Cutting the ruling family's expenditure was more difficult. Ceremonies were very expensive; seventy thousand rupees were spent on the wedding of Chhatrasalji's eldest sister in 1941, and even that was a mere seventh of the cost of her aunt's wedding in 1920. But the biggest drain was the allowances paid to the members of the family, which in 1942 absorbed twenty percent of the total state revenue and gave Digvijaysinhji's three brothers free electricity, water, telephones and

---

[25] Sir Maurice Hallett (Governor, United Provinces) to Sir Henry Craik (Political Adviser), 2 July 1942, NAI WISA, C-36-3/1942 Part II.

[26] Agency Memorandum, 2 Nov. 1942, NAI WISA C-36-3/1942 Part II. On the reorganization of the Agency in July 1944 (see Chapter Four), the Resident's supervisory functions passed to the Political Agent, Eastern Kathiawar; Agency Memorandum, 2 Sept. 1944, *ibid.*

palace guards, and paid for their sons' educations. Nicholson, Porbandar and Gaisford felt that the allowances could not be reduced, both because they had been gifts from deceased Thakor Sahebs and because of the size of the family. Linlithgow and his successor Wavell, however, stated that during a minority, allowances should only cover bare living expenses, and ordered cuts. Porbandar tried to block the reductions, at one point taking five months to answer a question from the Resident and at another not answering at all. Nevertheless, Nicholson did make progress: he limited the brothers' free electricity in December 1944, stripped them of free guards and telephones and free educations for their sons in May 1945, and cut off the cash allowances paid to their wives in December 1945. Other savings were gradually effected, and by June 1946 the allowances and easements enjoyed by the family had been reduced to 18.4 percent of the revenue. The savings allowed Nicholson to plan a programme of roads, buildings, and land reclamation, and to start construction of a school and a hospital. On the Viceroy's orders, he also established a full-fledged High Court[27] and a representative legislature, enacted laws regarding the administration of Limbdi town, and in July 1947 set up an Executive Council (comprising himself and two other members), which assumed executive and legislative authority over the state. Perhaps Nicholson's greatest triumph came in April 1943, when he successfully negotiated the return to Limbdi of the remainder of the refugees who had fled in the Hijrat four years earlier, and an end to the boycott of Limbdi cotton. Nicholson's reforms had certainly succeeded in their objective of quelling dissatisfaction with the state administration.

Meanwhile, arrangements had to be made for Chhatrasalji's education. His father had wished him to go to Eton, the most prestigious boys' school in England. In 1945, however, the Resident met with Nicholson and the boy's guardian, his uncle Ghanshyamsinhji, and they agreed that the Thakor Saheb would go to a preparatory school in England in 1948, but return to India four years later to enter the exclusive Doon School at Dehra Dun. Then,

[27] Since Nicholson's appointment in 1942, he and Fatehsinhji had constituted the High Court.

after discussions the following year, Porbandar and Hancock decided that Chhatrasalji's preparatory schooling would also be at Dehra Dun. This was probably connected with the coming of independence to India; Limbdi was the only salute state in Western India still under minority administration, and it was no doubt felt that its Thakor Saheb should not be out of the country when British paramountcy ended. Chhatrasalji's education was not the only aspect of the Limbdi minority to be affected by the impending lapse of paramountcy. The Political Department's decision in April 1947 to transfer power in minority administrations to regencies, preferably regency councils, raised the spectre of a resumption of control by Fatehsinhji, and Nicholson proposed that the incoming Limbdi council comprise Ghanshyamsinhji and his sisters-in-law, the late Thakor Saheb's widows Nandkunverba and Pravinkunverba. But neither Rani was willing to serve on the council, and they asked that their late husband's wishes finally be followed with the establishment of a regency comprising Fatehsinhji and Ghanshyamsinhji, and under the supervision of the Maharaja Rana Saheb of Porbandar. The Agency approved this proposal. In 1941, it had opposed the appointment of Porbandar to any official post on the grounds that his state was too far from Limbdi; now, however, it favoured his inclusion for the rather vague reason that this would "tend to stability."[28] As for the inclusion of Fatehsinhji, Nicholson was told that "whatever we may feel personally in the matter, we shall have to face the situation as it exists in Limbdi."[29] The Board of Regency (as it was now called) was constituted on 1 August 1947. Nicholson, not surprisingly, refused the Agency's request that he stay on as administrator in subordination to the board; and on 11 August 1947, three days before Independence, he relinquished his charge.

[28] E.F. Lydall (Secretary to Resident) to L.C.L. Griffin (Political Secretary), 29 May 1947, NAI, WISA, Eastern Kathiawar B-66-1(b)/1947.

[29] A.E. Drake (PA, Eastern Kathiawar) to Nicholson, 25 Apr. 1947, NAI WISA, Eastern Kathiawar B-66-1(b)/1947.

CHAPTER NINE

MALADMINISTRATION

The policy that the Paramount Power followed in cases of maladministration differed in one significant way from that used during minorities. Minority régimes did not necessarily alter the form of administration in the state concerned. By definition, however, any action taken to check misrule led to changes. The new policy of 1939 may have modified the definition of "maladministration," and hence the frequency of intervention against it; but it did not change the measures that were taken when such intervention did occur. Paramountcy was nowhere so visible as in its treatment of maladministration, which the British knew was a direct threat to their control in India, even as the rulers recognised intervention as a direct threat to their sovereignty. This may be seen in the case of Husseinyavarkhanji, the Talukdar of Sardargadh, who in 1934 was deposed in one of the few instances of British action against "maladministration" during the period of non-intervention in the internal affairs of the states; and in the events that in the 1940s occurred in Ambaliara and Kutch, ruled by two of many princes and chiefs whose powers were after 1939 curtailed on account of suspicions of misrule.

I

Sardargadh was a small taluka in Saurashtra, ruled by a branch of the Pathan dynasty of the major state of Junagadh.[1] Its chief, Husseinyavarkhanji (1903-1934), was less than a model ruler: two wives and a harem servant-girl sought British protection from his cruelty; he apparently arranged the murder of a Brahman whom he

---

[1] For Sardargadh, see *The Ruling Princes, Chiefs and Leading Personages*, pp. 155-158. This account of the deposition of Husseinyavarkhanji is based on IOC L/P&S/13/1571, R/1/1/2397(1) and R/2/639/320.

accused of poisoning his son; in 1921 he was involved in "incidents" of a kind that could not even be discussed in official correspondence.[2] More serious than these personal shortcomings, he manipulated justice (for example, framing and convicting innocent men against whom he had grievances), extorted money in the guise of customary gifts, and evicted his cultivators without compensation. The Agency periodically expressed concern over the Sardargadh chief's activities, but Husseinyavarkhanji was by no means alone in leading a scandalous personal life or conducting a state administration on less than ideal bases, and the policy of non-intervention made it very difficult to take any action against him. In 1932, the local Political Agent, J.C. Tate, believed that Husseinyavarkhanji had gone too far, and recommended suspending the chief's jurisdictional powers and deporting him from the taluka. The reason was that Husseinyavarkhanji had defied the Agency when it tried to stop him from embezzling money that rightly belonged to Zabardastkhanji, a relative who enjoyed a share of the taluka's revenues.[3] As far as Tate was concerned, if a ruler could disobey direct orders from the representatives of the Paramount Power, the whole basis of paramountcy was threatened. But Tate's superiors in the Agency knew that the Political Department would probably oppose intervention even in this case, and refused to approve the recommendation. Husseinyavarkhanji therefore remained in power, although Tate maintained a vigilant watch over him. In February 1933, however, the Political Agent finally managed to persuade the Agency to step in. The Sardargadh chief was ordered to hand over supervision of his administration to an Indian official of the Western India States Agency, who became Karbhari of the taluka and whom Tate detailed to investigate the complaints of the people of Sardargadh. Matters had at last reached a stage at which even the strictest exponents of non-intervention would admit that action was necessary. Husseinyavarkhanji had continued to

---

[2] J.C. Tate (AGG) to PD India, 9 Oct. 1933, IOC R/1/1/2397(1). Tate details Husseinyavarkhanji's misdeeds, except for "the incidents at Deolali related in the papers in the Bombay Government, Political Department, confidential file No. 1992."

[3] For the Zabardastkhanji case, see the correspondence in IOC R/2/629/195 and R/2/632/247.

obstruct Zabardastkhanji in his efforts to collect his share of the revenues. Worse, by early 1933, complaints from the people of Sardargadh had reached the press, and matters had to be corrected before political leaders used the reports as propaganda. Tate and the Agency would have preferred to take stronger measures, but they knew that the imposition of an Agency Karbhari was as far as Delhi would let them go.

A few weeks later, however, it came to light that Husseinyavarkhanji was guilty of more than misrule, and this gave the Agency the excuse it needed to suspend non-intervention and take decisive steps to end his nefarious activities. In July 1932, five Sindhi thieves fleeing from the Gondal state police had taken refuge in an acacia grove in Sardargadh. When he learned of their presence, Husseinyavarkhanji should have deported them to Gondal. Instead, he received them hospitably, and promised that in return for certain services, he would reward them and have the Gondal charges dropped. Among the services was burgling the house of his cousin Abdulrehmankhanji, one of the co-chiefs of the neighbouring Bantwa taluka, who had sided against Husseinyavarkhanji during a bitter family dispute.[4] For some reason, the Sardargadh chief believed that the burglary would convince the Agency that Abdulrehmankhanji was incapable of ruling and that his estate should be placed under management. On 24 September 1932, the gang broke into Abdulrehmankhanji's house and stole over two thousand rupees worth of property, including silver vessels, clothes, and firearms. They left the loot at a residence belonging to Husseinyavarkhanji, and for three months lived in the acacia grove at the expense of their patron. But matters did not turn out as Husseinyavarkhanji had anticipated. The Agency had not even considered punishing Abdulrehmankhanji for allowing his own house to be burgled; and as the Sindhis had not covered their tracks well, it was widely known both that they had robbed Abdulrehmankhanji and that they were hiding in Sardargadh. The Bantwa and Junagadh police sought the help of the Sardargadh authorities in catching the gang (Junagadh was both the home of the thieves and the largest neighbouring state), but on

[4] For the family dispute, which concerned the ownership of the village of Pajod in Sardargadh, see IOC R/2/632/241.

Husseinyavarkhanji's instructions were told by his own police that the men were not in the taluka. Nevertheless, by December, the superintendent of the Junagadh police knew that Husseinyavarkhanji had masterminded the burglary. He urged the chief to deport the gang, but Husseinyavarkhanji insisted that he knew nothing of the crime and secretly sent the Sindhis to Ahmedabad. The superintendent therefore ordered his officers to harass the thieves' families in Junagadh, to force the gang to return home. This, and the realisation that Husseinyavarkhanji could do nothing about the Gondal charges, had the desired effect, and in March 1933 the men went to Junagadh where they surrendered and confessed. Because the confessions implicated a ruler, Latimer, the Agent to the Governor-General, ordered the Agency police to take over the investigation of the burglary from the Junagadh authorities. On 20 April, he confined Husseinyavarkhanji to Rajkot (the headquarters of the Agency) and suspended him from any connection with the administration, which was assumed by the Agency Karbhari who had taken office in February. Latimer's object was to prevent the chief from hindering police investigations in Sardargadh, so that, if the confessions proved true, the evidence against him would ensure a conviction. A solid case was essential, as it had been decided that Husseinyavarkhanji must go. This was partly because for a century and a quarter, ever since Walker's security bonds of 1807-1808, the British had maintained peace among the rulers of Saurashtra.[5] If one ruler were allowed to harbour fugitives from another state, others might follow suit. Disorder would ensue, with all the resulting dangers to British rule, and the Paramount Power would show that it was unable even to prevent its vassals from committing crimes. More generally, "his administration has been for years past notorious for oppression and illegality, and ... the present opportunity of bringing him to book should not be foregone."[6]

The police found enough evidence to charge Husseinyavarkhanji with conspiring to commit burglary and harbouring fugitives from other jurisdictions, and Latimer ordered him to stand trial before the Kathiawar Sessions Judge. The Political Department now inter-

---

[5] See Chapter One.

[6] C. Latimer (AGG) to PD India, 20 Apr. 1933, IOC R/1/1/2397(1). For the notion of the British as bringers of peace, see Fisher, *Indirect Rule*, pp. 248-249.

vened to point out that as sovereigns in their own right, rulers could not be charged with criminal offences, and under the rules set down in 1920 Husseinyavarkhanji's conduct had to be judged by either a Commission of Enquiry or Latimer himself. The chief knew that the Agent to the Governor-General alone would be sure to convict him and he therefore asked for a Commission, perhaps hoping that its members could be induced to acquit him. Tate (who became officiating Agent to the Governor-General in May), however, made this unlikely by appointing Gordon, one of his own Political Agents, and Moos, the Sessions Judge, to the Commission, which was rounded off with Jorawarkhan, chief of Warahi; Jorawarkhan was only appointed after the rulers of Lakhtar, Sayla, Thana Devli, and Muli had in turn refused to serve, probably because they did not want to legitimise British interference in state affairs by participating in an enquiry into Husseinyavarkhanji's activities. Moreover, Lakhtar, Sayla, Thana Devli, and Muli were neighbours of Sardargadh in Saurashtra, while Warahi was far away in Banas Kantha. Jorawarkhan could therefore serve on the Commission without facing accusations that he was settling scores with a traditional rival.[7] Tate also dispensed with the services of the Agency's rather unskilled prosecutors, and accepted an offer to conduct the case against Husseinyavarkhanji from Popatlal Chudgar, a very capable Rajkot barrister, a founder of the Indian States' People's Conference and author of a book attacking the Indian states.[8] Husseinyavarkhanji was defended by a team of first-class lawyers, headed by Sir Chimanlal Setalvad of the High Court of Bombay.[9] Even Setalvad and his colleagues, however, could do no

---

[7] Even so, the British knew that it had been difficult for Jorawarkhan to serve on the Commission; his services were later rewarded when he was made a Companion of the Order of the Indian Empire, becoming the first petty Banas Kantha chief to receive such an honour (see Chapter Seven). Latimer to E.C. Mieville (Private Secretary to Viceroy), 10 Feb. 1934, IOC R/1/4/472, and 2 Feb. 1935, IOC R/1/4/474.

[8] P.L. Chudgar, *Indian Princes Under British Protection: a study of their personal rule, their constitutional position and their future* (London, 1929).

[9] Setalvad's memoirs do not mention his defence of Husseinyavarkhanji; Setalvad, *op. cit.* It may be noted in passing that the engaging of Chudgar and Setalvad as opposing counsel in the hearing is an illustration of the employment opportunities that capable lawyers might find in matters connected with the Indian

more than assert that the allegations against the chief had been trumped up by his enemies, and they produced no evidence for this claim. Husseinyavarkhanji therefore sought to prevent a conviction by other means. Before the Commission opened, he offered the Agency's Chief Medical Officer five hundred rupees to certify that he was too ill for an enquiry, and his son's British tutor suggested that they bribe Moos to deliver an acquittal. Both endeavours failed. The hearings began on 17 July 1933. A week later, Setalvad reported that the chief had become unwell, and on 31 July the Commission was therefore adjourned for two weeks. The day the hearings resumed, Husseinyavarkhanji offered to leave Saurashtra for two years, in return for an end to the enquiry, claiming that "serious nervous breakdown is sure to supervene as the result of the mental and physical strain involved under present conditions."[10] But the Chief Medical Officer found Husseinyavarkhanji to be in good health, and Commission, prosecution and police agreed that acceptance of Husseinyavarkhanji's proposal would amount to an acquittal. He would then return to Sardargadh, and take revenge on all those who had hitherto testified before the enquiry. For this reason, dropping the enquiry

> would ... be tantamount to betrayal of the witnesses who have so far conquered their dread of the Chief as to testify to his misdeeds in reliance on the protection of the Agency authorities; and render it impossible for any such action to be taken against a Ruling Chief for many years to come.[11]

Not surprisingly the chief's proposal was rejected, and the hearings continued. Husseinyavarkhanji did not attend any of the remaining sessions. On 21 September 1933, the Commission of Enquiry rendered its verdict. It found that Husseinyavarkhanji had ordered the burglary, although the only proof of this was the thieves' own testimony. Far more damning was the evidence of the many taluka officials and villagers who made it abundantly clear that the chief

---

states.

[10] Sardargadh to Tate, 14 Aug. 1933, IOC R/1/1/2397(1).

[11] J.T. Tanner (Deputy Inspector General of Police, Western India States Agency) to G.B. Williams (Secretary to AGG), 16 Aug. 1933, IOC R/1/1/2397 (1).

had sheltered the Sindhis even though he knew they were wanted in Gondal, Junagadh and Bantwa, and

> Never before in our experience has a case been more conclusively proved than the present one. No comment would be too strong for our condemnation of the part played by the Chief in harbouring the Sindhis and instigating the ... theft. Had he been before us as an accused person in a criminal trial we should have dealt with him severely. He has grossly abused his position as Chief and is in our opinion totally unfit to be entrusted with the exercise of jurisdictional powers.[12]

Both Tate and the Viceroy, Lord Willingdon, concurred in the Commission's recommendation that Husseinyavarkhanji be deposed and deported from Sardargadh. The former chief was sent to Ahmednagar, 130 miles east of Bombay, where he was placed under surveillance so that he could not harm the witnesses who had appeared at the Commission, and was succeeded as chief by his son Gulammoinuddinkhanji.

Despite the policy of non-interference, Husseinyavarkhanji had to be punished for what in British India would have been serious criminal offences. On those grounds alone, however, he might not have suffered deposition. The harsh penalty was influenced by other considerations, most of which had also played a part in the decisions to lay charges in the first place and to reject the chief's proposal to leave Saurashtra. The Paramount Power wanted to show other Saurashtra rulers that the gravest consequences would result if they threatened the peace of the peninsula. Moreover, as Latimer had noted in ordering a full investigation, Husseinyavarkhanji's long history misconduct was widely known; the commission's verdict provided a convenient excuse for ending his government permanently, despite the policy of non-intervention. Finally, and perhaps most important, Husseinyavarkhanji was the first ruler ever to be tried by a Commission of Enquiry; the need to ensure that the threat of Commissions could continue to check maladministration made his deposition inevitable, both so that witnesses in future cases would know that there was no danger of reprisals by the ruler they were testifying against, and so that other rulers would realise that

---

[12] Report of the Commission of Enquiry, 21 Sept. 1933, IOC R/1/1/2397(1).

Commissions (which had been established in response to a princely request) were to be taken seriously.

II

Ambaliara was a non-salute state in Mahi Kantha. In the age of non-interference between the wars, Thakor Keshrisinhji was what the Paramount Power considered a good ruler, and in 1930 he was rewarded with enhanced judicial powers.[13] By early 1942, however, some of his subjects were complaining of maladministration. Their chief grievance was heavy taxes, which they challenged in court. The Agency sent A.N. Mitchell, the Political Agent, to investigate the complaints. Perhaps Keshrisinhji's government really was worse than it had been a decade earlier, or charges of maladministration were taken more seriously after the abandonment of non-interference in 1939. It seems more likely, however, that the Agency acted mainly because the tax suits were sure to bring the discontent in Ambaliara to the notice of the press, and thus give unfavourable publicity to the Indian states. At any rate, Mitchell found that over half of the state revenue was absorbed by Keshrisinhji and his family, and concluded

> that the administration is being mainly run for the benefit of the Thakor and not for his people; that he has been levying every possible sum from the people in order to pay for expensive marriages; that some of his demands on the people are of disputed legality; and that discontent and agitation may be expected to continue as long as this form of administration continues.[14]

The Political Department ordered the Resident to draw up a programme of administrative reforms, and to force Keshrisinhji to

---

[13] For Ambaliara, see *The Ruling Princes, Chiefs and Leading Personages*, pp. 452-454 and R/2/638/309. This account of the imposition of management on Ambaliara is based on IOC R/1/1/3840 and R/1/1/4110. For judicial powers, see Chapter Eleven.

[14] A.N. Mitchell (PA, Sabar Kantha) to V.M.H. Cox (Secretary to Resident), 2 Mar. 1942, IOC R/1/1/3840.

implement them. It was March 1942. Sir Stafford Cripps was in the midst of his unsuccessful attempt to secure Congress support for the British war effort, and Delhi may have hoped to win Congress over with a hard line on maladministration. The Agency, however, did not think that such drastic action was warranted. Mitchell, and nine months later his successor Willoughby, discussed administrative reforms with Keshrisinhji, but neither man was willing to force the Thakor to take their advice. The Cripps Mission and later the Quit India rebellion (which began in August 1942) may have seemed far away from the isolated states of Mahi Kantha. Moreover, Willoughby noted that most of Keshrisinhji's subjects seemed satisfied with the administration, and that the Thakor would only be alienated by efforts to make him change his ways. This would be poor thanks for a ruler who "In spite of his many failings ... has the reputation of being intensely loyal to the British Government. Always courteous, a good host, and quite likeable."[15]

This probably explains why three successive Residents did not produce the programme of reform demanded by Delhi. A draft was finally submitted by the fourth, Gaisford, in February 1943. Despite Mitchell's findings, Gaisford denied that there was serious misrule in Ambaliara. He noted that all of the complaints had emanated from one village, where several wealthy supporters of the Congress leader Vallabhbhai Patel "aimed more at stirring up trouble in the State and embarrassing the Thakor rather than at effecting the redress of real grievances."[16] But if this were true, it seems odd that on Gaisford's advice, Keshrisinhji was told that the Agency would henceforth have to approve the appointment of his Karbhari, and that he must limit his privy purse to twenty percent of the revenue and improve his administration in general. Gaisford probably felt that while the accusations against the Thakor were exaggerated, Congress's involvement made it necessary to eliminate even the slightest grounds for criticism, before the rebellious nationalists

---

[15] V.W.D. Willoughby (PA, Sabar Kantha) to Cox, 1 Dec. 1942, IOC R/1/1/3840. At least one Political Agent was not so impressed with Keshrisinhji; see Sir Edward Wakefield, *Past Imperative: My Life in India 1927-1947* (London, 1966), pp. 146-152.

[16] P. Gaisford (Resident) to Sir Kenneth Fitze (Political Secretary), 22 Feb. 1943, IOC R/1/1/3840.

used the situation in Ambaliara to win support in the states. But even then, Gaisford did nothing to ensure that Keshrisinhji complied with his directive, presumably on the same considerations as had previously limited the Agency's activities in the state. In the spring of 1943, under the Attachment Scheme, all of the Paramount Power's rights in Ambaliara passed to Baroda, which therefore became responsible for preventing maladministration.[17] Baroda vainly ordered Keshrisinhji to follow Gaisford's directives. In October 1943 the exasperated Dewan of Baroda, Krishnamachari, asked the Agency's permission to deport the Thakor and take over the management of his state. But Gaisford was unwilling to enforce his own orders, even indirectly. He turned down the request, and merely secured a promise from Keshrisinhji voluntarily to implement the desired reforms. This of course had no effect, and in February 1944 Gaisford agreed that Baroda must assume charge of Ambaliara, apparently mainly because Krishnamachari was now receiving so many complaints from Keshrisinhji's subjects that it was clear the charges of maladministration had not all been manufactured by Congress. Moreover, Congress could only benefit if the grounds for popular complaint were not removed; and the Thakor was asserting that the ruling in December 1943 that the Attachment Scheme was illegal had nullified Baroda's authority over his state. By attacking an important project of the Political Department, the ruling had greatly embarrassed the British, who could not let themselves be further embarrassed by allowing a chief to use it as an excuse for misgovernment. Nevertheless, Krishnamachari could not act immediately. First Delhi insisted that he wait until the British Parliament had confirmed the legality of attachment (which happened in March), and then the Thakor simply ignored all communications from Baroda for several months. Keshrisinhji was finally removed from power in September 1944.

In December 1944 and again in February 1945, Keshrisinhji tried to regain the government of his state by promising to implement the desired reforms, but his demands were rejected by the Baroda authorities. Still, Baroda *did* want to restore him provided it could ensure that he did not revert to maladministration. Many petty chiefs

---

17 See Chapter Six.

were angered by the realisation that the Attachment Scheme had actually served to annex small states to their larger neighbours. The Political Department consistently denied that this was true, but by taking direct control of the Ambaliara administration, Baroda had seemed to confirm the suspicion. Krishnamachari's successor Mitter wanted to end such criticism, and in January 1946 he reinstated the Thakor after the latter agreed to appoint a Baroda nominee as his Karbhari and to give Baroda control over the state police and budget.

III

It has been seen that Kutch, the premier state of the Western India States Agency, conducted its tariff policy on a different basis from the other maritime states of Western India.[18] Unlike the Saurashtra states, Kutch always refused to maintain the British tariff at its ports, and this meant that all merchandise that crossed the Viramgam Line from Kutch into British India had to pay full duty at the frontier. As a result, there was very little trade between Kutch and British India, and most of what the state imported from overseas was consumed locally.[19] Then, in 1930, Maharao Khengarji III of Kutch opened a new port at Kandla, which he hoped would follow the Nawanagar port of Bedi in attracting a large share of the import trade of north-western British India. He requested permission from the Government of India to build a rail line to carry merchandise to markets on the other side of the Viramgam Line. Delhi, however, knew that low duties combined with a railway would invite merchants to import goods to Kandla and smuggle them across into British India, and consequently refused to allow a rail line unless the Maharao agreed to impose British customs duties. Khengarji

---

[18] See Chapter Five. For Kutch, see *The Ruling Princes, Chiefs and Leading Personages*, pp. 15-33. This account of the imposition of a British Dewan in Kutch is based on IOC R/1/1/3701, R/1/1/3825, R/2/597/10, R/2/597/16 and R/2/599/31.

[19] Until the beginning of the nineteenth century, Kutch was a great commercial centre. Tod, *op. cit.*, pp. 448-453, notes that the state's trade declined sharply after the establishment of British rule.

declined, and as a result Kandla received only those foreign imports that were consumed within Kutch.[20] During the 1920s and 1930s, Delhi therefore had no interest in the collection of import duties in Kutch, and (unlike the other maritime states of Western India) Kutch was allowed to administer its customs without any interference from the Paramount Power, although in 1934, when Delhi feared that Japanese cotton piece-goods were being landed in Kutch and then smuggled into British India, a British special officer examined the measures that Kutch took against smuggling (and found the situation satisfactory).[21] But the outbreak of the Second World War, and the new attitude towards the princes from the late 1930s, combined to change this. In 1940, Indian intelligence learned that wheat, and probably other things as well, was being smuggled out of Kutch to the Italians in East Africa.[22] It was bad enough that the lax Kutch customs service was unable to stop the export of commodities that under wartime regulations should not be taken out of India, but it was intolerable that foodstuffs were going directly from an Indian state to Britain's enemies. Delhi decided to end immediately its policy of non-intervention in the Kutchi customs administration. The first step was to determine exactly what measures were necessary to end smuggling from Kutchi ports. H.E.St G. McClenaghan, a top customs official from Bombay, was accordingly ordered to prepare a full report on the Kutch customs administration. McClenaghan spent two months in the state at the beginning of 1941. He found that while Khengarji had had no knowledge of the smuggling, such activity was inevitable because the state customs service was understaffed, badly trained, and so poorly paid that its officers had to supplement their incomes by taking bribes. McClenaghan advocated three principal reforms to remedy this situation: the establishment of a properly organized and well-paid customs service; the adoption by Kutch of British Indian rates of duty and customs law, at least for the duration of the war; and the

---

[20] See Rushbrook Williams, *op. cit.*, pp. 46-54; *East India (Constitutional Reforms), Report of the Indian States Enquiry Committee (Financial), 1932*, pp. 131-132.

[21] See IOC L/P&S/13/1469.

[22] M. Worth (Secretary to Resident) to the Dewans of the Maritime States of Western India, 6 Jan. 1941, IOC R/2/596/9.

revival of the post of Political Agent (abolished after the establishment of the Western India States Agency), to supervise customs. All of this would necessitate virtual British control over Kutch's import trade.

The Resident, Gibson, noted that Khengarji would never agree to the reestablishment of the Political Agency, which under the agreement concluded in 1925[23] would effectively have required his consent. But Gibson did agree that a new customs service was essential and that Kutch should adopt British Indian tariffs and customs law; and he warned that no reforms would be possible unless the Maharao first dismissed his weak, seventy-year-old Dewan, Rao Bahadur Rana, who was utterly unable to maintain control over the state administration. When all of this was reported to Delhi, the Political Adviser, Sir Francis Wylie, and the Viceroy, Lord Linlithgow, concurred in the need for an overhaul of the Kutch customs service and Rana's departure. But they also felt that reforms of the sort proposed by McClenaghan would have no effect unless they were accompanied by a thorough housecleaning at all levels of the state government; otherwise, smugglers would always be able to find cooperative officials who would help them evade even an efficient customs service. They also concluded that no Indian could be trusted to implement such a housecleaning, which would only be possible if Kutch were under the complete control of a *British* officer of the Political Department.[24] The old Maharao was accordingly informed "that [the] administration of Cutch is such that under modern conditions [the] existing state of affairs can no longer be permitted [to] continue;" he was told that he must either appoint a British political officer as Dewan, or subject his administration to investigation by a Commission of Enquiry.[25] Not surprisingly,

---

[23] See Chapter Four.

[24] The previous year, Khengarji had been forced to dismiss a Dewan who had first provoked popular agitation through his misgovernment, and then failed to suppress it; the Maharao had been allowed to choose the minister's successor, and appointed the unfortunate Rana. See IOC R/1/1/3307 and R/2/599/31.

[25] Telegram PD to E.C. Gibson (Resident), 12 June 1941, IOC R/2/599/31. Khengarji consulted the prime minister of Bikaner K.M. Panikkar during the dispute. In his memoirs, Panikkar gave a somewhat misleading account of the crisis: he claimed that the Paramount Power had in fact decided to depose the Maharao, because "his administration was not progressive enough to suit the conditions of the

Khengarji was furious at these orders, and complained that "I do not deserve this treatment."[26] He procrastinated for as long as possible, perhaps hoping that the matter would be forgotten; when this failed, he launched a campaign to obtain more lenient terms. With the help of such rulers as the great Ganga Singh of Bikaner, veteran leader of princely India, he secured modification of the original orders: Delhi agreed to let the Maharao prepare a list of two or three political officers whom he would accept as Dewans, and the Viceroy would then decide which of them should replace Rana. Linlithgow eventually selected W.F. Webb, a Political Agent in the Punjab, who in September 1941 began a one-year term as Dewan (later increased to two years).

Khengarji had been on the throne for sixty-five years. He was one of the last surviving princes to have been a personal friend of Queen Victoria; he had represented India at the League of Nations, and had been a leading member of the Chamber of Princes. When he learned that he would be forced to appoint a British Dewan, he called his treatment "a serious slur on his honourable career of over 50 years as a Ruler and an encroachment on his rights as such."[27] His attitude is understandable. Delhi believed that the Maharao had appointed a bad Dewan in Rana; worse, it did not trust him to choose a satisfactory replacement. In other words, the Paramount Power considered Khengarji incapable of filling the most important post in Kutch, and thus by implication of ruling his state. This was a heavy blow to the izzat of a man who prided himself on his inherited ability to govern, and whose reign had hitherto seemed to demonstrate his talents.[28] But the Political Department had not merely humiliated the Maharao of Kutch; as the Maharaja of Bikaner warned, "every Prince in India will be greatly pained by such an action and alarmed by it...."[29] Delhi must have anticipated this reaction, and only a few years earlier it would probably have been

---

day." K.M. Panikkar (translated by K. Krishnamurthy), *An Autobiography* (Delhi, 1979), p. 122.

[26] Note by Gibson on discussions with Kutch, 22 July 1941, IOC R/2/599/31.

[27] Note by Gibson on discussions with Kutch, 21 July 1941, IOC R/2/599/31.

[28] This is probably why the incident is not mentioned in Rushbrook Williams, *op. cit.*, the only full-length English history of Kutch, which is very partial to Khengarji.

[29] Bikaner to Lord Linlithgow (Viceroy), 11 Aug. 1941, IOC R/1/1/3701.

careful not to provoke such resentment.[30] But Delhi's abandonment of efforts to win the princes' friendship, while intended to enable the British more easily to redress supposed popular grievances and thus forestall political activity, also made it possible to take firm measures to deal with the customs crisis in Kutch.

While he reformed the state government, Webb implemented McClenaghan's recommendations by creating an efficient customs service and introducing British tariffs and customs law.[31] To modernise the customs service, he decided to place it under a British officer (again, an Indian was not trusted with so important a task), with orders to make whatever changes were necessary. The man chosen, A.C. Whitcher, hitherto Collector of Customs at Chittagong, assumed charge in December 1941. By the time he retired two years later, Whitcher had consolidated and expanded the Kutchi customs regulations and begun to build up a trained customs service, and he felt that "the foundations of a real State Customs Department have been laid."[32] Meanwhile, old Khengarji had died in January 1942. The new Maharao, his son Vijayarajji, was a "modern" ruler more to the liking of the Paramount Power, and for many years he had made clear his desire to reform the administration of Kutch.[33] Vijayarajji cooperated fully in the programmes that Webb and Whitcher were implementing, and the following year was rewarded by being allowed to choose successors to the two Britons; the reforms were considered sufficiently secure that all acquiesced

---

[30] The only comparable actions between the wars occurred in 1932-1933, when the Maharajas of Jammu and Kashmir and Alwar (also leaders of princely India) were removed from power. Even these comparisons are not entirely apt. Jammu and Kashmir and Alwar were both guilty of provoking uprisings in their states, while Khengarji had merely allowed his customs service to lose control of smuggling. See Ramusack, *Princes of India*, pp. 171-174, 179-180. (Such actions on account of alleged misrule must be distinguished from steps taken against a ruler for personal or criminal transgressions, as with the forced abdication of the Maharaja of Indore in 1926.)

[31] According to Panikkar, the most pressing reforms were implemented not by Webb, but by Panikkar and Khengarji; Panikkar, *Autobiography*, p. 123.

[32] A.C. Whitcher, "Reorganisation of the Kutch State Customs Department. Progress Report" (Oct. 1943), IOC R/2/597/16.

[33] See, for example, Vijayarajji (Heir-Apparent of Kutch) to Gibson, 16 Dec. 1939, IOC R/2/599/31. Panikkar commented that Vijayarajji "was obviously in a hurry to ascend the *gaddi*" (throne). Panikkar, *Autobiography*, p. 122.

when Vijayarajji selected Indians for both posts. The subsequent Dewans of the state aroused no complaint from the Paramount Power.

In 1942, Webb and Whitcher acted on McClenaghan's other recommendation by setting import tariffs at the rates levied in British India. McClenaghan had felt that this measure would only be necessary for the duration of the war, but the Political Department decided to make it permanent by concluding a customs agreement with Kutch, and ordered Webb to negotiate one on behalf of the Maharao. Delhi hoped that such an agreement would accomplish two objects: it would bring Kutch into line with the other maritime states of Western India which (except for Bhavnagar) all had such agreements, and it would help the minority administration then governing neighbouring Dhrangadhara across the Little Rann in its campaign to slash expenditure. So long as foreign goods paid low duties at Kutchi ports, smugglers would be tempted to carry them into British India through Dhrangadhara. The state therefore had to maintain expensive frontier patrols. But if a customs agreement guaranteed that Kutch would always levy British rates, smuggling would cease and the patrols would become unnecessary. Maharao Vijayarajji also wanted a customs agreement, although for a different reason. For twelve years, his father's modern port of Kandla had languished, as its imports were kept out of British India by both a tariff wall and the lack of a rail link. A customs agreement would eliminate the first of these obstacles, and the Maharao hoped that if he accepted Delhi's conditions, he would be rewarded with permission to build a railway out of Kutch. In January 1943, Vijayarajji (accompanied by Webb, Whitcher, and a top state official, Mukerjea) met with officials of the Railway Board and the Commerce and Revenue and Political Departments to begin negotiations on a customs agreement. No settlement was reached, however. The Maharao was prepared to follow the other maritime rulers in adopting the certificate system and handing over to Delhi a portion of the duties levied at his ports, but he demanded a larger share of the total collection than the central government would allow. Other states derived most of their income from land revenue. Much of Kutch, however, was held by semi-autonomous nobles of the bhayat, who kept the revenue from their lands;[34] to compensate for this, Vijayarajji wanted to retain thirty-five lakhs of rupees from customs duties on goods that were reexported to British India. In 1934, Nawanagar had only been allotted five lakhs out of the huge income of Bedi, and Delhi would not accept the Kutchi demand. Moreover, the Railway Board rejected Kutch's request for a rail link, which it feared would divert traffic from the lucrative Government of India State Railways. Since the lifting of the Viramgam Line in 1917, Saurashtra state railways had taken over much of the import trade that had formerly travelled on British lines from Bombay and Karachi. No insuperable objections had been raised to this, though; by letting state railways carry as much traffic as they could handle, Delhi had earned enough princely goodwill to cancel out any diminution of the Railway Board's earnings. But because the Paramount Power was no longer actively fostering its alliance with the princes, the Political Department now had to yield to the objections to a Kutchi line that were raised by Railways and Commerce and Revenue.[35] The Maharao apparently did not conceal his zeal for a customs agreement, and this made it obvious that he would not jeopardise a settlement by abandoning British Indian rates of duty at his ports. Delhi's principal objective in seeking an agreement had been to ensure that Kutch did not restore its former low tariff, but an agreement would necessarily involve some concessions on the part of the central government. On the other hand, so long as it held out to Vijayarajji the possibility of a settlement without actually entering into negotiations, Delhi could preserve high tariffs yet not have to yield anything. Despite the Maharao's repeated requests for further talks, it was therefore three years before the Paramount Power consented to a second meeting. This took place in April 1946; Kutch undertook to keep the British tariff, and Delhi promised to consider a rail line to Kandla. During the spring and summer of 1946, discussions were held on the division of customs earnings and on the railway line, but no agreement was reached before Nehru's provisional government took office in September.

---

[34] See Chapter One.

[35] This is sufficient comment on Hurd's generalisation that "the British were more inclined toward the builders of roads and railroads than were the Princes...." Hurd, *op. cit.*, p. 130.

The new authorities showed no interest in continuing negotiations with Kutch. In January 1947 the Maharao's heir-apparent and Sir Conrad Corfield, the head of the Political Department, accordingly decided "to pursue the Cutch (*sic*) agreement as part of the wider problem" of the lapse of British paramountcy, and discussions on customs and the railway ceased.[36]

---

[36] T.B. Creagh Coen (PD) to Sir Cyril Hancock (Resident), 14 Feb. 1947, IOC R/2/597/16. After the integration of Kutch into the Indian Union, the rail link was built, and Kandla grew very rapidly; see Rushbrook Williams, *op. cit.*, pp. 46-54.

CHAPTER TEN

SUCCESSION

Minorities, however much they might be prolonged, had to end some time, and certain conditions had to be met before the Paramount Power would intervene against maladministration; but the British had a completely free hand in selecting a ruler to fill a vacant throne. Several considerations governed the Paramount Power's selection of an heir every time a ruler was deposed or died without a son, and each case was resolved with little reference to what had been done elsewhere. Depending on their needs of the moment, the British might install someone whom it could control all his life, and not merely until he reached adulthood; forever exclude from the succession a branch of the ruling family that had proved itself disloyal to British rule, or incompetent in the tasks of administration; or simply choose the candidate whom it considered best qualified to rule, a welcome change from having unquestioningly to accept the eldest son of a deceased ruler. Admittedly, disputed successions were comparatively rare, and this means that there are too few examples to make it possible to delineate patterns. Nevertheless, British policy towards questions of succession reveals something of the prevailing trends in what was perhaps the most obvious manifestation of paramountcy, the selection of a ruler. There were no true succession disputes in Western India between 1916 and 1947, in the sense of conflict among candidates for a throne, all with equally good claims. Nevertheless, on several occasions, the Paramount Power did intervene to determine a succession that was in question in some way, and this chapter examines three such cases, in Rai Sankli, Bagasra, and Nawanagar. These studies illustrate the range of situations that might confront the Agency under the general heading of "disputed successions," and the considerations that guided the Paramount Power in its selection of a new ruler.

TABLE FOUR

THE RULING FAMILY OF BAGASRA

- Samat
  - Harsur
    - Laxman
      - Harsur
        - *Ram*
  - Godad
    - Bhaya
      - Mulu
        - *Ram*(P)
        - *Vira*(P)
    - Matra
      - Godad
        - Matra
          - *Godad*
          - *Samat*
  - Vajsur
    - Valera
      - *Vajsur*(P)

TABLE FIVE

THE RULING FAMILY OF NAWANAGAR

- *Vibhaji II* (1852-95)
  - Kalubha
    - Lakhubha(H)
  - *Jaswantsinhji* (1895-1906)
  - (chosen)
    - *Ranjitsinhji* (1907-33)
- Jivansinhji
  - *Ranjitsinhji* (1907-33) (also under Jivansinhji)
  - Juvansinhji(H)
    - Pratapsinhji(H)
    - Digvijaysinhji(H)

I

In 1922 Gopaldas, Talukdar of the tiny state of Rai Sankli, was deposed for disloyalty to the Paramount Power. An open supporter of Congress, he had been so caught up in Gandhi's Non-Cooperation campaign that he had missed ceremonies marking a visit to Saurashtra by the Governor of Bombay.[1] The Agent to the Governor of Bombay in Kathiawar, then in charge of Rai Sankli, at first proposed to recognise Gopaldas's eldest son Suryakant as the new ruler, but rejected this course when Suryakant declared that he held the same political views as his father did. The Bombay Political Department held that Gopaldas would raise his other three young sons to share his politics. It accordingly did not let any of them succeed to the chiefship, which therefore had to pass to Gopaldas's nearest heir. Bombay concluded that this heir was Gopaldas's brother Chaturbhai.

It has already been suggested that during the 1920s and 1930s, the Paramount Power ceased imposing its own candidates in disputed successions and sought to give its selection of new rulers the appearance of objectivity by relying on the laws of primogeniture. And here, there was a possible difficulty, since there were grounds for denying that Chaturbhai was next in line for the throne. This was because Gopaldas had originally succeeded on the death of his maternal grandfather, Ambaidas, who had had no sons and consequently had adopted Gopaldas. This meant that the deposed chief had succeeded as Ambaidas's adopted son, not as his daughter's son. According to Bombay's information, however, in Rai Sankli the succession could go through the female line–in other words, Gopaldas had derived his title from both his adoption and through his mother, Ambaidas's daughter. Since Chaturbhai was the son of the same mother, he enjoyed the same right, and he was also "loyal

[1] For Rai Sankli, see *The Ruling Princes, Chiefs and Leading Personages*, p. 430. This account of the Rai Sankli succession case is based on IOC R/2/600/41 and R/2/628/157; NAI FPD, 165-P/1924-25 and 165(2)-P/1926. For Gopaldas's life, see Aparna Bose, "Darbar Gopaldas Kashibhai Desai (1887-1951)," in S.P. Sen, editor, *Dictionary of National Biography* (4 volumes, Calcutta, 1972-1974), 1:426-427. In 1921 Rai Sankli had an area of 6 square miles and a population of 659.

and suitable."[2] But in 1923, a distant cousin of Gopaldas, Shivabhai (a railway station manager), submitted a petition to the governor of Bombay, protesting that Gopaldas had derived his title solely through his adoption, and that his brother Chaturbhai (not having been adopted) had no such rights; as the nearest blood relative of Ambaidas in the male line, Shivabhai claimed the succession for himself. The central Political Department consulted with the Legislative Department in New Delhi on the question. After considering the history of the family and other precedents, the Legislative Department reported that Shivabhai clearly had a much stronger claim that Chaturbhai, but added that it seemed "to be contrary to law as well as equity to deprive these children [of Gopaldas] as well as their descendants for ever of their inheritance in favour of a distant agnate like the appellant."[3] This was actually wrong–as the Bombay Political Department asserted, "The Gadi [throne] having become vacant by the misconduct of Gopaldas, the question who should be recognised as successor was entirely one for Government to decide...,"[4] and the Bombay government's choice had been Chaturbhai. Delhi, however, favoured removing Chaturbhai from the throne; perhaps after that,

> the best solution would be to recognise the succession of one of the sons of the deposed Chief, who has not yet identified himself with his father's political views.... the selection of one of them to succeed would involve minority administration, possibly for many years, and the fact that the arrangements for the education of the young Chief would rest with officers of Government might give opportunities of inculcating a proper sense of his duties towards the Paramount Power.[5]

---

[2] J.E.B. Hotson (Political Secretary Bombay) to Sir John Thompson (Political Secretary India), 19 Nov. 1923, NAI FPD, 165-P/1924-25.

[3] Minute by illegible (Legislative Department), 5 Aug. 1924, NAI FPD, 165-P/1924-25.

[4] Hotson to D.B. Binning (Shivabhai Amin's counsel), 1 Feb. 1924, NAI FPD, 165-P/1924-25.

[5] G.D. Ogilvie (PD India) to Hotson, 4 Sept. 1924, NAI FPD, 165-P/1924-25.

A month later, with the establishment of the Western India States Agency, authority over Rai Sankli passed from Bombay to the government of India. Watson, Delhi's new Agent to the Governor-General, agreed with his Political Department that Gopaldas's sons could not be excluded from the succession on the assumption that they would grow up to be disloyal. He was not, however, prepared to take one of the boys away from his father and place him under British control (which would have been a gross violation of the rights of a royal parent, and set a very dangerous precedent for a Paramount Power that claimed to favour non-intervention). Instead, he recommended that after the deposition of Chaturbhai, the chiefship should remain vacant until the sons had formed mature political views. When the eldest son reached his majority, the Agency was to determine whether he should succeed. If it deemed him disloyal, Rai Sankli would remain under management until the next brother attained *his* majority, and so on until an acceptable chief was found. "Many changes will have taken place by that time and it is, therefore, premature now to consider how the succession among collaterals should be determined."[6] The Delhi Political Department agreed, and deposed Chaturbhai and placed Rai Sankli under Agency management, over the furious protests of Shivabhai.

Watson and Delhi said that they did not want to deny Gopaldas's sons their inheritance merely because they *might* become nationalists. But nowhere else did the British deliberately leave a throne vacant for what in the end turned out to be over twenty years, no matter what the circumstances. Moreover, if they had really wanted a loyal son to succeed one day, they might have taken custody of the boys and indoctrinated them appropriately. But Gopaldas retained charge of his sons, which guaranteed that they would become "disloyal" and thus ineligible for the throne. A scrupulous regard for the sons' rights does not satisfactorily explain why the Paramount Power deposed Chaturbhai and placed the chiefship in abeyance. It is true that the people of Rai Sankli were reported to be happy under Agency management,[7] but this too does not explain what happened. Gopaldas was removed from the government during

[6] C.C. Watson (AGG) to Thompson, 18 Oct. 1924, NAI FPD, 165-P/1924-25.

[7] R.K.M. Battye (PA, Eastern Kathiawar), Tour reports on Rajpur and Rai Sankli, early 1943, IOC R/2/600/41.

the age of non-interference, when the Paramount Power was reluctant to take charge even of genuinely misruled states, and there had been no complaints about Chaturbhai's short reign. Quite possibly Rai Sankli, with fewer than seven hundred inhabitants, could not really afford its own administration, but it was by no means the smallest state in India, and until the implementation of the Attachment Scheme in 1943 the British were committed to preserving even the pettiest estates. Perhaps removing the sons from the succession would have made Gopaldas more of a martyr to the nationalist cause than deposition had already done; or appointing Chaturbhai as Talukdar would only confuse matters, since an independent Congress government would certainly restore the former chief. But Congress would probably not have found the exclusion of the sons any worse than the deposition, and it is most unlikely that in 1924 the Political Department was contemplating a speedy British withdrawal from India. The most plausible explanation of Watson's decision is this. It seems that no matter whom he chose, Shivabhai or Chaturbhai, Watson might be accused of returning to the old policy of arbitrarily selecting a new ruler and excluding the proper heir. Indeed, the question had been further complicated when another member of the family, Vithaldas, presented a claim to be next in line after Gopaldas and his sons, and he was soon followed in this by Shivabhai's brother Chhotabhai and yet another member of the house, Shantilal. If, however, at least one of the claimants had died by the time all of Gopaldas's sons were ruled ineligible to succeed, a seemingly impartial choice would be easier (as the three other claimants would be reduced to two, or even one). Watson may therefore have decided to leave the chiefship vacant in the hope that time would make it easier to decide which claimant should succeed; he hinted at this when he commented that "If the above view is accepted, it will not be necessary to give any further hearing" to Chaturbhai.[8]

A desire to postpone a ruling on the various claims to the throne certainly motivated British policy over the next twenty years (although it is unclear whether it originated from the knowledge that a choice would be difficult, or merely from lethargy.) If they had

[8] Watson to Thompson, 18 Oct. 1924, NAI FPD, 165-P/1924-25.

really intended to ascertain the loyalty of each of Gopaldas's sons as he reached adulthood, Watson and the Political Department would have chosen an age of majority for each of the boys, perhaps at the usual age of between eighteen and nineteen, and the Agency would have decided whether each son would be allowed to succeed as soon as he reached that age, on the basis of either his history or an interview. But none of this was done. In 1930-1931 the two eldest sons, Suryakant and Mahendra, were jailed for participating in Gandhi's Civil Disobedience Campaign–unlike the rival claimant Shivabhai, who for twenty years bombarded the Agency with obsequious reports of his own loyalty to British rule. But not until the 1930s did the Agency even ascertain the sons' birthdates, a prerequisite to deciding when they were adults. And no age of majority was set, which meant that the Agency could arbitrarily decide when it was time to rule on the sons' fitness. Suryakant and Mahendra were therefore twenty-five and twenty-one years old when in 1936 their inevitable exclusion from the succession came, and that was only after a police report had made further delay impossible by branding them "sworn enemies of the Government."[9] In 1939, when the next son, Bhupendra, was twenty, the Resident declared that twenty-one would henceforth be considered the age of majority in Rai Sankli. This was in keeping with Delhi's new policy towards minorities, but it also allowed further postponement of a decision. In any case, seven months after Bhupendra's twenty-first birthday, the Political Agent and the Resident agreed that for the present they would not rule on his fitness to govern, allegedly in order to avoid trouble (probably in connection with Gandhi's Individual Satyagraha); but it seems that they were merely avoiding action. By 1943, however, the danger had apparently passed, and Bhupendra and his twenty-year-old brother Yogendra, both open supporters of Congress, were disqualified from succeeding. With the four sons all excluded from the throne, the Paramount Power had to find a chief from among the other members of the ruling family, and the Resident, Gaisford, told the Political Agent, Battye, to make the choice. As Chaturbhai, Shivabhai and Vithaldas, the three claimants of 1924, were all still alive, the task was no easier

---

[9] Police report on Gopaldas's family, 1935, IOC R/2/600/41.

than it had been nineteen years earlier. But Gaisford found a solution: he added Gopaldas's fifth and youngest son Balendra to the list of candidates for the succession. Balendra had not previously been considered because he had been born in 1930. Treating a son born so long after his father's deposition as eligible to succeed violated both precedent and the policy declared by Watson and Delhi in 1924, but Gaisford concocted an absurd analogy involving the accession of a boy who had been adopted by a Rani after her husband's death. Battye of course made the correct choice: as Balendra's loyalty could not be determined until he had reached his majority, the succession would have to remain in abeyance until 1951. The Agency must have known that by then it would no longer be responsible for Rai Sankli, and that it would be up to other authorities to decide who was chief. And when India became independent, Nehru swiftly resolved the conflicting claims by dismissing all of them and reinstating Gopaldas.

II

In the early 1930s, the Kathi taluka of Bagasra had an area of ninety square miles and a population of twenty thousand. It was divided among six chiefs, whose names are printed in italics in Table Four; three of them had agreed that future succession to their shares would be by primogeniture (P).[10] In 1932, Ram Harsur (Ram son of Harsur) of the senior branch died without a son. This occasioned a dispute among his five kinsmen. Several of them demanded that the Agency apply primogeniture to the late chief's estate, but they disagreed whether Ram Mulu or Vajsur was the heir; the former was head of the next branch in seniority and would inherit under Anglo-Indian law, but the latter was heir according to classical Hindu law as the last great-grandson of the common ancestor of the Bagasra chiefs. Others wanted a partition, either *per capita* or *per*

---

[10] For Bagasra, see *The Ruling Princes, Chiefs and Leading Personages*, pp. 293-305. The figures for area and population do not include the small shares held by Godad Matra and Samat Matra. This account of the Bagasra succession dispute is based on IOC L/P&S/13/929, R/2/635/286 and R/2/639/317.

stirpes; the first would divide the territory equally among the surviving chiefs, while the second would give half to Godad's four descendants and half to his brother Vajsur's single descendant Vajsur Valera. Tate, the Political Agent, ruled out both Hindu law and per capita partition, as neither had ever governed inheritance among the Kathis. Many Kathi chiefs had instituted primogeniture under Anglo-Indian law, including three of the claimants, but Ram Harsur had not, and the lands of sonless members of the Bagasra family had always been partitioned per stirpes. Tate noted that "all such cases [of succession] have been decided, I believe, mainly on considerations of political policy."[11] He saw no considerations of this nature requiring the unity of the taluka, and recommended that the Agency approve a per stirpes partition. For thirty-five years, however, the Paramount Power had been trying to persuade the Kathi rulers to introduce primogeniture. It was true that this had hitherto meant having living Kathi rulers decree that on their deaths their lands would pass intact to the nearest heir by primogeniture, but it would set a bad example if the British now failed to implement primogeniture in an estate that was at their disposal. An identical case had recently arisen in Bilkha, the only one of the five major Kathi states whose ruling family had not previously instituted primogeniture. Its chief died without a legitimate son in 1923, and the government of Bombay ordered the partition of the state among the heirs. Rawat, the chief's nearest heir by primogeniture, had protested against this order, asking for the application of primogeniture which would make him sole heir to the state. C.C. Watson, who assumed office as first Agent to the Governor-General for the States of Western India in 1924, supported Rawat's claim, noting that "if Government fail to apply primogeniture it will act as a discouragement to those more enlightened Kathi rulers who see in the adoption of the policy the salvation of their estates in the future."[12] Watson eventually won the Political Department around to his views, and in 1927 the Secretary of State overturned the

---

[11] J.C. Tate (PA, Western Kathiawar) to G.B. Williams (Secretary to AGG), 27 Mar. 1933, IOC R/2/635/286.

[12] Watson to PD India, 19/22 Apr. 1926, IOC R/1/1/1494(1). For the Bilkha case, see IOC L/P&S/10/1119, R/1/1/1494(1), R/2/622/95 and R/2/622/96; NAI FPD 47(1)-P/1924.

earlier decision and ordered the succession of Rawat as chief of the entire state. Latimer, now the Agent to the Governor-General, used the same arguments to convince Tate that Ram Mulu should inherit the whole estate.[13] The Political Department agreed, and Ram Harsur's villages were merged into Ram Mulu's territory to show the Kathis that the Paramount Power was sincere in its desire to extend primogeniture to all of their estates in order to prevent the creation of new petty states.

III

In 1925, Ranjitsinhji, the bachelor Maharaja Jam Saheb of Nawanagar, informed the Agency that on his death he wished the succession to pass to his nephew Digvijaysinhji, an officer of the Indian Army and the second son of Ranjitsinhji's younger brother Juvansinhji.[14] But he wished neither to adopt his nephew nor to inform his family that Digvijaysinhji was his chosen heir: "Official adoption involves a lot of family trouble, jealousies and dangers; and I therefore think it prudent and more advisable to state to you my wishes leaving it to the good-will of the Government of India to fulfil them."[15] Ranjitsinhji died eight years later, in 1933, without having adopted Digvijaysinhji. It often took months for the Agency and the Political Department to find the heir to a ruler who died without a real or adopted son. But Latimer, the Agent to the Governor-General, happened to be in Nawanagar when the Jam Saheb died. He informed the Nawanagar royal family of Ranjitsinhji's wishes regarding the succession. At this point, L.F. Rushbrook

---

[13] Tate wrote of his change of opinion that "Having now had the advantage of reading the files ..., I admit that my views as P[olitical]. A[gent]. cannot be supported. I therefore unhesitatingly agree with Mr. Latimer's views." Note by Tate (now AGG), 18 June 1933, IOC R/2/635/286.

[14] For Nawanagar, see *The Ruling Princes, Chiefs and Leading Personages*, pp. 33-43. This account of the Nawanagar succession case is based on IOC L/P&S/13/1484, R/1/1/1634, R/1/1/2392(1), R/1/1/3020 and R/2/635/286A.

[15] Extract from Nawanagar to Watson, 28 Apr. 1925, in C. Latimer (AGG) to PD India, 5 Mar. (i.e. Apr.) 1933, IOC R/1/1/2392(1). Stern, *op. cit.*, pp. 226-227, notes that for similar reasons, Maharaja Sawai Madho Singh of Jaipur, who died in 1922, refused for some time to divulge the name of his adopted son.

Williams, Ranjitsinhji's British Foreign Minister, told Latimer that it was the invariable custom in Nawanagar to acclaim a new ruler immediately after his predecessor's funeral. The funeral was to be held the same afternoon; Latimer telegraphed Delhi, explained that Ranjitsinhji had wished Digvijaysinhji to succeed and that Rushbrook Williams had informed him that immediate recognition was necessary, and obtained the Political Department's approval for announcing Digvijaysinhji's accession at the funeral. But as the India Office later noted, Rushbrook Williams was "a somewhat unreliable source of information."[16] It was simply not true that custom required that the accession of a new Jam Saheb take place immediately on the death of an old one–Ranjitsinhji himself had not been recognised as ruler until over seven months after his predecessor had died. Why, then, did Rushbrook Williams force through recognition of Digvijaysinhji's accession? It seems that he acted at the suggestion of the late Jam Saheb's relatives, who agreed that Digvijaysinhji was the best man to rule Nawanagar. Unlike Latimer, however, the family knew that a mere desire on the part of Ranjitsinhji to be succeeded by his nephew did not make the latter the rightful ruler. For in default of a formal adoption, Digvijaysinhji was merely one of several of the late prince's kinsmen; if the Paramount Power followed its recent policy of finding heirs by primogeniture, at least two other men had a stronger claim to the throne. But by securing official recognition for Digvijaysinhji, Rushbrook Williams had made it difficult for the Agency to replace the new Jam Saheb with a less qualified but nearer relative. Table Five shows Ranjitsinhji's possible heirs (H); names of Jam Sahebs are printed in italics.

The question of the Nawanagar succession led to disagreement between the Political Department in Delhi and the India Office in London, neither of which showed any understanding of British policy in succession disputes. Sir Charles Watson, the head of the Political Department, explained his recognition of Digvijaysinhji by saying that Ranjitsinhji had "secretly" or "informally" adopted his nephew, without realising that he could easily have defended his actions on the grounds that the Paramount Power had the right to

[16] Note by P.J. Patrick (IO), 10 (?) May 1933, IOC L/P&S/13/1484.

choose whomever it wished to fill a vacant throne, and that it was free to take into account a sonless ruler's own wishes regarding the succession if it so desired. On the other hand, Sir Reginald Glancy, a senior India Office administrator, insisted that the Paramount Power was legally bound to install the late prince's next-of-kin as determined by primogeniture. He believed that this next-of-kin was Ranjitsinhji's younger brother Juvansinhji; the succession ought therefore to pass to the latter, and thence to Juvansinhji's eldest son Pratapsinhji. In other words, under the laws of primogeniture, Digvijaysinhji was third in line for the throne, rather than first, and if Pratapsinhji fathered a son, Digvijaysinhji's place in the order of succession would become even more distant. Here, Glancy showed that he was unaware that absolute reliance on primogeniture was a recent innovation with no force of law. At the same time, he demonstrated ignorance of Hindu custom, under which Juvansinhji was not considered to be Ranjitsinhji's brother at all. In 1877, the Paramount Power had allowed Jam Saheb Vibhaji to exclude his son own Kalubha from the succession, and confirmed his selection of his young kinsman Ranjitsinhji as his heir. (Ranjitsinhji was never formally adopted; but unlike Digvijaysinhji, he was officially confirmed as heir-apparent by the Paramount Power, which effectively amounted to an adoption.) One of Vibhaji's wives later bore Jaswantsinhji, who as a real son replaced Ranjitsinhji in the succession; but when Jaswantsinhji died in 1906, his virtual brother Ranjitsinhji was recognised as Jam Saheb. In other words, Ranjitsinhji had inherited the throne by adoption. Juvansinhji, of course, had not been included in the adoption, which had transformed Ranjitsinhji from his brother to a distant cousin. If Glancy had wanted to find Ranjitsinhji's nearest relation, he ought to have looked to Lakhubha, son of the disinherited Kalubha and in effect the late Jam Saheb's nephew. Lakhubha, who lived in Paris, did lay claim to the Nawanagar succession in 1933, but he had been ruled ineligible for the throne on account of his father's misdeeds in both 1877 and 1907, and his claim was speedily dismissed.

But to Glancy, the main concern was not whether Lakhubha or Juvansinhji should be the new Jam Saheb. His real fear was that by confirming Digvijaysinhji's succession, the Paramount Power would sanction the late Jam Saheb's desire to pass over his closest relatives and nominate his own successor. This would not be a serious problem in Nawanagar, but other rulers might cite the case as a precedent in demanding that they be allowed to pass over even their own eldest sons, overturning the laws of primogeniture which normally governed undisputed successions.[17] Nevertheless, in the end the India Office contented itself with making token protests, and let Delhi's recognition of Digvijaysinhji stand. There were probably several reasons for this. Ranjitsinhji had had solid grounds for selecting his nephew as his heir. All agreed that Digvijaysinhji was better suited to rule than his elderly father Juvansinhji or his brother Pratapsinhji, whose "character was not sufficiently robust for the position."[18] Moreover, the people of Nawanagar did not care about intricate problems of inheritance; they wanted a ruler, and were glad when Digvijaysinhji was quickly recognised. And if the throne remained vacant while various claims were studied, Nawanagar would have to be placed under Agency management. This would provoke criticism from the princes: not only was Nawanagar a wealthy state, but Ranjitsinhji had led princely opposition to British plans for federation, and a long period of management might be interpreted as a means of ensuring that no successor could do likewise. But the India Office almost certainly dropped its opposition to Digvijaysinhji's accession mainly because Latimer and his superiors in Delhi had publicly recognised Digvijaysinhji as Jam Saheb, thanks to Rushbrook Williams's intervention. It would have been impossible to replace Digvijaysinhji without humiliating the Agent to the Governor-General and the Political Department, thereby undermining their authority and the Paramount Power's image as an omniscient overlord. The Nawanagar family and Rushbrook Williams had known this, and had used their knowledge to guarantee that Ranjitsinhji's wishes were followed.

---

[17] It has already been noted that in 1926, the Begum of Bhopal was allowed to overturn the custom of primogeniture when she secured British acceptance of the succession of Hamidullah Khan; see Chapter Seven.

[18] Latimer to C.L. Corfield (PD India), 11 Mar. 1937, IOC R/1/1/3020.

PART FOUR: A MATTER OF HONOUR

CHAPTER ELEVEN

THE HONOURS SYSTEM IN PRINCELY INDIA

The honours system has played a major part in the history of both Britain and the British Empire, with kings, prime ministers, and proconsuls seeking to cement their position by bestowing titles and other distinctions on potential allies. Princely India was no exception, as the Paramount Power sought to influence the rulers of the Indian states with an elaborate system of honours. Titles, salutes and other distinctions were liberally conferred or withheld in an attempt to induce rulers to act at the behest of their overlords.[1] This was why when, in 1893, the Political Department revised the handbook used by its officers, a new chapter on titles and ceremonial was added, in view of "the great importance of these matters in Indian Political business."[2] At the same time, the honours system was not a one-way street. The rulers often had good reasons for seeking honours, and both parties tried to use the system to their own advantage–the rulers as way of asserting their sovereignty as manifested by izzat, and the Paramount Power as a tool in maintaining control and, in many cases, keeping the politicians from power.

I

The British use of honours in dealings with Indian rulers followed the practice of the Mughal emperors, who encouraged effort and

---

[1] See John Walker, *The Queen Has Been Pleased: The British Honours System at Work* (London, 1986); John Benyon, "Overlords of Empire? British 'Proconsular Imperialism' in Comparative Perspective," in *The Journal of Imperial and Commonwealth History*, 19, 2 (May 1991), pp. 164-202, at pp. 185-187. For honours in princely India, see Stern, *op. cit.*, pp. 121-123, 129, 165-166 and 194, and Dirks, *op. cit.*, pp. 386-389.

[2] Tupper, *op. cit.*, 1:v.

rewarded conspicuous loyalty among their feudatories with titles, clothes, emblems, and so forth.[3] For example, a favoured Raja ("king") might be promoted to Maharaja ("great king"); or, in what later became the Western India States Agency, the emperor Akbar conferred the title of Dewan on the Muslim king of what was then known as Jalor and later became Palanpur. Under Lord Hastings (1813-1823), the East India Company assumed the emperor's right of conferring titles on Indians, in a natural extension of the process by which it was assuming the traditional functions of an Indian sovereign. Most of the early Indian recipients of such honours at the hands of the Company were landowners and philanthropists, but from the 1840s rulers who had performed valuable services for their overlords (usually in wartime) were also rewarded.[4] One of the many ways in which the Paramount Power sought to secure princely support after the revolt of 1857 was to create a host of new honours, which were added to the stock of older ones that the British had inherited from the Mughals.[5] By the 1870s, the rulers of the states of Western India were players in an honours system that included not only the surviving Mughal honours (for example, regnal titles), but also precedence, judicial powers, salutes, orders of chivalry, and honorary military ranks, and rulers were more or less overtly encouraged to compete for honours by outdoing one another in

---

[3] For honours in the Mughal Empire, see Bayly, *op. cit.*, pp. 13-14, 107; P.S. Bedi, *The Mughal Nobility Under Akbar* (Jalandhar, 1985), pp. 102-105; Kolff, *op. cit.*, pp. 19, 30, 135-136. For the history of titles in India, see S.A.I. Tirmizi, "Introduction," in *Index to Titles (1798-1885) As Recorded in the Alqabnamas or Books of Titles and Forms of Address* (n.p. [New Delhi], n.d. [*ca* 1979]), pp. i-xxi. The honours conferred in the Mughal successor state of Hyderabad are enumerated in Hyderabad Government, Central Records Office, *The Chronology of Modern Hyderabad 1720-1890* (Hyderabad, 1954), pp. vi-viii.

[4] For Indian titles under the British, see Tupper, *op. cit.*, 3:205-233. The Company's assumption of Mughal prerogatives is noted in Bayly, *op. cit.*, p. 82.

[5] See Metcalf, *op. cit.*, pp. 223-224. In a well-known essay, Cohn presents the subsequent British use of honours in India (particularly at the Imperial Assemblage of 1877) as an example of Eric Hobsbawm's "invented traditions." Bernard S. Cohn, "Representing Authority in Victorian India," in Eric Hobsbawm and Terence Ranger, editors, *The Invention of Tradition* (Cambridge, 1983), pp. 165-209. This interpretation is highly questionable, for reasons explored in John Edmond McLeod, *The Western India States Agency 1916-1947* (PhD thesis, University of Toronto, 1993), pp. 306-310.

winning the notice of the Paramount Power: in 1930, the Political Agent for Eastern Kathiawar reported of the chief of the tiny state of Vithalgadh that "He is making a tremendous effort just now to bring himself to notice (offering to do pro-Gov[ernmen]t. propaganda etc., in the perennial hope I suppose of getting his [judicial] powers enhanced."[6]

The honours bestowed by the British as Paramount Power formed an elaborate network of distinctions. Precedence was central to this network, since (as will be seen) it often determined which other honours a ruler might receive. In a system reminiscent of the Mughal hierarchy of nobles, official Tables of Precedence ranked each ruler according to the history of his family and the importance of his state. Thus, the Nawab of the large state of Junagadh came first among the rulers of Saurashtra, while his cousin the Talukdar of Sardargadh was forty-fourth. Precedence decided how a ruler would be presented to the Viceroy or where he would sit at public ceremonies, but its real significance was that it showed exactly how important the Paramount Power considered him to be in relation to his neighbours.[7] Closely related to precedence were judicial powers. These were not normally regarded as honours, but, at least in Western India, the way in which they functioned and were perceived makes it reasonable to include them in this discussion; in 1930, the chief of Thana Devli requested enhanced powers, but made it clear that he wanted them "only for the sake of prestige and position which we chiefs value most."[8] This is because after the classification of powers in the states of Western India in the mid-nineteenth century, a ruler's judicial powers determined his precedence, First Class princes ranking at the top and unclassified petty chiefs at the bottom.[9] Precedence and powers also influenced a ruler's artillery salute, a European tradition that was transferred to

---

[6] A.J. Hopkinson (PA, Eastern Kathiawar), "Handing-over notes. Eastern Kathiawar Agency," 26 Sept. 1930, IOC MSS Eur D 998/5 (Hopkinson Collection). See Tupper, *op. cit.*, 3:237, on the use of honours as rewards and punishments.

[7] See Tupper, *op. cit.*, 3:235-236 and 239-241. The Tables of Precedence are in IOC R/2/649/444.

[8] Thana Devli to J.C. Tate (PA, Western Kathiawar), 28 Apr. 1930, IOC R/2/629/193.

[9] See Chapter Six.

India. In Britain, guns are fired on the arrival of royalty and major officials, the number of shots increasing with the rank of the person being greeted. In 1867, after several false starts, artillery salutes were extended to the rulers of the Indian states. The major princes were assigned salutes of between nine and twenty-one guns (the number was always odd), according to the size of their states and the history of their dynasties, while the mass of lesser chiefs received none. The criteria governing the allocation of salutes were vague and in any case not consistently applied, and the liberality of local political officers in dispensing salutes varied from region to region.[10] Nevertheless, rulers often valued salutes more than any other honour, for several reasons. They were impressive in a way that Tables of Precedence or judicial powers could never be, and on public occasions showed to all the ranking of different rulers (at least in the eyes of the British).[11] In this, they are comparable to the highest honour bestowed by the Mughals, the *Mahi Maratib* or Insignia of the Fish, which was also displayed at state ceremonies.[12] Salutes were also prized because from 1889 to 1947, only princes whose salutes were eleven guns or more were styled His Highness, and because in Western India from 1924 to 1943, salute determined whether a state was supervised by the Agent to the Governor-General (later Resident) himself, or by a subordinate Political Agent. The establishment of the Chamber of Princes in 1921 enhanced the value of both salutes and judicial powers, as full membership in the Chamber was confined to rulers with salutes of at least eleven guns, or unrestricted powers.[13]

---

[10] For the history of artillery salutes in India, see Tupper, *op. cit.*, 3:233-239; for their allocation, see Letter of the Government of India, 6 Feb. 1917, IOC R/2/598/25.

[11] Nihal Singh, *op. cit.*, pp. 164-165.

[12] The Mahi Maratib is described in Hyderabad Government, *Chronology*, p. 10. For the general context of honours in Muslim India, see J. Burton-Page, "Marātib," in *The Encyclopaedia of Islām* (2nd edition, Leiden 1960-), 6:536-537.

[13] For the title of Highness, see Tupper, *op. cit.*, 3:224; for political relations (the nature of British supervision), see Chapter Four; for membership in the Chamber, see *Handbook of the Chamber of Princes*, p. 1. Three weeks before independence, nine-gun princes were also made Highnesses; see NAI WISA, C-30-5/1947.

If they had remained fixed, titles, precedence, powers, and salutes would have merely showed how the Paramount Power ranked rulers. But each of these distinctions could be augmented or decreased at the will of the British, and this transformed them into honours for which princes could compete. In fact, the competition was enhanced by the fact that each honour except precedence could be either a personal distinction (it would lapse on the death of the recipient) or an hereditary one. Moreover, regnal titles could be personal (prefixed to the ruler's name, as *Maharaja* Shri Lukhdhir-ji) or dynastic (placed before the name of the state, as *Maharaja* of Morvi); and salutes could be general (fired everywhere), or local (enjoyed within prince's own state).[14] Such subdivisions multiplied the number of rewards that the British could bestow on rulers, which was increased still further by two other honours that were always personal, and did not in any way affect the rulers' precedence. These were membership in an Order of Chivalry and honorary military rank, which both resemble the Mughal system of *mansabs* (military commands). An Indian was first knighted in 1842, but no prince was so honoured until 1861, when the Viceroy Lord Canning established the Order of the Star of India for rulers, notables from British India, and important British officials in India. In 1878, a second Indian Order was established, the Order of the Indian Empire, and the supply of knighthoods was further enlarged with the creation of the Royal Victorian Order and the Order of the British Empire (both of which were for all inhabitants of the British Empire, and not merely those connected with India). There was also the Order of the Crown of India for women, which was occasionally bestowed on the wives and mothers of rulers.[15] The final

[14] In a sense, local salutes were pointless, since within his own state a prince could fire whatever salute for himself he wished. This meant that a local salute would only ever be used if there happened to be a British military station within the state, and the ruler visited it. Minute by F.F. Pearson (PD India), 23 Jan. 1924, NAI PSV, Honours Branch, 133-H/1945.

[15] See Michael Maclagan, *'Clemency' Canning: Charles John, 1st Earl Canning, Governor-General and Viceroy of India 1856-1862* (London, 1962), pp. 282-287; Ray, *Princely States and the Paramount Power*, pp. 45-47; Arthur Jocelyn, *Awards of Honour: The orders, decorations, medals and awards of honour of Great Britain & the Commonwealth from Edward III to Elizabeth II* (London, 1956), pp. 35, 38, 39, 40-41.

distinction for princes, the honorary rank of officer in the army, was first conferred in 1877. It usually recognised some sort of military contribution to the Paramount Power, and it came to be accepted that a ruler's rank should bear some resemblance to the size of his state forces. During the Second World War, a few princes (though none in Western India) were made honorary officers of the Royal Air Force, although a proposal at the same time to grant honorary Commissions in the Royal Indian Navy was turned down, as granting them would "raise a fresh cause for jealousy and comparisons among Rulers"[16] (the Paramount Power wanted healthy competition for honours, but not angry resentment over their conferral).[17] For many years, the Paramount Power was much less willing to grant non-honorary commissions that would make members of ruling families into professional officers. This later changed, and Digvijaysinhji, who succeeded as ruler of Nawanagar in 1933, served eleven years in the Indian Army and retired as a Captain.[18] Although never hereditary, chivalric and military distinctions were also subdivided. Each Order comprised two classes of knights (Knight Grand Commander or Grand Cross, and mere Knight Commander), and one or more lower categories (for example, Companion) which did not carry the title of Sir. As the Orders were also ranked in relation to each other, this created an elaborate hierarchy: a Knight Grand Commander of the Order of the Star of India (GCSI) outranked a Knight Grand Commander of the Order of the Indian Empire (GCIE); he in turn came before a

---

[16] Minute by illegible, perhaps L.C.L. Griffin (Secretary to Crown Representative), 11 Feb. 1944, IOC R/1/4/391. One Maharashtrian chief with naval experience did hold an honorary commission in the R.I.N.

[17] For honorary military rank see Tupper, *op. cit.*, 3:141-143. For the rules that governed the conferment of honorary Commissions, see IOC L/P&S/15/116 and R/1/4/386; NAI PSV, 176-H/1943 and PSV, Honours Branch, 133-H/1945 and 127-H/1946. No one ever thought to decide which army the ranks were in. Shortly before the lapse of British paramountcy in 1947, the Maharaja of Jammu and Kashmir enquired whether his commission as a Lieutenant-General was in the British or the Indian Army (if it were in the latter, he wished to resign it). The Political Department, General Headquarters, and the India Office were unable to answer this query. See NAI PSV, Honours Branch, 127-H/1946.

[18] See Chandar S. Sundaram, "Preventing 'Idleness:' The Maharaja of Cooch Behar's proposal for officer commissions in the British Army for the sons of Indian Princes and Gentlemen, 1897-1898," in *South Asia*, 18, 1 (June 1995), pp. 115-130

Knight Commander of the Order of the Star of India (KCSI), who was the superior of a Knight Commander of the Order of the Indian Empire (KCIE); a lowly Companion of the Order of the Star of India (CSI) nevertheless was higher in precedence than a Companion of the Order of the Indian Empire (CIE). This is why, for example, in 1948 one prince protested to the government of independent India that in the last set of honours bestowed on the rulers of the Indian states (announced on 1 January 1948), he had received only a KCIE, while his four predecessors had all held a KCSI as their initial honour.[19] And honorary Commissions could give the recipient any of the ten officers' ranks in the Army: in descending order, General, Lieutenant-General, Major-General, Brigadier-General (later Brigadier), Colonel, Lieutenant-Colonel, Major, Captain, Lieutenant and Second Lieutenant.

II

Some rulers never showed much interest in the Paramount Power's honours system. In fact, when the British introduced their chivalric honours to princely India, they often met with hostility. This was partly because knighthoods brought the recipients nothing more concrete than silver and silver gilt insignia, which paled in comparison to the jewelled ornaments of gold and the hereditary estates with which Indian rulers had traditionally expressed esteem. The first prince in Saurashtra to receive a knighthood was Ranmallsinhji II of Dhrangadhara, in 1869. He was most reluctant to accept the distinction, and only acquiesced after much urging by his courtiers who pointed out that refusal would grossly insult the Paramount Power and Queen Victoria. But he first made a resolution to undertake a pilgrimage to Benares and to undergo cleansing, and he also purified the new insignia of knighthood with milk and Ganges

[19] See NAI WISA, Confidential Branch C-38-1/1948. This prince requested, and eventually received, the honorary rank of Major as compensation; NAI WISA, Confidential Branch C-35-3/1948.

water.[20] But such views were rarely expressed. In any case, the honours system could not have existed if many rulers had not found distinctions to be desirable. And clearly they did. At a banquet given by the Thakor Saheb of Sayla in 1927 to celebrate the enhanced judicial powers that he had just received, the Agent to the Governor-General observed that:

> The poet has said "Man never is but always to be blessed" and another even more pessimistic has adjured us to call no man happy until he is dead. I hesitate therefore to describe our genial host this evening as the perfectly happy man. He will however perhaps allow me to congratulate him on having climbed a step or two on the ladder of his ambitions and on having obtained at least some of his cherished desires.[21]

It is obvious that enhanced judicial powers increased a ruler's authority over his subjects at the expense of the local Agency, and a higher salute might entitle him to full membership in the Chamber of Princes and thus place him among the leaders of princely India. Honours might also bring financial benefits. In 1940 the local Political Agent visited the petty state of Virpur, whose ruler was strongly lobbying for enhanced jurisdictional powers.

> I am afraid I didnt [*sic*] take it very seriously. When I said "why should you be so anxious to be able to give 7 years imprisonment, instead of, as at present, 3 years," it appeared to boil down to this,

---

[20] H.H. of Dhrangadhara. In 1871, the Maharaja of Indore informed the former Secretary of State Lord Derby that he saw no value in "mere title and empty orders without a corresponding grant of land." L.A. Knight, "The Royal Titles Act and India," in *The Historical Journal*, 11, 3 (1968), pp. 488-507, at p. 507. One Maharana of Udaipur felt that the great GCIE was an award for lowly bureaucrats rather than princes. Charles Allen and Sharada Dwivedi, *Lives of the Indian Princes* (London, 1984), pp. 96-97. And see Scindia, *op. cit.*, p. 118, for the Maharaja of Baroda's refusal to wear the insignia of the GCSI that he had received.

[21] C.C. Watson (AGG), speech at Sayla, 1927, IOC Photo Eur 84 (Watson Collection).

> that the enhanced status improves the value of your daughters in the marriage market, and thus helps you to economise over dowries.[22]

To many observers, however, the distinctions seem to have been worthless, and some scholars have therefore called the whole honours system a British trick: the elaborate gradations of powers and salutes meant nothing to the rational Paramount Power, but as they appealed to the princes' Oriental vanity they could be used to induce rulers to pursue particular policies at no cost to the British.[23] But this view is quite wrong, except that it recognises that honours were intended to influence princes as rewards and punishments. In the first place, the British did and still do value titles and other distinctions, which are sufficiently prized in Britain to this day that the government can use them to gain supporters. And if anything, the Britons serving in India were much more sensitive to matters of protocol and honours than were their compatriots at home.[24] In the nineteenth century, Indian rulers sometimes found that they could win over the British Residents at their courts by conferring titles on them. And in 1934, the forthcoming visit to Jamnagar (the capital of Nawanagar) of a British Field Marshal threw the entire staff of the Western India States Agency into turmoil, because no one knew whether the Field Marshal or the Agent to the Governor-General

---

[22] Hopkinson, private letter, 28 Jan. 1940, IOC MSS Eur D 998/14 (Hopkinson Collection). Also, the lower a chief's jurisdiction, the greater the percentage of his revenues that he had to contribute to the Agency's thana funds which paid for police and judicial services.

[23] See P.J. Rich, "Indo-British Influence on the Arabian Gulf," in *Indo-British Review*, 18, 1 (1990), pp. 143-153, especially pp. 145, 147, and the work that seems to have played a major role in moulding modern India's image of the princes, Dass, *op. cit.*, especially pp. 101, 175-178, 224-225, 266-277. The inaccuracy of this interpretation is noted by Stern, *op. cit.*, pp. 121-122.

[24] For the attitude of the nineteenth-century British aristocracy, see David Cannadine, *The Decline and Fall of the British Aristocracy* (New Haven and London, 1990), p. 13, and Michael W. McCahill, "Peerage creations and the changing character of the British nobility, 1750-1830," in *English Historical Review*, 96, 379 (Apr. 1981), pp. 259-284, at pp. 266-268. For modern Britain, see Walker, *op. cit.*; and for the British in India, see Allen, *Plain Tales from the Raj*, pp. 90-99.

enjoyed higher precedence.[25] A Resident who nominated a prince for a knighthood was not merely playing on the prince's vanity in order to secure a collaborator, since he himself looked forward to receiving one in the same Order of Chivalry. In Western India in the mid-1940s, for example, Englishmen and Indians alike used the full titles of both *Lieutenant-Colonel His Highness Maharaja Jam Shri Sir Digvijaysinhji Ranjitsinhji Jadeja, GCSI, GCIE, ADC, Maharaja Jam Saheb of Nawanagar*, and *the Honourable Lieutenant-Colonel Sir Cyril Percy Hancock, KCIE, OBE, MC, Resident at Baroda and for the States of Western India and Gujarat*, on all official correspondence. The British recognised the political uses to which honours could be put; but they always considered them to have an intrinsic value, and believed that receiving one really was an "honour." Perhaps paradoxically, the Paramount Power saw honours as both a cheap means of controlling princes *and* something more than empty vanities.

It is easy to write off the fondness that many princes had for honours as snobbishness, but this misses the point. Among other things, as a social élite, they had no need of marks of distinction to boost their standing. Rather, the most important reason that the princes valued honours was the maintenance of izzat. The translation of this term as "personal honour" shows that in England, as in India, there have always been close links between the abstract concept of honour and the concrete honours system. An honour was a sign of respect from the only people who could really make their opinion matter, the British. (Although they tried to use them to manipulate rulers, the British had a genuine regard for honours, and therefore would not grant them to utterly unworthy individuals.) But more important, in some sense an honour was given not only to the recipient himself, but to his whole family and the state that he ruled; so by receiving a new title, an enhanced salute, or a knighthood, a prince fulfilled his duty of upholding the izzat of his dynasty and realm: all rulers "are equally interested in preserving, untarnished, the honour of their Dynasty–they jealously guard the dignities associated with their Persons and office–they would rather die than

[25] Fisher, *Indirect Rule*, p. 302; H.A.N. Barlow (Under-Secretary to AGG), private letter, 11 Feb. 1934, SAS Barlow Papers, II.26.

part with any of the emblems of authority that they have inherited or acquired...."[26] This attitude was well stated in 1945 by the Maharao of Kutch, when he was (unsuccessfully) lobbying for his salute of seventeen guns to be raised to nineteen guns:

> For the enhancement of the Izzat of my State, I put this consideration first. If the Salute were made one of a permanent 19 guns, I should consider that I gain something for my State, of which I shall always be proud.[27]

This is why, as will be seen, ruling families with long histories of rivalry now occasionally competed in accumulating honours as a means of earning izzat:

> There is a suggestion that H[is]. H[ighness]. of Panna should be made a Captain in the Army, and that H.H. of Alirajpur should get either the same rank or his son that of Lieutenant. There is also another suggestion that if H.H. of Alirajpur receives anything, then H.H. of Baria would expect promotion to Major.
>
> Now H.H. of Baria is junior in the Army to H.H. the Nawab of Palanpur. If the former is promoted to Major, then the latter should certainly receive promotion, and I think he would be hurt if he wasn't promoted.[28]

III

The official citations that accompanied honours usually said that a prince or chief was being recognised because he was a good ruler and loyal to the Paramount Power. But the honours system was more complex than that, and good government alone hardly ever brought distinctions. The reason is simple. Most states were admin-

---

[26] Nihal Singh, *op. cit.*, p. 146.

[27] Kutch to Lord Wavell (Viceroy), 8 Oct. 1945, NAI PSV, Honours Branch, 169-H/1945.

[28] H.D.H.Y. Nepean (Military Adviser, Rajputana State Forces) to C.P. Hancock (Secretary to AGG), 26 Nov. 1928, IOC R/2/619/59. McCahill notes exactly the same phenomenon among the British aristocracy of the late eighteenth and early nineteenth centuries, as would-be peers fiercely competed with one another in acquiring titles; McCahill, *op. cit.*, pp. 260-261, 272-273, 276-279.

istered as well as their resources permitted. If this had consistently earned honours, there would have been few rulers in all India who did not possess a host of distinctions. Naturally a truly bad ruler was unlikely to receive an honour, but good administration was a mere prerequisite to the conferment of a distinction and in itself was not sufficient to earn one. Similarly, it has already been seen that necessity compelled most rulers to be at least passively loyal to the British,[29] yet they did not thereby automatically win distinctions. Good administration and loyalty *did*, however, provide convenient explanations of why a given ruler had been singled out for recognition, and such explanations were necessary because honours were apparently often conferred for reasons that neither princes nor Paramount Power wished to publicise–as part of Delhi's efforts to court the princes at times when British control was particularly threatened. But as the British would not want to be seen bribing princes, and recipients of honours would not want to be accused by other rulers of accepting bribes, the cover of good administration and disinterested loyalty was favoured by both parties. On certain occasions, the Paramount Power was particularly lavish with honours. A prime example occurred at the end of the First World War: in 1918 and again in 1921, at the recommendation of local political officers and governments, rulers whose contributions had been particularly noteworthy were rewarded for their participation in the Allied war effort with new titles, enhanced salutes, and chivalric distinctions.[30] In general, rulers stood their best chance of receiving honours when the Paramount Power believed that its authority was especially threatened. It is striking how many distinctions were bestowed across India during the First World War and its aftermath (up to 1921), the Round Table Conferences (1930-1932) and the Civil Disobedience movement (1930-1933) and the crisis over federation (1933 to about 1936).[31]

This does not mean that honours were only given to secure support during crises. Occasionally honours really were bestowed

---

[29] See Chapter One.

[30] For the honours conferred in connection with the First World War, see IOC R/1/1/623B.

[31] See John McLeod, "The English Honours System in Princely India," in *Journal of the Royal Asiatic Society*, 3rd series, 4, 2 (July 1994), pp. 237-249.

to recognise good government, though usually only after a long reign. And top-ranking princes would receive such honours as knighthoods virtually without effort, as recognition of their status. On the other hand, whatever the British may have thought, in the honours race it was often rulers who were managing the Paramount Power rather than the reverse. An adroit prince knew exactly when he should present requests for the honours that confirmed or enhanced his izzat. He did not have to promise anything, but merely gave the impression that, if his requests were granted, he would support the British in whichever crisis or project they were currently dealing with. He could thus use his understanding of the honours system to win much of what he wanted.[32] Given an understanding of how the system worked, patience, and a bit of luck, however, a ruler could secure almost any honour for which the size and importance of his state rendered him eligible.

This raises the important question of eligibility. If a ruler decided, for whatever reason, to enter the competition for honours, he would first approach the Agent to the Governor-General (later Resident) and explain why he deserved a particular honour. If the Agent found the request to be justified, he would recommend to the Political Department that it be granted; the case would then be considered by the Department, the Viceroy, the Secretary of State, and finally the King. (All honours might also be conferred on British initiative as well. In fact, princes rarely lobbied for knighthoods or for Commissions; the Agent to the Governor-General made the initial recommendations for the former, while candidates for the latter were usually proposed by the British supervisor of the Indian State Forces.) But honours were not dispensed on demand, and the claim could be turned down at any stage of this procedure, and for any reason. Usually, however, the grounds were either that a ruler had done nothing to deserve the honour he sought, or that he was ineligible to receive it. It is in the area of eligibility that the interrelated nature of honours is most apparent. An understanding of the system therefore requires some explanation of the criteria that

---

[32] In much the same way, among British aristocrats in the late eighteenth and early nineteenth centuries, "The influence derived from the dispersal of patronage, even in the form of a peerage, was insufficient to dictate or enforce political obedience" if this was not in the recipient's interests. McCahill, *op. cit.*, p. 281.

governed eligibility. For while it is true that "those whose powers are much circumscribed are more particular in regard to their prestige [as demonstrated by the accumulation of honours] than those whose internal sovereignty is absolute, or practically supreme,"[33] it was also the case that honours often merely reflected the relative importance of the states. Major princes could be certain of accumulating several knighthoods during their reigns, while petty chiefs had no hope of obtaining such distinctions. In this case, honours confirmed the izzat already possessed, rather than enhancing it.

The most important consideration in determining eligibility was precedence.[34] Thus, between 1910 and 1934 the regnal titles of all rulers in the Western India States Agency with salutes of at least eleven guns were revised, and they were promoted to Maharao (the Rao of Kutch in 1918), Maharajas (the rulers of Bhavnagar in 1917, of Nawanagar, Porbandar and Dhrangadhara in 1918, and of Morvi and Gondal in 1926) or Maharana (the Raj Saheb of Wankaner in 1934) (these may be called "maha" titles) if they were Hindus, and Nawab if Muslims (the Dewan of Palanpur in 1910), while nine-gun chiefs remained Thakor Sahebs. Moreover, while eleven-gun princes often received Grand Commanderships and military rank, nine guns brought no more than Knight Commanderships, and even that was rare. The pattern continued in the lower ranks: chiefs with Third and Fourth Class judicial powers were usually styled Thakor (not Thakor Saheb) and were never awarded any chivalric distinction higher than a Companionship, and their inferiors were Talukdars and received no Orders whatsoever.[35] The career of

---

[33] Nihal Singh, *op. cit.*, p. 146.

[34] It has sometimes been asserted that precedence itself was determined by salute. This is backwards: salute, like other honours, was influenced by precedence; Tupper, *op. cit.*, 3:235-236.–The conferral of honours according to precedence is discussed in McLeod, *Western India States Agency*, pp. 294-297.

[35] This reflects the situation that existed in Britain until the rise of the notion of honours as a form of reward: before about 1880, a man's rank (as determined by landed wealth, political power, and inherited title) normally determined the honours that he might receive. W.D. Rubinstein, *Elites and the Wealthy in Modern British History: Essays in Social and Economic History* (Sussex and New York, 1987), pp. 223-230. This view challenges that put forward by McCahill, *op. cit.*, pp. 259-260, 269-276.

Thakor Saheb Bhagwatsinhji of Gondal illustrates the links among the various honours. In 1888, he was rewarded for ruling well by having his powers enhanced from the Second Class to the First, which promoted him from eleventh in precedence in Saurashtra to seventh. At the same time, his salute was increased from nine to eleven guns. Three years later he received the title of Maharaja as a personal distinction (it was made hereditary in 1926), and in 1897 his Knight Commandership was transformed into a Grand Commandership. Only the higher precedence and salute came automatically with the enhanced powers; the Thakor Saheb had to "earn" the other honours. But if he had remained a Second Class Chief, he would almost certainly never have been eligible to become a Maharaja or a Grand Commander, no matter what his other qualifications were.

The Gondal case also shows that in what in 1924 became the Western India States Agency, judicial powers were the most valuable distinction that a ruler could receive, since by raising his precedence they enabled him to compete for other honours. Rulers therefore often began their quest for honours by lobbying for enhanced powers. Outside of princely Gujarat, however, precedence was not affected by other distinctions, and enhanced powers were merely one of the honours for which a ruler became eligible if his precedence were raised. This meant that in other Agencies, powers were a distinction like titles or knighthoods, granted or withdrawn without altering the local Table of Precedence and thus the whole honours system. Most princes did not object to the recognition of good government by the grant of enhanced powers, but they felt that altered jurisdiction did not justify a new place for a ruler in the precedence system. The Paramount Power tried to minimise resentment by confining new hereditary honours to rulers at the top of one Class or the bottom of another, or simultaneously giving the same distinction to all of the men whose states were about equal in importance. For example, the rulers of Morvi and Jafarabad received First Class powers in 1887-1888, when they were the only eleven-gun Second Class Chiefs in Saurashtra, and the Raj Saheb of Wankaner was granted enhanced powers in 1929 when he was the highest-ranking nine-gun prince. Nevertheless, the example of the Thakor Saheb of Gondal could always be held up as an example of the evils of the system, as the grant of First Class powers in 1888 had promoted him over four rulers who had outranked him in the Table of Precedence, and opened his way to honours unavailable to them. The system also raised another problem: the British became increasingly reluctant to grant higher powers to low-ranking chiefs, even if their courts were considered capable of exercising them, because this would upset the Order of Precedence. By the 1920s, many rulers in Western India therefore wanted the abolition of the Class System which based precedence on powers. In 1924, for example, the Rani regent of the Third Class state of Jasdan commented that

> This exact and sustained classificatory correspondence both of guns and powers of internal jurisdiction invests the nomenclature with an impressiveness and indeed a practical finality which is likely to be extremely prejudicial to all the ruling princes of the third and also of the fourth class.[36]

By this time, the British had their own reason for wanting to divorce precedence from powers: if a prince had to win each of his distinctions separately, rather than obtaining several automatically after receiving enhanced powers, the number of separate honours at the disposal of the Paramount Power would be increased, and presumably the opportunities for influencing rulers as well. In 1924, the government of Bombay approved a proposal to abolish the class system, but nothing was done in view of the impending the transfer of Western India to the control of the government of India. But in 1925, following transfer, the Western Indian Table of Precedence was fixed, so that in the future it would not be affected by changes in judicial powers. To make clear the separation of powers and precedence, even the designations of the old Classes of powers and chiefs were abolished. Rulers were henceforth distinguished merely as salute or non-salute rather than according to Class (though the gradation of powers was kept). Three years later the

---

[36] Regent Rani Saheba of Jasdan to H.S. Strong (PA, Western Kathiawar), 31 Aug. 1924, NAI WISA, P-125/1924. Her request for enhanced powers for Jasdan (by far the largest non-salute state of Saurashtra) was rejected, because of the difficulties it would raise in connection with precedence; see IOC R/2/624/123A and NAI WISA, P-125/1924. Third and Fourth Class rulers governed the principal non-salute states (those listed in Table One).

Class system was also abolished in Mahi Kantha, which was administered by Bombay until it became part of the Western India States Agency in 1933.[37] Precedence alone henceforth determined which honours rulers received. This was not apparent for several years, and the grant of unrestricted powers to the Raj Saheb of Wankaner in 1929 was followed by an eleven-gun salute in 1931 and a "maha" title in 1934.[38] But the Paramount Power soon began to confer distinctions separately. Between 1927 and 1935, five of the seven old Third Class chiefs of Saurashtra were given what had been called Second Class powers, but without any change in their precedence or salute.[39] The Thakor of Khirasra was in a similar situation: in 1868, his great-grandfather was demoted from the Fourth Class to Seventh Class as punishment for not maintaining order in his state. In the process, he went from thirtieth to seventy-second in the Table of Precedence. In 1930, after years of lobbying, the chief's ancestral powers were restored, but he did not regain his precedence.[40] Each honour now had to be earned: the remaining nine-gun princes of Western India all received unrestricted powers in 1930, but their salutes and titles were not affected by the change. It will be seen in the next chapter that in 1945, after much exertion, one of them, the Thakor Saheb of Palitana, was made a Maharaja as a personal distinction, whereas in earlier days an hereditary Maharaja-ship would probably have swiftly followed the enhanced powers. Indeed, after the early 1930s, the Paramount Power bestowed few hereditary honours. Seventy years of promotions meant that all salute princes enjoyed full powers, and most non-salute chiefs had the maximum powers with which their rudi-

---

[37] For the abolition of the Class system in the Western India States Agency, see IOC R/1/1/1504(1) and R/2/622/103; and in Mahi Kantha, see J.R. Martin (Political Secretary Bombay) to Commissioner, Northern Division, 10 Nov. 1928, IOC R/2/633/268.

[38] See Chapter Twelve.

[39] The chiefs were those of Lakhtar and Sayla in 1927 (see IOC R/2/622/97 and R/2/622/99), Jasdan and Thana Devli in 1932 (IOC R/2/624/123A, R/2/629/ 192, R/2/629/193 and R/2/632/243, and NAI WISA P-125/1924), and Manavadar in 1935 (IOC R/2/632/250). The enhanced powers were granted to the Thana Devli ruler as a personal distinction, and as an hereditary one to the others.

[40] See IOC R/2/622/102, R/2/626/133 and R/2/639/321, and NAI FPD, 226-R/1930. Some years later, the Thakor was restored to his old place in the Table.

mentary judicial systems could cope. In the previous fifteen years, the number of hereditary Maharajas, Maharaos or Maharanas in Western India had increased from one to nine (until 1917, the Maharaja of Idar had been alone in this category), and none of the remaining Thakor Sahebs was important enough to deserve a higher title. Only two of the top thirteen rulers in the Agency had never received an addition to their original salute, and most princes possessed the highest salute that the importance of their states warranted. This meant that even with the abolition of the linked Class System, it was difficult to justify the grant of new hereditary distinctions.

It was noted above that hereditary honours were usually bestowed in such a way that the recipient's fellow rulers did not feel slighted. Fortunately, before the First World War princes rarely met their brethren from other Agencies, and paid little attention to their powers, titles or salutes. This meant that in conferring such honours, the Paramount Power had merely to take account of the feelings of the rulers in, say, Saurashtra. But the creation of the Chamber of Princes in 1921 brought together rulers from all over India, and in the 1930s the prospect of federation made even closer relations seem imminent. During the 1920s and 1930s, a number of rulers received enhanced titles or salutes in order to bring them up to the level of princes of similar importance elsewhere in India, as frequent contacts among rulers raised the spectre of new grievances over status. This, however, created problems; if an eleven-gun prince in Western India were given an enhanced salute, rulers everywhere might protest that they were entitled to the same promotion. There was also the problem that, under the 1935 constitution, the states' seats in the Federal Assembly were to be based partly on salutes, and changes would upset all of this. The Paramount Power therefore decided to grant no new titles or salutes until the federation had actually come into being. Thus, in 1931 the Raj Saheb of Wankaner became the last Western Indian prince to receive an enhanced permanent salute, once a common honour. Over the next sixteen years, the Nawab of Radhanpur and the Maharaja of Morvi lobbied for thirteen-gun salutes. They were unsuccessful, despite the fact that they were the only Saurashtra princes whose original eleven guns had never been augmented; and the Paramount Power rejected repeated requests for salutes from the non-salute chiefs of Sayla, Jasdan, and Manavadar, even though several of the requests were supported by political officers in Western India.[41] Rulers now received only personal distinctions, usually knighthoods. Even military support was no longer lavishly rewarded. The India Office urged Delhi to mark victory in the Second World War with the same sort of large-scale distribution of honours as had occurred in 1918, and recommended enhanced salutes, new titles, and even the remission of all tribute paid to the Paramount Power by the states. But Political Department and the Viceroy, Lord Wavell, decided against these plans, which would "open a question of such complexity ... excite the numerous jealousies which individual Princes harbour on this subject ...," and "must cause grave dissatisfaction to a large number of Rulers and satisfaction to a much smaller number."[42] The Viceroy was therefore prepared only to give chivalric honours and honorary military ranks.

Nevertheless, the honours system played a part in the rulers' quest for sovereignty, and the Paramount Power's for control, throughout the history of the Western India States Agency. The next chapter examines the role of honours in the lives and reigns of two princes from Saurashtra.

---

[41] See IOC R/2/633/267 and R/2/598/25 (Morvi); IOC R/2/643/366 (Radhanpur); IOC R/2/636/297 (Sayla); IOC R/2/598/24, R/2/629/192, R/2/633/260 and R/2/649/439 (Jasdan); IOC R/2/629/197, R/2/632/250 and R/2/651/489A (Manavadar).

[42] Lord Wavell (Viceroy) to L.M.S. Amery (Secretary of State), 27 June 1945, and Sir Evan Jenkins (Private Secretary to Viceroy) to Sir David Monteath (IO), 2 Sept. 1945, both NAI PSV, Honours Branch, 133-H/45.

CHAPTER TWELVE

A TALE OF TWO PRINCES

Non-salute rulers had little opportunity of receiving any honours, except perhaps enhanced judicial powers; they might seek to improve their chances by securing salutes, but after the 1870s these were rarely conferred on chiefs who did not already possess them. The great princes also could not fully participate in the honours race: they usually already enjoyed such distinctions as "maha" titles and full powers, and received others (for example, Grand Commanderships) almost automatically. This meant that when the Paramount Power did want to reward them, it had to devise special honours. For example, in 1918 Delhi wished to recognise the war services of the Nizam of Hyderabad, the premier prince in India. He already held two Grand Commanderships and a twenty-one gun salute, and could imagine no title higher than Nizam. He therefore received the unique designations "His Exalted Highness" and "Faithful Ally of the British Government." The operation of the honours system is thus best observed among the middle-ranking states, those whose rulers enjoyed salutes of between nine and fifteen guns, and this chapter examines the careers of two nine-gun princes from Saurashtra, important enough to be eligible for honours but not so important that there were none left to give them.

I

Amarsinhji (1879-1954) succeeded as Raj Saheb of Wankaner in 1881, and took charge of the administration at the end of his minority in 1899. His Second-Class state had an area of just 400 square miles and a population of only thirty thousand, and his salute was a mere nine guns, but as the representative of the senior branch of the Jhala clan of Rajputs he considered himself the equal of the leaders of the great Rajput dynasties. He was particularly jealous of the status of the Raj Saheb of Dhrangadhara, whose branch of the family was junior to his own but since the seventeenth century had headed the Jhalas. Amarsinhji must have known that, after being held by the Dhrangadhara line for three hundred years, the leadership of the Jhalas would never be regained by the Wankaner family. But if he could not be the Dhrangadhara prince's superior, he could try to be his equal. Knowing that the distribution of honours showed rulers their place in the Paramount Power's hierarchy, Amarsinhji apparently resolved to assert his equality by winning as many distinctions as his rival. Although he never overtook his fellow Raj Saheb, the Wankaner prince was remarkably successful in his quest for honours. Between 1911 and 1935, he won four personal and four hereditary distinctions, and was transformed from a nine-gun, Second Class Raj Saheb into a Maharana with an eleven-gun salute and full judicial powers. A study of his career shows both how rulers lobbied for honours, and how the British tried to use distinctions to manage them.[1]

The first step came in 1911, when George V knighted many princes to mark his proclamation as emperor at Delhi. Among those honoured was Amarsinhji, who received a KCIE. At the time, he was first in precedence among the Second Class chiefs of Saurashtra, none of whom had yet been knighted, and his knighthood may well have been intended to induce the rulers of his class to enter the competition for honours, rather than to single him out for recognition. Then, during the First World War, Amarsinhji was one of a number of rulers who saw active service (he served in an ambulance corps in Flanders). In 1918 he was rewarded with an honorary commission as a Captain in the army, and the addition of two guns to his salute as a personal distinction. This made him an eleven-gun prince and therefore entitled him to the designation of His Highness. He seemed on the verge of attaining equality with the Raj Saheb of Dhrangadhara, who also had a salute of eleven guns (though permanent rather than personal) and a knighthood.

---

[1] For the history of Wankaner and an outline of Amarsinhji's life, see *The Ruling Princes, Chiefs and Leading Personages*, pp. 231-236. This account of Amarsinhji's quest for honours is based on IOC L/P&S/13/1747, R/1/4/24, R/1/4/25, R/1/4/90(1), R/1/4/111(1), R/2/617/1, R/2/626/135 and R/2/643/358; NAI FPD, Honours Branch, 10(18)-H/1927 and 100(4)-H/1929; FPD, Political Branch, 221-P/1929 and 312-P/1926.

Amarsinhji no doubt anticipated that the First-Class powers already enjoyed by Ghanshyamsinhji of Dhrangadhara would quickly follow the enhanced salute. But at the same time, his rival was also honoured for war services: Ghanshyamsinhji was made a Maharaja, and his salute was increased to thirteen guns. Even worse, these distinctions were hereditary, not personal. Amarsinhji was not merely failing to keep up in the race for honours; he was actually falling behind. Wankaner's permanent salute was now four guns less than Dhrangadhara's, rather than just two, and while both rulers had hitherto been Raj Sahebs, Ghanshyamsinhji had joined the select company of Maharajas. It seems to have been the honours conferred on Dhrangadhara in 1918 that spurred Amarsinhji to lobby actively for distinctions. In 1919 he began his campaign with a memorial to Sir George Lloyd, the Governor of Bombay, whose government then had jurisdiction over Saurashtra. The memorial requested First Class powers, a permanent salute of eleven if not thirteen guns (to which the personal salute of two guns would be added), and the title of Maharaja. All this would restore to Amarsinhji the same title as his rival, and a permanent salute of only two fewer guns. If necessary, the Raj Saheb was willing to forego the enhanced powers and Maharaja-ship, and would settle for the eleven guns and the title of Mahara*na*; the latter designation was customarily applied to important Jhala rulers, but without the recognition of the Paramount Power.[2] Lloyd, however, rejected all of Amarsinhji's requests. The Raj Saheb had done nothing to deserve further recognition only a year after he had received two honours, and he could not be given a "maha" title when the rulers of Morvi and Gondal, who outranked him in the Table of Precedence, remained Thakor Sahebs. The episode showed Amarsinhji that he must space his requests for distinctions, present good grounds for receiving them, and not demand honours that would promote him over rulers with higher precedence. Then, in 1921, Lloyd *did* ask the king to bestow on Amarsinhji the hereditary personal title of Maharana. The Governor could use the complex gradations of the honours system to grant one of the Wankaner prince's requests without slighting other rulers. A

---

[2] Although it was borne by the ruler of Udaipur, widely regarded as the highest-ranking Rajput prince in India, the title "Maharana" was normally considered inferior to that of "Maharaja."

personal title (not to be confused with a personal distinction) was the designation placed before a ruler's name; Raj Saheb Shri Sir Amarsinhji (Shri is an honorific) would now become Maharana Shri Sir Amarsinhji. But his dynastic title would remain Raj Saheb of Wankaner, so the Thakor Sahebs of Morvi and Gondal could not complain that he now enjoyed a higher title than they did. Moreover, the personal title would only be used on the occasions when Amarsinhji was addressed by his full style. Any resentment that arose could be soothed by explaining that the Wankaner prince had not received a fresh honour, but merely official sanction for a designation already in use. Lloyd ignored Amarsinhji's requests for enhanced powers and a higher salute, teaching the Raj Saheb that his lobbying was most likely to succeed if he sought one distinction at a time.

Despite these excuses, however, Lloyd *was* nominating Amarsinhji for a new honour. If he had simply wanted the king to sanction the customary use of the personal title Maharana, his recommendation would have included the Jhala Thakor Sahebs of Limbdi and Wadhwan, who were also addressed as Maharana. But the personal titles of these princes were not altered; indeed, in 1926 Delhi reprimanded Daulatsinhji of Limbdi (who had unsuccessfully requested recognition of the title) for styling himself Maharana on his visiting card.[3] Why, then, had Lloyd changed his mind and decided that Amarsinhji deserved an honour after all? The Raj Saheb had done nothing to warrant fresh recognition, and the Governor probably wanted to win Amarsinhji's future allegiance rather than reward his past conduct. Gandhi's Non-Cooperation movement was in full swing, and 1921 also saw the inauguration of the democratized central and provincial legislatures; perhaps Lloyd hoped that an honour would persuade Amarsinhji to join wholeheartedly in the British struggle against the Nationalists. This, however, seems unlikely: if the Governor had been seeking princely allies, he would surely have approached rulers of larger and more important states than Wankaner. It is more likely that Lloyd wished to enlist Amarsinhji not against Congress, but against the government of India. Amarsinhji was not one of the rulers who actively

[3] See IOC R/2/619/27.

supported the transfer of the Bombay states to central control,[4] and the Governor likely hoped that the new title would win the Raj Saheb over to his side, dividing the princes and making it easier to kill the proposal. Moreover, as has already been seen, some rulers desired transfer because they believed Delhi would be more liberal in dispensing honours than Bombay had been. Amarsinhji's title may have been intended to show that they were wrong and that transfer was therefore unnecessary. Whatever the reason, it does seem clear that Lloyd was courting Amarsinhji, who now learned that requests for honours were best made when the Paramount Power especially needed princely support. But then, on 17 November 1921, the Prince of Wales began his tour of India at Bombay. The rulers of the principal states in the Bombay Presidency were assembled to meet him. Because of their number, it had been decided that only those with salutes of eleven guns or more would be individually presented to the prince. Several nine-gun rulers, including Amarsinhji (who was excluded because his eleven guns were only personal), threatened to boycott the reception for the royal visitor unless they too were presented. Although in the end the malcontents did attend the function, Lloyd considered their threat an insult to the Prince of Wales, and hence to the King-Emperor. He would not allow Indian princes to treat his sovereign with such disrespect; and, having decided that Amarsinhji had led the protest (it is unclear with what justification), withdrew his recommendation that the Raj Saheb receive the title of Maharana. Amarsinhji learned that even the slightest offence was grounds for the Paramount Power to withhold a promised distinction. Nevertheless, Amarsinhji had allies. Delhi's Political Secretary, Sir John Wood, considered the protest over the arrangements at the royal reception to have been justified, and not a reason for denying the Raj Saheb his new title, and the Viceroy, Lord Reading, unsuccessfully asked Lloyd to reconsider the punishment. Wood and Reading may have believed that Amarsinhji had been ill-treated, or they may have wanted to beat the Governor at his own game, and secure a supporter of transfer. In any case, in 1924 the first stage of transfer was carried out with the establishment of the Western India States Agency.

---

[4] See Chapter Four.

Given his support of Amarsinhji against Lloyd three years earlier, Reading was bound to renew the recommendation for the personal title of Maharana, which was granted only two months after the government of India assumed charge of Western India.

Amarsinhji had won the first battle in his campaign for equality with Ghanshyamsinhji. He waited until a decent interval had elapsed, and then began to prepare the ground for his next assault. The first stage came in 1926, when he re-submitted to Wood's successor Sir John Thompson the requests that he had prepared in 1919. He pointed out that "Wankaner State's long-standing grievance is that its dynastic position has not properly appreciated from the beginning and consequently it has suffered in precedence, powers, salutes and honours..." as other states received promotions that were denied to Wankaner.[5] He made it plain that his objective was merely to keep his complaints in the view of the Political Department, and that he was fully aware that Thompson would not even consider his request unless it had been submitted through the Agent to the Governor-General. In 1927, however, an fresh honour came to Amarsinhji. Certain rulers were allowed a "return visit" by the Viceroy, which meant that if they paid their respects to the Viceroy at his residence or camp, he would call on them immediately afterwards wherever they might be staying. The principles on which return visits were allocated were somewhat arbitrary, but all Saurashtra princes with permanent salutes of eleven guns or more enjoyed the privilege. Amarsinhji asked for the right to a return visit in 1924. He was initially turned down, but in 1927 the request was granted (as a personal distinction) in view of the Raj Saheb's personal salute. The following year, Amarsinhji advanced to the next stage by presenting to Kealy, the Agent to the Governor-General, a suggestion that his permanent salute be increased to eleven guns, which he felt he deserved on account of his good administration and the proud history of his family. With the two personal guns he had been granted in 1918, his salute would total thirteen guns, equal to his rival's. Kealy was apparently unmoved by the proposal, as he did not act on it. But his successor Keyes felt

[5] "Short Notes regarding Wankaner State's long-standing grievance," NAI FPD, Political Branch, 312-P/1926.

that it had been wrong to increase Dhrangadhara's permanent salute while leaving Wankaner's untouched, and soon after taking office in 1929 forwarded Amarsinhji's request to Delhi. Keyes, however, knew that the Political Department would not grant brazen demands for higher salutes; if these were conferred merely for good government and ancient lineage, a host of princes would deserve the honour. Enhanced judicial powers, on the other hand, were a suitable reward for an able ruler, and Keyes therefore recommended that Delhi recognise Amarsinhji's good administration by giving him full powers, what until 1925 had been called First Class. He casually added that this would automatically necessitate a higher salute. In recent years the Political Department had granted unrestricted powers to several full members of the Chamber of Princes who did not already enjoy them,[6] and it agreed that the time had come to enhance Amarsinhji's jurisdiction. In August 1929, the Raj Saheb was accordingly granted full powers. But Keyes was wrong in thinking that this enhancement would increase Amarsinhji's salute, as since 1925 rulers' powers had ceased to govern their salutes.[7] Sir Charles Watson, the former Agent to the Governor-General and now Political Secretary, decided that Amarsinhji's permanent salute would remain at nine guns, since an enhancement "would at once raise similar claims in many other directions, which would be difficult to resist. This must wait ... until we have some big occasion such as may justify reopening this question."[8] But Amarsinhji wanted equality with Dhrangadhara as soon as possible. Seven months after receiving enhanced powers, he again requested a higher salute (preferably a permanent thirteen guns, although he would accept eleven if necessary). He now appealed to the British sense of fair play: "I have been ruling over my State for nearly 32 years and my administration is recognised by responsible officers of Government as good and progressive, but ... During these 32 years

---

[6] See IOC R/2/627/140. Full members were those princes who sat in the Chamber individually, rather than electing a representative member. By and large, and always in the Western India States Agency, the full members were the salute rulers.

[7] See Chapter Eleven.

[8] Minute by Sir Charles Watson (Political Secretary India), 17 July 1929, NAI FPD, Honours Branch, 100(4)-H/1929.

I am honoured only once by the Insignia of K.C.I.E., in 1911."[9] This time, Watson ignored Amarsinhji's Captaincy, personal salute, Maharana-ship, return visit privileges, and enhanced powers, and agreed that the Raj Saheb had not obtained the recognition he deserved, especially in view of the forthcoming Golden Jubilee of his accession in 1881. Watson successfully put Amarsinhji's claim before Lord Irwin, who in five years as Viceroy had made only two changes to the Table of Salutes, but who now agreed that Amarsinhji's long and successful reign, the enhanced powers that he had recently received, and his place in his clan, should be recognised with an enhanced salute. The India Office protested that such an action would surely reopen other claims, but Delhi replied that "Lord Irwin thought that his having made this one recommendation only for an enhanced dynastic salute during his term of office would both emphasise his belief in the strength of the case and would make it easier for his successor to resist claims based upon it as a precedent."[10] Whitehall caved in when the government of India submitted its unanimous agreement, and in September 1931 the King declared the Raj Saheb's personal salute of eleven guns to be permanent. Amarsinhji's loud (though unfounded) complaints that he had been overlooked in the dispensation of honours apparently secured a distinction that had only recently been refused him. It does, however, seem significant that the salute was enhanced at a time when the British were probably more eager for Indian allies than at any time since 1857, both at the Round Table Conferences in England and in the face of the Civil Disobedience movement in India. Amarsinhji may have benefited from an attempt by Delhi to show rulers the rewards of cooperating with the Paramount Power, and during the next year the grant of enhanced salutes to two more princes marked the end of a decade of British reluctance to alter salutes.

Amarsinhji was angry that the enhanced permanent salute did not bring his personal salute to thirteen guns (personal salutes always lapsed when permanent ones were increased). Still, the new honour restored the position that had existed before 1918, when Wanka-

---

[9] "Notes on the complaint of Wankaner State regarding the enhancement of its dynastic Salute of guns," undated (Nov. 1930), IOC R/1/4/90(1).

[10] Watson to P.J. Patrick (IO), 16 July 1931, IOC L/P&S/13/1747.

ner's permanent salute was only two guns less than Dhrangadhara's. He now turned to his dynastic title, and in March 1931 suggested that he too should be made a Maharaja. The Political Department, however, was in the midst of securing Whitehall's approval for the enhanced salute, and ignored this request. Amarsinhji resumed his efforts in 1934. He again complained that he had not received the honours he deserved, and added that it was not right that he was the only eleven-gun Hindu prince in Saurashtra who was not a Maharaja. He secured the support of the Agent to the Governor-General, Latimer, and the Political Secretary in Delhi, Glancy, who agreed that his salute entitled him to a "maha" title. Wankaner was not sufficiently important for Amarsinhji to become a Maharaja, but on Glancy's recommendation the Raj Saheb's personal designation of Maharana was added to his dynastic title, making him the Maharana Raj Saheb of Wankaner. This was close enough to the Dhrangadhara title of Maharaja Raj Saheb to satisfy Amarsinhji. Only two months elapsed between Amarsinhji's request for a higher title in February 1934 and its conferment in April. He had benefited from the backing of Latimer and Glancy, who supported the demand because they felt it was justified: in 1926 the rulers of Morvi and Gondal had been made Maharajas partly because they were then the only full-powered, eleven-gun Hindu princes in Saurashtra who did not yet possess the title, and this precedent made it awkward to refuse a similar promotion to Amarsinhji.[11] But the Raj Saheb had probably also chosen the right moment for his request. He was now a member of the Standing Committee of the Chamber of Princes, and the Political Department may have hoped that gratitude over the conferment of the new title would encourage him to lobby the Chamber to support federation at a time when the scheme was being heavily criticized, or at least that his fellow rulers would see the advantages of cooperating with the Paramount Power. Amarsinhji had now won all of the honours that he had been seeking since 1919: full judicial powers, a permanent eleven-gun salute, and a "maha" title. In late 1934, he asked that his personal salute of two additional guns be restored, which would bring his salute to thirteen guns, and finally give him full equality

[11] For the Morvi and Gondal titles, see below.

with Ghanshyamsinhji. This time, however, he was flatly turned down, in view of the Political Department's decision to withhold hereditary honours until the federation had come into being.[12] Amarsinhji's failure was to some extent compensated with a KCSI in 1936, to reward his "great and intelligent interest in the scheme of Federation...."[13]

After the defeat over his personal salute, Amarsinhji withdrew from the campaign for honours. He had been on the throne for fifty-five years, and probably knew he had received all of the distinctions that the importance of his state warranted. He had consistently sought distinctions for reasons of family honour, rather than to gratify personal vanity. Eight Saurashtra states ranked above Wankaner in the order of precedence, but Amarsinhji saw the honours race as a means of catching up to his hereditary rival Dhrangadhara, and not merely as a route to accumulating whatever titles or privileges were available. His requests for honours never suggested that he desired equality with the premier states of Junagadh, Nawanagar, Bhavnagar and Porbandar, or even with Morvi, Gondal and Jafarabad (his immediate superiors in the Table of Precedence): his sights were always set single-mindedly on Dhrangadhara. To Amarsinhji the honours race really was a competition, in which he was responsible for restoring his family's proper place in the Jhala clan. He failed to achieve his goal of becoming the equal of Ghanshyamsinhji of Dhrangadhara, but through persistence, a good understanding of the way in which honours were bestowed, and luck, he had come much closer to success than anyone could have predicted in 1919.[14]

---

[12] See Chapter Eleven.

[13] Sir Courtenay Latimer (AGG) to E.C. Mieville (Private Secretary to Viceroy), 25 Aug. 1935, IOC R/1/4/476.

[14] In fairness to Amarsinhji, it must be noted that he was careful to ensure that he enjoyed only those honours to which he was entitled. In 1931, he pointed out that Agency correspondence had wrongly given him the rank of Major, when in fact he was only a Captain. See NAI WISA G-8(e)/1931.

II

Thakor Saheb Bahadursinhji (1900-1964) succeeded to the throne of Palitana in 1905 and was invested with ruling powers in 1919. Between his accession and 1926, every Saurashtra prince above him in precedence received an hereditary honour of some sort: new salutes and titles for Nawanagar, Bhavnagar, Porbandar and Dhrangadhara; a salute alone for Junagadh, and titles alone for Morvi, Gondal and Wankaner; enhanced powers for Jafarabad. It was reasonable to assume that similar recognition would soon come his way. Indeed, Bahadursinhji had perhaps more right to an enhanced title, powers or salute than Amarsinhji. Palitana had almost half as many people again as Wankaner and a higher revenue, and was four hundred years older. As he ranked immediately after Amarsinhji in the Saurashtra order of precedence, he could have received all of the honours granted to the Wankaner prince without being promoted over the heads of other rulers. Yet Bahadursinhji was much less successful than Amarsinhji in the quest for honours, and by 1947 his efforts had secured only two knighthoods and one title (a mere personal distinction at that).[15]

His campaign began in 1926, when the Thakor Sahebs of Morvi and Gondal were made Maharajas. This was done mainly because their former designation did not reflect their true rank. Not only were they the only eleven-gun princes in Saurashtra who were mere Thakor Sahebs, but in most of northern India, a Thakur (as the title is spelled in Hindi, Thakor being the Gujarati form) was a mere landlord. With the frequent contacts among states that followed the establishment of the Chamber of Princes in 1921, the Morvi and Gondal Thakor Sahebs feared that rulers from Rajputana and Central India would mistake them for petty noblemen rather than important princes. Delhi agreed that this concern was justified, and

---

[15] For the history of Palitana and an outline of Bahadursinhji's life, see *The Ruling Princes, Chiefs and Leading Personages*, pp. 197-202. This account of Bahadursinhji's quest for honours is based on IOC R/1/1/1844(1), R/1/4/135 and R/2/598/26; NAI FPD, Honours Branch, 100-6(H)/1929, 129-H/1932 and 153-H/1930; FPD, Political Branch, 113-3-P/1925. IOC R/2/626/128, which deals with Bahadursinhji's request for the title of Maharaja in 1927, is missing.

granted the higher title.[16] This left Bahadursinhji as the highest-ranking Thakor Saheb in Western India. In 1927 he argued that he too was liable to be taken for a landlord unless he were made a Maharaja. As the Paramount Power did not usually grant "maha" titles to nine-gun rulers, he also asked that his salute be enhanced to eleven guns. His demand was, however, rejected. Bahadursinhji had committed several errors that Amarsinhji had learned to avoid: he had requested two distinctions simultaneously, and ones that would have promoted him over a ruler who outranked him (Amarsinhji was still a mere Raj Saheb with a permanent salute of only nine guns); he had not chosen a time when the British were actively seeking princely allies; and in less than eight years' reign, he had done nothing that could be used to rationalise an enhanced title or salute. The following year, however, Kealy, the Agent to the Governor-General, proposed that the streamlining begun with the promotion of the Morvi and Gondal rulers to Maharaja in 1926 be completed by conferring higher titles on the five remaining salute Thakor Sahebs in the Western India States Agency (the princes of Palitana, Dhrol, Limbdi, Rajkot, and Wadhwan). These were only nine-gun rulers. Kealy knew that there was little chance of their being given "maha" titles, and he therefore proposed the conferment of the title of Rana Saheb (on the Jhala rulers of Limbdi and Wadhwan) or Raja Saheb (on the other three). This proposal, like others for the grant of such titles, required the approval of the Viceroy. When it was put to Lord Irwin, he commented that "'Thakur Sahib' is an interesting historic survival, which it would be a pity to merge in the better known 'Raja' and 'Rana.'" He was nevertheless prepared to sanction the new titles, but only if Watson (the Political Secretary) ascertained that the rulers still wanted them after an explanation of the Viceroy's views.[17] For two and a half years, however, Watson was for some reason unable to find the opportunity to canvass the princes' opinion, and Kealy was accordingly informed several times that his proposal was under consideration. Kealy may have had in mind recent events in Palitana. In 1926, Bahadursinhji had proposed to levy a head-tax on pilgrims to

---

[16] See IOC R/2/622/107.

[17] Minute by Watson, 8 May 1928, NAI FPD, Honours Branch, 153-H/1930.

Shetrunjaya, a hill in Palitana held sacred by the Jains. The Jains claimed that he had no right to do so, and reacted angrily. The government of India intervened in the resulting dispute, and Watson (then Agent to the Governor-General) imposed a settlement that was accepted by the Thakor Saheb but not by the Jains (it lifted the planned levy, but only for ten years, and also reaffirmed Bahadursinhji's right to tax Jain pilgrims).[18] Kealy may have supported Bahadursinhji's request for an honour in order to show Jains all over India that the Paramount Power did not intend to make any further concessions to them in the Shetrunjaya case, even though the Jains' response to the situation had been to boycott the pilgrimage to the hill. Lord Irwin did not grant the request, but he did eventually intervene in the Shetrunjaya dispute. On his insistence, Bahadursinhji and the Jains reached a new agreement that both parties found acceptable (it rescinded the tax for thirty-five years instead of ten, and recognised the right of the Jains to call for the help of the Paramount Power in any future disputes over the hill). This reconciled the Jains not only to the Palitana administration, but more important to the government of India which had backed the original settlement. In 1929, Kealy's acting replacement Keyes proposed that the Thakor Saheb's contribution to the resolution of the dispute be recognised with the title of Raja, the grant of full judicial powers as a personal distinction, and a personal salute of eleven guns. Keyes's recommendation posed a dilemma for Watson, who was now Political Secretary. Bahadursinhji's role in the settlement of the Shetrunjaya dispute deserved recognition, as he had helped defuse a confrontation between Delhi and one of India's wealthiest communities; when the dispute was at its height, Lord Birkenhead, the Secretary of State, had commented ominously that "we do not, in addition to other religious disputes, want a Jain question on our hands."[19] Indeed, in the Shetrunjaya case, Bahadursinhji had done more to earn a distinction than Amarsinhji had

[18] For the Shetrunjaya dispute, see IOC R/1/1/1648; NAI WISA, Political Branch, P-59(1)/1928; FPD, Political Branch, 113-2-P/1925, 113-3-P/1925, 439-P/1927, and 604-P/1927.

[19] Telegram Lord Birkenhead (Secretary of State) to Lord Irwin (Viceroy), 30 July 1926, NAI FPD, Political Branch, 113-3-P/1925. For the Jains' anger, see NAI WISA, P-59(1)/1928.

ever done. Still, Watson would not "support a recommendation for additional guns as yet owing to the usual reasons against reopening this form of reward...."[20] However, the Nawab of Rampur in what is now Uttar Pradesh also wanted a personal salute of two extra guns, and Watson decided that he would consider the Rampur and Palitana claims together once he had disposed of more pressing business. As to Keyes's other recommendation, Kealy's proposal of a general promotion of the Saurashtra Thakor Sahebs to Raja or Rana was still before the Political Department. Watson therefore felt that there was no point in considering Bahadursinhji for a new title while there remained the possibility that four other rulers would shortly similarly be promoted. The Political Department was prepared to consider the question of enhanced powers, but the only immediate recognition that the Thakor Saheb's services received was a KCIE, granted on New Year's Day, 1930, to reward his handling of the Jain controversy.[21]

Bahadursinhji might still have received an increased salute and powers once a suitable interval had elapsed. Bad luck, however, deprived him of both honours. The Nawab of Rampur died in June 1930. The Political Department decided that this provided an excuse to allow his request to lapse, and (rather unfairly) Bahadursinhji's lapsed with it. And in August 1930, the Political Department granted hereditary unrestricted judicial powers to all nine-gun princes in Western India who did not already have them, in order to give them equality with other full members of the Chamber of Princes.[22] Bahadursinhji had received full powers, but because he happened to have a salute of nine guns and not as a special honour.[23] The following year, Watson finally sounded out Bahadursinhji on Kealy's proposed general promotion of the Thakor Sahebs to Rajas and Ranas; but "When he heard that there was no prospect that the

---

[20] Minute by Watson, 3 July 1929, NAI FPD, Honours Branch, 100-6(H)/1929.

[21] Watson to G. Cunningham (Private Secretary to Viceroy), 4 Oct. 1929, IOC R/1/4/463.

[22] See IOC R/2/627/140.

[23] The grant of enhanced powers occurred during Gandhi's Civil Disobedience campaign, but it had been approved by the Political Department before the campaign began and was not apparently intended to win princely support.

titles of 'Maharaja' or 'Maharana' would be given in place of 'Thakore Sahib' he seemed inclined to think that it might be better to stick to the old nomenclature. Their only difficulty had been that of being confused with the Thakores in Rajputana and he admitted that with wider and more frequent association with other States this difficulty was disappearing."[24] Rather foolishly, perhaps, Bahadursinhji had turned down a fresh title that the Paramount Power was prepared to give. Although his previous requests for an enhanced salute had been rejected, and Watson had personally told him that he would under no circumstances receive a "maha" title, Bahadursinhji in 1932 once more demanded an eleven gun salute and a Maharaja-ship, which he claimed he needed to "command sufficient respect and dignity" from the tens of thousands of Jains who visited Shetrunjaya each year.[25] But the Agent to the Governor-General did not even forward the submission to the Political Department. The persistent Bahadursinhji nevertheless repeated his request in 1933 and 1934, though with no more success, thanks to Delhi's new policy on titles and salutes. By the summer of 1938, however, the federal scheme was in crisis, and it was apparent that it would have to be drastically amended before the princes would accept it. Bahadursinhji may have finally realised that such difficulties often induced the Paramount Power to grant honours, and again demanded a Maharaja-ship and an eleven-gun salute, as well as a second knighthood. In view of the possible danger to the federation, the first two requests were denied, but Bahadursinhji *was* granted a KCSI in recognition of his place as ruler of the "1st among the nine-gun salute States in Kathiawar."[26] It is quite likely that this was to suggest the advantages of federation to his fellow nine-gun rulers of Western India. At the same time, a knighthood for the Maharaja Jam Saheb of Nawanagar sent a signal to the other princes of the Agency, whose leader *he* was.

In the nineteen years since the end of his minority, Bahadursinhji had received two knighthoods. Nineteen years after *his* minority ended, on the other hand, Amarsinhji of Wankaner had held a knighthood, a Captaincy, and a personal salute of eleven guns (with

---

[24] Minute by Watson, 13 Feb. 1931, NAI FPD, Honours Branch, 153-H/1930.
[25] Palitana to Kealy, 24 July 1932, NAI FPD, Honours Branch, 129-H/1932.
[26] E.C. Gibson (Resident) to F.H. Puckle, 3 Sept. 1938, IOC R/1/4/482.

the title of Highness). Amarsinhji had had two advantages: a war, in which he won two distinctions, and the fact that the Paramount Power had been much more willing to grant titles and salutes before the problems of federation arose. Bahadursinhji may have hoped that the outbreak of another war and the suspension of federal negotiations in 1939 would make it easier for him to obtain his title and salute, and he again requested them in 1941. This time, even the Resident did not support him, as the Thakor Saheb had done nothing to deserve further honours so soon after receiving his KCSI. Like most rulers, Bahadursinhji contributed financially to the war effort, but (unlike Amarsinhji twenty-five years earlier) he was not in uniform, and he had no state forces to send overseas. This made it difficult to reward him for military services, and he had to find other grounds for requesting distinctions. He still did not fully understand the workings of the honours system, however. In 1944, he suggested that a quarter-century of good government be marked with an honour. Having finally realised that he would receive only one distinction at a time, he gave the Paramount Power a choice of awarding him an enhanced salute, a Maharaja-ship, or a third knighthood. The Resident, Hancock, agreed that Bahadursinhji's reign did deserve recognition. But there was a problem: Wavell's policy on war rewards ruled out an enhanced salute for Bahadursinhji, and as he already had a KCIE and a KCSI, a new knighthood would have to be a Grand Commandership, which was not normally awarded to nine-gun princes. After some prodding by Hancock, Delhi agreed that Bahadursinhji might be made a Maharaja as a personal distinction. The title was granted in June 1945, in recognition of the Thakor Saheb's successful administration and his contributions to the war effort.

On the surface, Bahadursinhji appears to have lacked Amarsinhji's focus; he accepted that he was inferior to the head of his own clan, the Maharaja of Bhavnagar, and merely wanted to gain prestige by acquiring honours. But in his own way, Bahadursinhji was actually as consistent as Amarsinhji in what he wanted: almost every one of his requests was for an eleven-gun salute and the title of Maharaja. This is why he was not satisfied with the two knighthoods with which the Paramount Power tried to quiet him. The rival to whom *he* wanted to catch up was the body of eleven-gun Maharajas, rather than a single ruler. He believed that he had wrongly been denied the salute that the size and antiquity of his state warranted, and that he had as much right to a "maha" title as any other prince in Saurashtra. It is possible that other distinctions would have subsequently come to Bahadursinhji, but the independence of India two years after the conferral of the Maharaja-ship brought the Paramount Power's elaborate honours system to an abrupt end. On 1 January 1947, at the request of Jawaharlal Nehru's interim government, Wavell announced that no honours would henceforth be conferred on Indians living in British India, except for medals for gallantry and humanitarian work, and for the police and fire services. Rulers and subjects of the Indian states remained eligible for honours until after independence.[27] The last set of chivalric distinctions was bestowed on rulers on 1 January 1948, although the awards were backdated to 14 August 1947, the day before independence. Perhaps symbolically, in that same month of January 1948, the government of India began to eliminate the princely sovereignty that had loomed so large in the rulers' quest for honours, by overseeing the merger of the states of Saurashtra into the United State of Kathiawar.

[27] See NAI PSV, Honours Branch, 127-H/1946 and 364-H/1946.

EPILOGUE

On 14 August 1947, the Union Jack over the Residency at Rajkot was lowered for the last time. The Baroda, Western India and Gujarat States Agency was no more; British paramountcy over the Indian states had ended, and India was an independent nation.[1] One of the three players in political life in the Indian states had left the scene. Or had it? The state politicians assumed that with the departure of the British, they would acquire the power that they had sought for so long. But this did not happen. The Congress leaders of free India quickly distanced themselves from the All-India States' People's Conference, and assumed the role of the Paramount Power. In July 1947, the Ministry of States had been established as the successor to the old Political Department, and Sardar Vallabhbhai Patel, its first Minister, announced the incoming government's policy towards the princes:

> I should like to make it clear that it is not the desire of the Congress to interfere in any manner whatever with the domestic affairs of the States. They are no enemies of the Princely Order, but, on the other hand, wish them and their people under their ægis all prosperity, contentment and happiness. Nor would it be my policy to conduct the relations of the new Department with the States in any manner which savours of the domination of one over the other; if there would be any domination, it would be that of our mutual interests and welfare.[2]

Patel confirmed that free India would indeed recognise the sovereignty of the rulers of the Indian states, who were asked merely to cede to the new government control over their defence, foreign affairs, and communications. During the first two weeks of August,

---

[1] See the description of the end of the Agency by the last Secretary to the Resident, Edward Lydall, *Enough of Action* (London, 1949), p. 252.

[2] Sardar Vallabhbhai Patel (Minister of States), statement of 5 July 1947, in Government of India. Ministry of States, *White Paper on Indian States*, pp. 157-159. For the Ministry of States, see Menon, *op. cit.*, pp. 88-91 and *passim*.

most of the salute princes of Western India acceded on these three subjects, and after independence the chiefs of the principal non-salute states also acceded. A few rulers were reluctant. The Nawab of Radhanpur did not sign the instrument of accession until September; the Nawab of Junagadh acceded to Pakistan, and his kinsmen the chiefs of Manavadar, Bantwa and Sardargadh announced their intention of doing the same thing. Pressure was duly placed on Junagadh, Manavadar, Bantwa and Sardargadh, and by November the rulers of all four states had left for Pakistan and their territories were under the administration of the government of India.

Meanwhile, the Ministry of States had appointed Regional Commissioners to replace the British Residents as agents of paramountcy. The Regional Commissioner for Baroda and the States of Western India and Gujarat was responsible for the former Baroda, Western India and Gujarat States Agency, and he and his staff carried on the traditions of their British predecessors (even down to using Agency stationery for their correspondence).[3] The Ministry resisted pressure from the state political leaders to transfer power to them, for example in Junagadh after control of the state was assumed by the government of India in November 1947. It looked as if relations between the rulers and the new Paramount Power would continue on the same basis as before, with a balance between the sovereignty of one side and control by the other. Many rulers certainly thought so, and carried on in their quest to enhance the reality or the symbols of their sovereignty. In September 1947, the Maharaja of Baroda renewed his claim to jurisdiction over the other states of Gujarat, now requesting the title of "King of Gujarat and Kathiawar;" and in November 1947, the Rao of Vijaynagar unsuccessfully asked that the Ministry of States grant him an artillery salute.[4] But something had changed: Patel might be unwilling to step in and force the rulers to hand over power to the politicians; but the

---

[3] See the correspondence of the office of the Regional Commissioner, which is filed with the Agency records in NAI WISA.

[4] For the establishment of government management in Junagadh and the Baroda request, see Menon, *op. cit.*, pp. 124-150, 418. For Vijaynagar, see NAI PSV, Honours Branch, Class B, 67-H/1947. Copland, *Princes of India*, especially pp. 226-228, notes that at the time of independence, the states were by and large flourishing, and not in any imminent danger of internal collapse.

close links that had grown up between the Indian National Congress and the All-India States' People's Conference during the previous decade meant that the new government of India would not allow the rulers to suppress political agitation in the states. As a result, the rulers found themselves under unprecedented pressure from local political leaders. The first to give in was the Maharaja of Bhavnagar. By January 1948, matters in his state had reached the point at which he judged it best not to resist any further, and he appointed a new government made up of politicians and responsible to a legislature.

As it turned out, however, Bhavnagar was to be the only state in the former Western India States Agency to enjoy responsible government. In late 1947, opinion in Patel's Ministry of States had turned against continued monarchical rule in the states. This was not so much because the Minister and his colleagues wanted an immediate handover to the politicians, as because they had realised that the continued popularity of the sovereign rulers threatened the control of India by the Congress Party. This could not be publicly admitted by a democratic government. Fortunately, the new nation's need for administrative uniformity and democratization provided the Ministry with a convenient excuse for eliminating the states.[5] In Western India, the princes of Saurashtra had since June 1946 been discussing plans to unite the entire peninsula into a single state. Patel took up this idea, and immediately after the establishment of responsible government in Bhavnagar his Ministry began to press the rulers to bring about the proposed union. This had the desired effect, and on 22 January 1948 the rulers of the salute states and the principal non-salutes states signed a covenant providing for the merger of their territories into a new United State of Kathiawar, with a popular ministry composed of the leading AISPC politicians of the peninsula. The new state formally came into being three weeks later. The Ministry now turned to the rulers of the Banas Kantha and Mahi Kantha states, who in April 1948 agreed to the merger of their states in Bombay; state political leaders moved into positions of power as local Congress bosses.

---

[5] See McLeod, "A Model Prince?" For a variant view, see Copland, *Princes of India*, pp. 261-265.

And in May, the Maharao of Kutch agreed to hand over his state to the central government. The princes and chiefs of Western India had lost their battle for sovereignty, while, in the interests of control, the new overlord had granted power to the politicians.[6]

But the past should not be studied with hindsight, and during most of the period examined in this book, the rulers were able to secure much that they believed to be essential to the maintenance of their sovereignty. Until 1948, they preserved that sovereignty against all attempts by the politicians to gain power, and they also enlarged their sovereign authority at the expense of the British Paramount Power. This trend began with Lord Minto's speech in 1909; in 1917, the government of India issued the resolution that restored to the states control over most aspects of minority administration, and at the same time the lifting of the Viramgam Line recognised the princes' sovereign right to collect customs on all imports that arrived at state ports; in 1918, the Montagu-Chelmsford report recommended the transfer of the states from provincial to central control and the institution of direct relations, which would both reduce the scope for British interference in state affairs and enhance the princes' stature as partners in the government of India; and in 1920, the procedure for investigating accusations of maladministration was altered in such a way as to give the rulers considerably more leeway than they had hitherto enjoyed. The symbolic side of the rulers' quest for sovereignty was recognised with the plethora of honours granted to mark the states' contributions to the First World War. This first wave of victories ended around the time of the creation of the Western India States Agency in 1924, and three years later the princes suffered a major defeat with the reimposition of the Viramgam Line. But the 1930s saw further concessions to the princes: the completion of transfer to central control in 1933; the settlement of the customs dispute with the maritime states of Saurashtra (except Bhavnagar) in 1936;

---

[6] For the proposals to unite Saurashtra in 1946-1947, see IOC L/P&S/13/828, L/P&S/13/984 and R/2/571/28; NL AICC, non-categories file 2, 1947, and SPC, file 267. The broader context is discussed in Copland, *Princes of India*, pp. 213-214, 230-231. The classic account of the creation of the United State and the merger of the mainland Gujarat states and Kutch is Menon, *op. cit.*, pp. 175-198, 205-208, 300-301.

Delhi's rejection of the Baroda plans for absorbing the smaller states, which by abandoning Lord Canning's guarantees of territorial integrity would have caused consternation across princely India.

This success, however, was entirely dependent on the Paramount Power's willingness to heed the concerns of the rulers. That willingness in turn depended on the aims of British policy in India, which were influenced by the current assessment of the place of the politicians. This book has suggested that until 1930, the British seem to have believed that they could control India and, with the help of the princes, relegate to a minor role the politicians who were striving for power. So long as this belief dominated, the princes were courted, as allies against the politicians. The constitutional changes of the 1930s, however, made it clear that the politicians, more particularly Congress, were an unstoppable force in much of India, who under the new constitution would inevitably come to power in most of the provinces (as they were to do in 1937). At the same time, politicians remained relatively weak in the states, and British policy now aimed at finding ways of balancing Congress in the semi-autonomous federal India of the future, particularly with the states as a non-Congress counterweight within the federation. For a decade, the British continued concessions to the rulers. But this did not accomplish its goal. By 1939 the princes had rejected federation, political activity was beginning in the states, and it was clear that Indian independence was fast approaching. British policy therefore shifted to one that aimed merely at controlling the situation. This included eliminating perceived grievances among the rulers' subjects to stop the spread of politicization. Another part of it was making the states viable units that might survive after the politicians came to power with the end of British rule, which was only possible if the policy of seeking the princes' friendship were abandoned; and from then until 1947, the states' sovereignty was often ignored. As a result, after 1939 the rulers lost many of the gains that they had made in the previous thirty years, as exemplified by the pressure on Bhavnagar after 1939 to give up its treaty right of keeping all customs duties collected in the state; the implementation of the Attachment Scheme in 1943; the abandonment of direct relations in the Western India States Agency in 1944; the imposition of tight British control on extended minorities, and frequent intervention in cases of alleged maladministration.

Throughout, the history of the states and their people was shaped by the relationship between princes and Paramount Power, which in turn was determined by each party's pursuit of its goals. Those goals, however, were quite different, perhaps even incompatible, except in that they shared the objective of restraining the politicians. This is disguised by the fact that, at least to some extent, each side spoke in terms intended to appeal to the other. Thus, knowing that the Political Department's primary goal was to secure the rulers' cooperation in British policies, princes often referred to their loyalty to the imperial connection, even as they sought to reduce the force of that connection–hence the Jam Saheb's angry reminder of his wartime assistance when he protested the abolition of direct relations. (Of course, the rulers often had to make demonstrations of loyalty merely to retain their thrones, let alone win any concessions.) By the same token, the Paramount Power portrayed its bids for princely support as honest attempts to boost the rulers' sovereignty, as when in 1933 Lord Willingdon told the princes that the transfer of the Bombay states was shortly to be completed partly to ensure that an autonomous provincial administration did not interfere in their affairs. But in the end, it was all for nothing, and neither the rulers nor the Paramount Power attained their objectives, despite the tenacity with which both fought for them.

APPENDIX ONE

RULERS OF THE PRINCIPAL STATES OF WESTERN INDIA 1916-1947

BAJANA, Maleks of: Jivankhanji 1903-1920; Kamalkhanji 1920-1948

BHAVNAGAR, Thakor Saheb, from 1917 Maharajas of: Bhavsinhji 1896-1919; Krishnakumarsinhji 1919-1948

BILKHA, Darbars of: Kanthad 1909-1923; Ravat 1928-1948

CHUDA, Thakors of: Jorawarsinhji 1908-1920; Bahadursinhji 1920-1948

DHRANGADHARA, Raj Saheb of, from 1918 Maharaja Raj Sahebs (Maharajas Sriraj) of: Ghanshyamsinhji 1911-1942; Mayurdhwajsinhji (later Meghrajji III) 1942-1948

DHROL, Thakor Sahebs of: Daulatsinhji 1914-1937; Zorawarsinhji 1937-1939; Chandrasinhji 1939-1948

GONDAL, Thakor Saheb, from 1926 Maharajas of: Bhagwatsinhji 1869-1944; Bhojrajji 1944-1948

IDAR, Maharajas of: Dowlatsinhji 1911-1931; Himmatsinhji 1931-1948

JAFARABAD, Nawabs of Janjira and: Sidi Ahmad Khan 1879-1922; Sidi Muhammad Khan 1922-1948

JASDAN, Darbars of: Vajsur 1912-1919; Ala 1919-1948

JETPUR, Darbars of: Mulu 1899-1936; Surag 1936-1948

JUNAGADH, Nawab of: Mahabatkhan 1911-1947

KHIRASRA, Thakors of: Balsinhji 1905-1920; Sursinhji 1920-1948

KOTDA SANGANI, Thakors of: Himmatsinhji 1913-1930; Pradumansinhji 1930-1948

KUTCH, Rao, from 1918 Maharaos of: Khengarji III 1876-1942; Vijayarajji 1942-1948

LAKHTAR, Thakors, from 1927 Thakor Sahebs of: Karansinhji 1846-1924; Balvirsinhji 1924-1940; Indrasinhji 1940-1948

LATHI, Thakors of: Pratapsinhji 1900-1918; Prahladsinhji 1918-1948

LIMBDI, Thakor Sahebs of: Daulatsinhji 1908-1940; Digvijaysinhji 1940-1941; Chhatrasalji 1941-1948

MALIA, Thakors of: Raisinhji 1907-1930; Harishchandrasinhji 1930-1939; Bhupendrasinhji 1939-1948

MALPUR, Raols of: Jaswantsinhji 1914-1923; Gambhirsinhji 1923-1948

MANAVADAR, Khans of: Fatehuddinkhan 1888-1918; Ghulam Moinuddinkhan 1918-1947

MANSA, Raoljis of: Takhtasinhji 1889-1934; Sajjansinhji 1934-1948

MOHANPUR, Thakors of: Himmatsinhji 1882-1916; Takhtasinhji 1916-1927; Sartansinhji 1927-1948

MORVI, Thakor Sahebs, from 1926 Maharaja of: Waghji 1870-1922; Lukhdhirji 1922-1948

MULI, Thakor of: Harishchandrasinhji 1905-1948

NAWANAGAR, Jam Saheb, from 1918 Maharaja Jam Sahebs of: Ranjitsinhji 1907-1933; Digvijaysinhji 1933-1948

PALANPUR, Nawabs of: Sher Mahomed Khan 1877-1918; Taley Mahomed Khan 1918-1948

PALITANA, Thakor Saheb of: Bahadursinhji 1905-1948

PATDI, Desais of: Dolatsinhji 1913-1928; Raghuvirsinhji 1928-1940; Naransinhji 1940-1941; Pratapsinhji 1941-1948

PORBANDAR, Rana Saheb, from 1918 Maharaja Rana Saheb of: Natwarsinhji 1908-1948

RADHANPUR, Nawabs of: Jalaluddinkhanji 1910-1936; Murtazakhanji 1937-1948

RAJKOT, Thakor Sahebs of: Lakhajiraj 1890-1930; Dharmendrasinhji 1930-1940; Pradyumnasinhji 1940-1948

SAYLA, Thakors, from 1927 Thakor Sahebs of: Vakhatsinhji 1881-1924; Madarsinhji 1924-1938; Karansinhji 1938-1948

THANA DEVLI (AMARNAGAR), Darbars of: Lakshman 1883-1922; Amra 1922-1948

THARAD, Thakors of: Dolatsinhji 1910-1921; Bhimsinhji 1921-1948

VADIA, Darbars of: Bawa 1875-1930; Surag 1930-1948

VALA, Thakors of: Vakhatsinhji 1875-1943; Gambhirsinhji 1943-1948

VIJAYNAGAR, Rao of: Hamirsinhji 1916-1948

VIRPUR, Thakors of: Suraji 1851-1918; Hamirsinhji 1918-1938; Dilipsinhji 1938-1945; Narendrasinhji 1945-1948

WADHWAN, Thakor Sahebs of: Jaswantsinhji 1910-1918; Jorawarsinhji 1918-1934; Surendrasinhji 1934-1948

WANKANER, Raj Saheb, from 1934 Maharana Raj Saheb of: Amarsinhji 1881-1948

WAO, Ranas of: Chandansinhji 1884-1924; Harisinhji 1924-1948

APPENDIX TWO

PRINCIPAL BRITISH OFFICIALS IN THE WESTERN INDIA STATES AGENCY

(Officiating officeholders are marked with an asterisk.)

Agents to the Governor-General in the States of Western India:

10 Oct. 1924-15 July 1926	C.C. Watson
16 July-Nov. 1926	A.D. Macpherson*
21 Nov. 1926-17 Oct. 1927	C.C. Watson
18 Oct. 1927-22 Apr. 1928	E.H. Kealy*
23 Apr.-18 May 1928	E.H. Kealy
19 May 1928-2 Apr. 1929	H.S. Strong*
3 Apr.-23 Oct. 1929	T.H. Keyes*
24 Oct. 1929-1931	E.H. Kealy
15 Aug. 1931-1932	A.H.E. Mosse*
14 Aug. 1932-15 Feb. 1933	C. Latimer*
16 Feb.-26 May 1933	C. Latimer
27 May-13 Oct. 1933	J.C. Tate*
14 Oct. 1933-5 June 1936	Sir Courtenay Latimer
6 June-1 Nov. 1936	J. de la H. Gordon*
2 Nov. 1936-28 Feb. 1937	Sir Courtenay Latimer*
1-31 Mar. 1937	Sir Courtenay Latimer

Residents for the States of Western India:

1 Apr.-10 Oct. 1937	Sir Courtenay Latimer
11 Oct. 1937-15 May 1939	E.C. Gibson*
16 May 1939-31 Jan. 1941	E.C. Gibson
1 Feb.-14 Mar. 1941	G.B. Williams*
15 Mar. 1941-Mar. 1942	Sir Edmund Gibson
4 Mar.-3 Apr. 1942	M.C. Sinclair*
5-14 Apr. 1942	R.W. Parkes*
Apr.-Nov. 1942	Sir Edmund Gibson
2 Nov. 1942-2 Jan. 1944	P. Gaisford*
3 Jan.-6 Sept. 1944	P. Gaisford

7 Sept.-4 Nov. 1944	C.P. Hancock*

Residents at Baroda and for the States of Western India and Gujarat:

5 Nov. 1944-4 July 1945	C.P. Hancock*
5 July 1945-6 May 1947	Sir Cyril Hancock
7 May-14 Aug. 1947	L.G. Coke-Wallis

Secretaries to the Agent to the Governor-General, from 1937 the Resident:

10 Oct. 1924-19 Jan. 1925	J. de la H. Gordon
20 Jan. 1925-23 Mar. 1926	C.L. Corfield
26 Mar. 1926-18 Sept. 1929	C.P. Hancock
Sept. 1929	C.G. Snelling
1-21 Oct. 1929	R.L. Bazalgette*
22 Oct. 1929-8 Nov. 1932	G.F. Squire
9 Nov. 1932-1 Oct. 1933	G.B. Williams
2-11 Oct. 1933	Kunwar Daya Singh Bedi*
12-20 Oct. 1933	G.B. Williams
21 Oct. 1933-3 Mar. 1935	W.F. Campbell
7 Mar. 1935-21 Mar. 1936	A.A. Russell
22 Mar. 1936-16 Mar. 1938	C.W.L. Harvey
17 Mar.-4 May 1938	W. Le B. Egerton
5 May 1938-29 Nov. 1939	E.W. Fletcher
30 Nov. 1939-20 Sept. 1941	M. Worth
21 Sept.-24 Oct. 1941	R.W. Parkes*
25 Oct. 1941-30 Apr. 1944	V.M.H. Cox
1-14 May 1944	V.M.H. Cox
15 May-4 Nov. 1944	J.R. Cotton
21 Mar. 1944-31 May 1945	D.Y. Fell
1 June-17 Oct. 1945	J.R. Cotton
4 Nov. 1945-11 May 1946	J.R. Cotton
12 May 1946-1947	E.F. Lydall
23 Apr.-14 Aug. 1947	E.W.M. Magor*

Political Agents, Palanpur, from 1925 Banas Kantha Agency:

10 Oct. 1924-29 Sept. 1925	E. O'Brien
30 Sept. 1925-22 Mar. 1926	H.S. Strong
23 Mar. 1926-9 Feb. 1928	H.M. Wightwick

10 Feb.-31 Oct. 1928	B. Reilly
1-9 Nov. 1928	G.B. Williams*
10 Nov. 1928-20 Mar. 1931	H.M. Wightwick
21 Mar. 1931-31 Mar. 1933	G.P. Murphy

Political Agents, Sabar Kantha Agency:

1 Apr.-26 May 1933	G.P. Murphy
27 May-5 Dec. 1933	H.M. Wightwick
6 Dec. 1933-17 Mar. 1935	G.B. Williams
18 Mar. 1935-20 Apr. 1936	E.W. Fletcher
21 Apr.-7 Aug. 1936	C.E.U. Bremner
Aug.-Dec. 1936	Rao Saheb Sunderlal N. Desai*
13 Dec. 1936-31 Jan. 1937	C.E.U. Bremner
16 Feb.-26 Sept. 1937	E.B. Wakefield*
27 Sept.-30 Oct. 1937	O.C.B. St John
31 Oct. 1937-22 Oct. 1938	D.R. Smith
23 Oct. 1938-6 Nov. 1941	L.W. Wooldridge
7 Nov. 1941-21 Jan. 1942	G.B. Williams*
22 Jan.-10 Mar. 1942	A.N. Mitchell
18 Mar. 1942-31 July 1943	V.W.D. Willoughby

Political Agents, Western Kathiawar, from 1926 Western Kathiawar Agency:

10 Oct. 1924-28 Sept. 1925	H.S. Strong
29 Sept.-24 Oct. 1925	J. de la H. Gordon*
25 Oct. 1925-24 Mar. 1927	A.H.E. Mosse
25 Mar.-28 Nov. 1927	L.E. Lang
29 Nov. 1927-12 May 1928	E.C. Gibson
28 May 1928-24 Feb. 1929	A.S. Meek
25 Feb. 1929-27 May 1933	J.C. Tate
27 May 1933-17 Oct. 1934	G.P. Murphy
18 Oct. 1934-20 Mar. 1936	C.W.L. Harvey
21 Mar. 1936-14 Apr. 1937	T.B. Creagh Coen
15 Apr.-18 June 1937	O.C.B. St John
21 June-1 Oct. 1937	T.B. Creagh Coen
2 Oct. 1937-16 Mar. 1938	W. Le B. Egerton
17 Mar.-9 June 1938	O.C.B. St John
10 June 1938-26 June 1939	C.K. Daly
29 Mar. 1939-8 Apr. 1940	A.J. Hopkinson

9 Apr. 1940-31 Jan. 1941	G.B. Williams
15 Mar.-15 Sept. 1941	G.B. Williams
16 Sept. 1941-3 Mar. 1942	M.C. Sinclair
4 Mar.-3 Apr. 1942	R.W. Parkes
4 Apr. 1942-5 Sept. 1943	M.C. Sinclair
27 Oct. 1943-6 Nov. 1944	M.C. Sinclair
7 Nov. 1944-14 Aug. 1947	P.C. Hailey

Political Agents, Eastern Kathiawar, from 1926 Eastern Kathiawar Agency:

10 Oct. 1924-26 Jan. 1925	H. Wilberforce-Bell
27 Jan. 1925-2 Dec. 1926	J. de la H. Gordon
3 Dec. 1926-23 Oct. 1928	D. de M.S. Fraser
24-31 Oct. 1928	C.P. Hancock*
1 Nov. 1928-12 Nov. 1930	A.J. Hopkinson
13 Nov. 1930-17 Mar. 1931	K.A.G. Evans-Gordon
18 Mar.-23 Aug. 1931	P.G. Loch
24 Aug.-12 Nov. 1931	R.L. Bazalgette
13 Nov. 1931-9 Mar. 1932	Fisher
10-13 Mar. 1932	G.F. Squire*
14 Mar. 1932-13 Nov. 1934	J. de la H. Gordon
14 Nov. 1934-2 May 1935	K.A.G. Evans-Gordon
3 May-12 Aug. 1935	J. de la H. Gordon
13 Aug. 1935-7 Apr. 1938	H.M. Poulton
5 May-26 Oct. 1938	W. Le B. Egerton
27 Oct. 1938-1940	H.M. Wightwick
19 Apr.-27 May 1940	A.J. Hopkinson
28 May-8 Aug. 1940	F.F. Pearson
9 Aug. 1940-17 Sept. 1941	D.G.H. de la Fargue
18 Sept. 1941-17 Apr. 1942	G.B. Williams
13 Apr.-27 Sept. 1942	R.W. Parkes
28 Sept.-5 Nov. 1942	Harishwar Dayal*
6 Nov.-7 Dec. 1942	R.W. Parkes
8 Dec. 1942-15 Jan. 1943	Harishwar Dayal*
16 Jan.-31 Aug. 1943	R.K.M. Battye

Political Agents, Eastern Kathiawar Agency and for Sabar Kantha:

1 Sept. 1943-30 Apr. 1944	V.W.D. Willoughby
1 May 1944-15 Apr. 1946	V.M.H. Cox

16 Apr.-15 May 1946	P.C. Hailey
16 May-10 Dec. 1946	V.M.H. Cox
11 Dec. 1946-11 June 1947	A.E. Drake
12 June-14 Aug. 1947	P.C. Hailey

SELECT BIBLIOGRAPHY

Adam, Colin Forbes. *Life of Lord Lloyd*. London, 1948.

Aitchison, C.U. *A Collection of Treaties, Engagements and Sanads Relating to India and Neighbouring Countries*. 5th edition, 14 volumes. Calcutta, 1929-1933.

Allen, Charles. *Plain Tales from the Raj: Images of British India in the Twentieth Century*. Calcutta, 1992.

— and Sharada Dwivedi. *Lives of the Indian Princes*. London, 1984.

Arora, A.C. "British Government and Minorities of Native Chiefs (1858-1905): A Case Study of Bahawalpur State," in *The Panjab Past and Present*, 10, 1 (Apr. 1976), pp. 108-119.

—. "British Rule and Minority Arrangements in the Phulkian States, 1858-1905," in *Bengal Past and Present*, 92, 1 (1973), pp. 89-103.

Ashton, S.R. *British Policy Towards the Indian States 1905-1939*. London, 1982.

Bawa, V.K. *The Last Nizam: The Life and Times of Mir Osman Ali Khan*. New Delhi, 1992.

Bayly, C.A. *Indian Society and the Making of the British Empire* (*The New Cambridge History of India*, II.1). Cambridge, 1988.

Bedi, P.S. *The Mughal Nobility Under Akbar*. Jalandhar, 1985.

Coen, T. Creagh. *The Indian Political Service: A Study in Indirect Rule*. London, 1971.

Cohn, Bernard S. "Representing Authority in Victorian India," in Eric Hobsbawm and Terence Ranger, editors. *The Invention of Tradition*. Cambridge, 1983, pp. 165-209.

Copland, Ian. "The Baroda Crisis of 1873-77: A Study in Governmental Rivalry," in *Modern Asian Studies*, 2, 2 (1968), pp. 97-123.

—. *The British Raj and the Indian Princes: Paramountcy in Western India, 1857-1930*. Bombay, 1982.

—. "Congress Paternalism: The 'High Command' and the Struggle for Freedom in Princely India, c. 1920-1940," in *South Asia*, new series, 8, 1 and 2 (June-Dec. 1985), pp. 121-140.

—. *The Princes of India in the Endgame of Empire, 1917-1947*. Cambridge, 1997.

Dass, Diwan Jarmani. *Maharaja: Lives, Loves and Intrigues of Indian Princes*. Delhi and Bombay, 1970.

Dirks, Nicholas B. *The Hollow Crown: Ethnohistory of an Indian Kingdom*. Cambridge, 1987.

East India (Constitutional Reforms). Report of the Indian States Enquiry Committee (Financial), 1932. Cmd 4103. London, 1932.

East India (Constitutional Reforms). Report on Indian Constitutional Reforms. Cd 9109. London, 1918.

East India (Fiscal Commission). Report of the Indian Fiscal Commission 1921. Cmd 1764. Simla, 1922.

East India (Indian States). Report of the Indian States Committee 1928-1929. Cmd 3302. London, 1929.

Fisher, Michael H. *Indirect Rule in India: Residents and the Residency System 1764-1858*. Delhi, 1991.

—. "Indirect Rule in the British Empire: The Foundations of the Residency System in India (1764-1858)," in *Modern Asian Studies*, 18, 3 (1984), pp. 393-428.

Fitze, Sir Kenneth. *Twilight of the Maharajas*. London, 1956.

Gaekwad, Fatesinghrao P. *Sayajirao of Baroda: The Prince and the Man*. Bombay, 1989.

Gandhi, M.K. *An Autobiography or the Story of My Experiments with Truth*. Ahmedabad, 1992.

—. *The Indian States' Problem*. Ahmedabad, 1941.

Gauba, K.L. *His Highness, or the Pathology of Princes*. Lahore, 1930.

Gazetteer of the Bombay Presidency. 27 volumes in 35. Bombay, 1877-1904.

Gibson, James. "Glimpses of a Passing Landscape," in *Indo-British Review*, 18, 2 (n.d.), pp. 27-48.

Government of India. Ministry of States. *White Paper on Indian States*. 2nd edition. Delhi, 1950.

Haksar, Kailas Narain. "The Indian States and the Sea-Customs Duties," in *The Asiatic Review*, 23, 4 (Oct. 1927), pp. 579-584.

Handbook of the Chamber of Princes (Narendra Mandal), A. Simla, 1942.

Hardiman, David. "Baroda: The Structure of a 'Progressive' State," in Robin Jeffrey, editor. *People, Princes and Paramount Power: Society and Politics in the Indian Princely States*. Delhi, 1978, pp. 107-135.

Hitchcock, John T. "The Idea of the Martial Rajput," in Milton Singer, editor. *Traditional India: Structure and Change*. Philadelphia, 1959, pp. 10-17.

Hurd II, John. *Some Economic Characteristics of the Princely States of India 1901-1931*. PhD dissertation, University of Pennsylvania, 1969.

Hyderabad Government, Central Records Office. *The Chronology of Modern Hyderabad 1720-1890*. Hyderabad, 1954.

Imperial Gazetteer of India. 26 volumes. Oxford, 1908-1909.

India Office List, The. London, annually 1907-1937.

Jeffrey, Robin, editor. *People, Princes and Paramount Power: Society and Politics in the Indian Princely States*. Delhi, 1978.

Jocelyn, Arthur. *Awards of Honour: The orders, decorations, medals and awards of honour of Great Britain & the Commonwealth from Edward III to Elizabeth II*. London, 1956.

Knight, Lionel. "British Paramountcy and the Education of the Mysore Prince," in *Bengal Past and Present*, 92, 1 (1973), pp. 37-57.

Kolff, Dirk H.A. Naukar, *Rajput and Sepoy: The ethnohistory of the military labour market in Hindustan, 1450-1850*. Cambridge, 1990.

Kulkarni, V.B. *Princely India and the Lapse of British Paramountcy*. Bombay, 1985.

Lee-Warner, Sir William. *The Native States of India*. London, 1910.

Lydall, Edward. *Enough of Action*. London, 1949.

Manor, James. *Political Change in an Indian State: Mysore 1917-1955*. New Delhi, 1977.

Mathur, Vishnu Dayal. *States' People's Conference: Origin and Role in Rajasthan*. Jaipur, 1984.

Mayer, Adrian C. "Perceptions of Princely Rule: Perspectives from a Biography," in *Contributions to Indian Sociology*, n.s., 15, 1 and 2 (1981), pp. 127-154.

McCahill, Michael W. "Peerage creations and the changing character of the British nobility, 1750-1830," in *English Historical Review*, 96, 379 (Apr. 1981), pp. 259-284.

McLeod, John. "A model prince? Maharana Bhavani Singh and the end of India's states," in *History Today*, 45, 12 (Dec. 1995), pp. 41-46

—. "Indian States and British Courts: The Tripura Succession Dispute of 1862-1869," in *Indo-British Review*, 15, 2 (Dec. 1988), pp. 31-46.

—. "The English Honours System in Princely India, 1925-1947," in *Journal of the Royal Asiatic Society*, 3rd series, 4, 2 (July 1994), pp. 237-249.

—. "Towards the Analysis of Hindu Princely Genealogy in the British Period, 1850-1950," in *South Asia Research*, 6, 2 (Nov. 1986), pp. 181-193.

—. *The Western India States Agency 1916-1947*. PhD thesis, University of Toronto, 1993.

Memoranda on Native States in India 1912, together with a list of Independent Ruling Chiefs, Chiefs of Frontier States, and other Personages with their Proper Forms of Address. Calcutta, 1912.

Memoranda on the Indian States. Calcutta or Delhi, yearly 1930-1940.

Menon, V.P. *The Story of the Integration of the Indian States*. New York, 1956.

Metcalf, Thomas R. *The Aftermath of Revolt: India, 1857-1870*. Princeton, 1964.

Moon, Penderel, editor. *Wavell: The Viceroy's Journal*. London, 1973.

Nehru, Jawaharlal. *An Autobiography*. New Delhi, 1980.

—. *Glimpses of World History: being further letters to his daughter, written in prison, and containing a rambling account of history for young people*. New Delhi, 1982.

—. *Presidential Address. All India States' People's Conference February 1939, Ludhiana*. Allahabad, n.d.

Nicholson, A.P. *Scraps of Paper: India's Broken Treaties, Her Princes, and the Problem*. London, 1930.

Nightingale, Pamela. *Trade and Empire in Western India 1784-1806*. Cambridge, 1970.

O'Dwyer, Sir Michael. *India as I Knew It 1885-1925*. London, 1925.

Panikkar, K.M. (translated by K. Krishnamurthy). *An Autobiography*. Delhi, 1979.

—. *The Indian Princes in Council: A Record of the Chancellorship of His Highness the Maharaja of Patiala 1926-1931 and 1933-1936*. London, 1936.

Phadnis, Urmila. *Towards the Integration of Indian States, 1919-1947*. London, 1968.

Price, Pamela G. *Kingship and Political Practice in Colonial India*. Cambridge, 1996.

—. "Revolution and Rank in Tamil Nationalism," in *The Journal of Asian Studies*, 55, 2 (May 1996), pp. 359-383.

Ramusack, Barbara N. "Congress and the People's Movement in Princely India: Ambivalence in Strategy and Organization," in Richard Sisson and Stanley Wolpert, editors. *Congress and Indian Nationalism: The Pre-Independence Phase*. Berkeley, 1988, pp. 377-403.

—. *The Princes of India in the Twilight of Empire: Dissolution of a Patron-Client System, 1914-1939*. Columbus, 1978.

Ray, Bharati. *Hyderabad and British Paramountcy 1858-1883*. Delhi, 1988.

Ray, Mihir Kumar. *Princely States and the Paramount Power 1858-1876: A study on the nature of political relationship between the British Government and the Indian State*. New Delhi, 1981.

Rudolph, Susanne Hoeber. "The Princely States of Rajputana: Ethic, Authority and Structure," in *The Indian Journal of Political Science*, 24, 1-4 (Jan.-Dec. 1963), pp. 14-32.

— and Lloyd I. Rudolph. *Essays on Rajputana: Reflections on History, Culture and Administration*. New Delhi, 1984.

Ruling Princes, Chiefs and Leading Personages in the Western India States Agency, The. 2nd edition. Delhi, 1935.

Rushbrook Williams, L.F. *The Black Hills: Kutch in History and Legend: A Study in Indian Local Loyalties*. London, 1958.

Scindia, Vijaya Raje, with Manohar Malgonkar. *The Last Maharani of Gwalior: An Autobiography*. Albany, 1987

Setalvad, Chimanlal H. *Recollections & Reflections: An Autobiography*. Bombay, n.d. (*ca* 1946).

Sever, Adrian, editor. *Documents and Speeches on the Indian Princely States*. 2 volumes. Delhi, 1985.

Sharma, Hari. *Princes and Paramountcy*. New Delhi, 1978.

Singh, St Nihal. *The King's Indian Allies: The Rajas and their India*. London, 1916.

Singh, Shiv Kumar Prasad. *The Indian Ruling Princes and the National Movement: 1927-47*. New Delhi, 1991.

Spodek, Howard. "Urban Politics in the Local Kingdoms of India: A View from the Princely Capitals of Saurashtra (Kathiawar) under British Rule," in *Modern Asian Studies*, 7, 2 (1973), pp. 253-275.

Stern, Robert W. *The Cat and the Lion: Jaipur State in the British Raj*. Leiden, 1988.

Sugich, Michael. *Palaces of India: A Traveller's Companion Featuring the Palace Hotels*. London, 1992.

Sundaram, Chandar S. "Preventing 'Idleness:' The maharaja of Cooch Behar's proposal for officer commissions in the British Army for the sons of Indian Princes and Gentlemen, 1897-1898," in *South Asia*, 18, 1 (June 1995), pp. 115-130.

Tambs-Lyche, Harald. *Power, Profit and Poetry: Traditional Society in Kathiawar, Western India*. New Delhi, 1997.

Thomas, R. Hughes, editor. *Selections from the Records of the Bombay Government*, n.s., 12, 15, 25, 37, 39 (Bombay, 1855-1856).

Tirmizi, S.A.I., "Introduction," in *Index to Titles (1798-1885) As Recorded in the Alqabnamas or Books of Titles and Forms of Address*. n.p. (New Delhi), n.d. (*ca* 1979), pp. i-xxi.

Tod, James. *Travels in Western India, embracing a visit to the sacred mounts of the Jains and the most celebrated shrines of the Hindu faith between Rajpootana and the Indus; with an account of the ancient city of Nehrwalla*. London, 1839.

Tupper, C.L. *Indian Political Practice: A Collection of the Decisions of the Government of India in Political Cases*. 4 volumes. Calcutta, 1895.

Waghorne, Joanne Punzo. *The Raja's Magic Clothes: Re-Visioning Kingship and Divinity in England's India*. University Park, Pennsylvania, 1994.

Wakefield, Sir Edward. *Past Imperative: My Life in India 1927-1947*. London, 1966.

Walker, John. *The Queen Has Been Pleased: The British Honours System at Work*. London, 1986.

What are the Indian States? (All-India States' People's Conference Research Bureau, pamphlet no. 1). Allahabad, n.d. (1939).

Wild, Roland, *"Ranji:" The Biography of Colonel H.H. Shri Sir Ranjitsinhji Vibhaji, Maharaja Jam Saheb of Nawanagar*. London, 1934.

Wood, John R. "Rajkot: Indian Nationalism in the Princely Context: The Rajkot Satyagraha of 1938-9," in Robin Jeffrey, editor. *People, Princes and Paramount Power: Society and Politics in the Indian Princely States*. Delhi, 1978, pp. 240-274.

Zaidi, A.M., and S.G. Zaidi, editors. *The Encyclopaedia of the Indian National Congress*. 26 volumes to date. New Delhi, 1976-.

INDEX